THE LOVED BODY'S
CORRUPTION

THE LOVED BODY'S CORRUPTION

ARCHAEOLOGICAL CONTRIBUTIONS TO THE STUDY OF HUMAN MORTALITY

edited by

JANE DOWNES
and
TONY POLLARD

CRUITHNE PRESS

GLASGOW

cover: Johari Lee

1999

© individual authors

Cruithne Press
197 Great Western Road
Glasgow G4 9EB
Great Britain

British Library Cataloguing in Publication Data

A catalogue record for this book is available from the British Library

ISBN 1 873448 06 6

Set in Palatino by $J^{a^{zz}}$ Cornets

Printed and bound by Redwood Books, Trowbridge, Wiltshire

Contents

Owen Beattie graduated in archaeology from Simon Fraser University, British Columbia. His doctoral research was concerned with the physical anthropology of the prehistoric peoples of the north-western coast of the United States. Owen is currently a lecturer in the anthropology department at the University of Alberta and is best known for his work on the Franklin expedition, writing *'Frozen in Time'* with John Geiger.

Bill Bevan completed an MA in archaeology at the University of Sheffield after helping to develop the National Trust's Lake District Historic Landscape Survey. He is currently at the Peak District National Park Authority where he co-directs, along with John Barnatt and Mark Edmonds, the Gardom's Edge Pre-historic Landscape Project. Other current research includes Iron Age to Romano-British occupation of the southern Pennines, most recently producing a volume on the Iron Age of northern and western Britain.

Angela Boyle graduated in archaeology at the University of Glasgow before going on to obtain an MSc in human osteology at the University of Sheffield. For the past six years Angela has worked as an osteologist with the Oxford Archaeological Unit and is currently undertaking a part-time PhD at the Institute of Archaeology, University College London.

Margaret Cox is a lecturer in archaeology at the University of Bournemouth where she developed the MSc course in forensic archaeology. Margaret co-directed the Spittalfields project with Jez Reeve and carried out the osteological analysis of the excavated human remains. This experience provided the basis for her PhD and a well-received book on the project aimed at a general readership.

Jane Downes graduated in archaeology from the University of Manchester before going on to specialise in the study of Bronze-Age funerary practice, which is the subject of her PhD. Jane is director of the Orkney Barrows Project and an assistant director of ARCUS (Archaeology Research Centre, University of Sheffield).

Shawn Healey was awarded his PhD by Simon Fraser University and went on to carry out archaeological and anthropological fieldwork in Canada, the United States, Peru, and Mexico. He teaches anthropology at Red Deer College and its adjunct faculty at Senior University (Casper, Wyoming, USA).

John Hunter is a senior lecturer in archaeology at the University of Birmingham and before that taught at the University of Bradford. John has done much to develop a role for the archaeologist in forensic police work in Britain. He has excavated a variety of sites in the northern isles of Scotland, most recently publishing his work on Fair Isle.

Lucy Kirk graduated in archaeology from the Institute of Archaeology, University College London. She is currently studying part-time for an MSc in forensic archaeology at the University of Bournemouth whilst working as a field officer and human bone specialist with UCL's Field Archaeology Unit.

Mike Parker Pearson is a lecturer in archaeology at the University of Sheffield. As well as carrying out fieldwork on Madagascar he has been heavily involved with Sheffield University's Outer Hebrides Project. Mike has written on a wide variety of archaeological subjects, including the volume on Bronze-Age Britain in the popular English Heritage series.

Tony Pollard graduated in archaeology from the University of Glasgow, where he wrote his PhD thesis on the exploitation of marine resources in prehistoric Scotland. After working for several years with GUARD (Glasgow University Archaeological Research Division), he left to become the projects manager of the Field Archaeology Unit (Archaeology South-East), University College London, but is now happy to have returned to GUARD as senior project manager.

Jez Reeve co-directed, along with Margaret Cox, the excavation of the church crypt at Spittalfields, and has since written widely on the subject of post-medieval burial archaeology. She is head of English Heritage's London Archaeological Advisory Service and honorary chair of the Institute of Field Archaeologists.

Mel Richmond graduated in archaeology from the University of Glasgow and is currently a part-time technician with Glasgow University Archaeological Research Division. She is also a freelance archaeologist specialising in the analysis of post-medieval coffin furniture.

Charlotte Roberts began her career as a nurse, her involvement with people and illness and an interest in archaeology prompting her to give up nursing and study for a PhD in human osteology at the University of Sheffield. Charlotte is currently a lecturer in the department of archaeological sciences at the University of Bradford. Recently she co-edited a volume on forensic archaeology with John Hunter.

Ross Samson graduated in medieval history from the University of St Andrews and obtained his PhD in the department of archaeology at the University of Glasgow, where his research centred on secular Dark-Age architecture. Ross went on to found the Cruithne Press and is now a joiner.

Simon Stoddart is a lecturer in archaeology at the University of Cambridge and was formerly attached to the University of Bristol. He is assitant editor of *Antiquity*.

Helen Start graduated in archaeology and ancient history from the University of Birmingham, and went on to study toward an MSc in osteology, palaeopathology, and funerary archaeology at the Universities of Sheffield and Bradford. Helen is currently working as a research assistant at the University of Sheffield.

Nancy Wicker was awarded her PhD by the University of Minnesota, her main interest being Scandinavian medieval art. Since 1995 she has been an associate professor in the art department at Manakato State University. She is currently writing a book on the realtionship between goldsmiths, workshops, patrons, and their female clientele in early medieval art.

First to our ancestors who lie in barrows
Or under nameless cairns on heathery hills
Or where the seal-swim crashes on the island narrows

Or in Jacobean tomb, whose scrolls and skull
Carry off death with an elegant inscription,
The Latin phrasing which beguiles and dulls

The bitter regrets at the loved body's corruption
Or those who merely share the prayer that is
  muttered
For many sunk together in war's eruption,

To all, clay-bound or chalk-bound, stiff or scattered,
We leave the values of their periods,
The things which seemed to them the things that
  mattered,

— Auden and MacNeice: Their Last Will and Testament

Although the original impetus for this volume was provided by two conferences[1] centred on the theme of death, and archaeological approaches to it, this book aims to be more than a conference proceedings. To this end a number of the contributions are not based on conference presentations but were solicited by the editors from writers it was felt had something new to say about the subject. It became apparent to the editors reading recent literature and giving their own papers at these and other conferences that writing concerned with the archaeology of death represents a specific genre within the wider field of archaeological writing. Like any literary genre it has its own set of rules and approach to narrative, which in this case expresses itself through the presentation of data. The literature covers a broad spectrum of subjects, ranging from the physical remains of the dead to the role within society of funerary rites, and encompasses different approaches, from the purely 'scientific' to the more humanistic.

Where the majority of work so far published has dealt objectively with the issue of human remains as empirical archaeological data, an important remit of this book from the outset was to encourage archaeologists within the field of funerary archaeology and palaeo-pathological studies to write subjectively about their work. In attempting this the present volume probably has more in common with literature dealing with death within the social sciences, much of which is concerned with the idea of the individual, the body, and attitudes to mortality in the post-modern world (e.g. Todd 1993; Davies 1994; Palmer 1993; Lynch 1997).

The introduction of post-processual approaches has more than anything else led to an increased awareness that archaeology is more subjective than objective. This realisation has prompted a move toward a writing style that takes into account the experiences of the practitioner and the influence of the present, in which they are situated, on the writing of the past. Murray expresses this when writing on the archaeology of the contact period in Tasmania: 'In recent years, perhaps as a consequence of the self-reflective turn in archaeology, and concern for the social and political implications of their practice, archaeologists have been more outspoken about their emotion' (1993, 504).

Although the editors were attracted to the idea of moving away from traditional styles of archaeological writing, where the tendency has been to objectify human remains as data and treat them like any other find or artefact from an archaeological site, they are fully aware that our own twentieth-century western perceptions of death and the dead are unlikely to have been shared by our more distant ancestors or people from other cultures. Very recently one of the editors was involved with the management of a large-scale excavation of a seventeenth- to nineteenth-century Quaker burial ground in Greater London (see Kirk and Start, this volume) during which some 350 burials were excavated. Like the majority of excavations carried out today this was a commercial contract project with the work carried out for a developer who wished to build houses on the site. A meeting between the archaeologist and the developer is worth recounting within the present context. The conversation moved away from the issue of funding to a programme which had been on television the night before (the third of the Horizon programmes on Ice Mummies) which obviously directed thoughts to our mutual experience of the burial ground excavation. He asked how digging up all those bodies had affected the archaeologists and was told that many had reported strange dreams and dramatic mood swings, both of which they put down to their day-to-day work of digging up the dead. The developer replied to this that working with the bones of the dead would not really bother him because of his religion. Only then did he explain that he was actually a Buddhist, which in itself surprised the archaeologist and made him re-assess, for a short time at least, his attitude toward developers, who tend not to display the sensitivities one would associate with Buddhism. More importantly it served to reinforce the importance of belief and ideology on the way we view the past. Buddhism, an eastern religion, places no importance on the material remains of the dead – for believers bones are bones and that is the end of it, the soul is elsewhere.

Eschatology is of prime concern in many cultures, and must have been so in the past (see papers by Downes and Samson, this volume). In the Hindu Balinese beliefs Connor rightly points out that the word cremation has been interpreted as 'the reduction of the body to ashes and not a process of spiritual purification' (1995, 539). Although we may be aware of the importance of the fate of the soul and the nature of the afterlife, as archaeologists our focus is on the physical remains. It is perhaps oversimplifying matters to assert that this is a direct reflection of a lessening of western beliefs in an afterlife, but our own ideas about death necessarily colour the way we interpret burial and funerary evidence. The hidden and private nature of death in contemporary western society is thought to increase problems of confronting our own deaths, the dying, and the remains of the dead. Sociologists have over the past few years been developing Giddens' notion of death as a threat to 'ontological security', bringing chaos and disorder (cf. Clarke 1993; Shilling 1993) to the individual and society. The archaeologist's fascination with the dead could be seen as a desire on their part to confront death and the dead.

The encounter with the dead for the archaeologist, or anthropologist, can shock and disturb. For the archaeologist it can appear to be the closest, most immediate contact we can have with the past. The moment makes us feel as if we are invading privacy, give us the impression that all at once we are seeing the person as though sleeping, their possessions around them, perhaps wearing jewellery and clothing. In these items we seek to glimpse the intentions and feelings of the bereaved. Even though it is now widely accepted that we cannot equate the manner in which a person is buried with their status, it is still tempting to view the burial and accompanying artefacts as similar to a headstone in that the persons age, sex, identity, position in life, occupation, and the regard with which they were held by family and community can be read.

Contributors to this volume were encouraged to take account of their own experiences and emotions in dealing with their subject matter. It is the nature of this encounter which must influence the way archaeologists write about death. This experience is rarely made explicit or discussed in archaeological literature, a failing which may be a result of a general reluctance within western society to confront mortality. When reading the papers contained within this volume it will become apparent that some authors have taken to this approach more readily than others, though this of course does not in any way reduce the value of their contribution.

This book has essentially been an experiment in writing archaeology, and like many experiments (a term which sits somewhat uneasily with a project motivated by the post-processualist ethos) had an unpredictable result. This is only to be expected given the range of contributors which include anthropologists, archaeologists, and practitioners in both disciplines who have different types of contact with material – from those who study mortuary rites to those who specialise in osteology, palaeopathology, forensic pathology, and forensic archaeology. Variation in the types of human remains – ranging from graves where no bone survives, through the 'dry' bones of skeletons cremations, to well-preserved bodies with soft tissue surviving – is bound to provoke differing responses.

The first papers in the volume tackle the subject from anthropological and ethno-archaeological perspectives. A fitting introduction is provided by Healey's overview of what death is and means to a variety of different cultures. Culturally specific accounts of funerary rites appear in the contributions by Parker Pearson, who discusses the burial rites and funerary architecture of the Tandroy of southern Madagascar, and Downes who considers Hindu Balinese cremation within the context of the archaeological interpretation of cremation rites.

The influence of anthropological or ethno-archaeological approaches on archaeology can be seen in the papers which follow. Bevan discusses Iron-Age burials in East Yorkshire, placing an emphasis on their land-scape context, while Stoddart et al. consider changes in mortuary practices in Neolithic Malta. Infanticide has been the cause of heated archaeological debate and attracted a high media profile over recent years and is here discussed by Wicker, in the context of Iron-Age Scandinavia. Pollard's paper looks at the role of the sea as grave, con-sidering issues such as place, memory, and loss, and concludes by drawing on his own experiences to argue for the presence of prehistoric cenotaphs dedicated to those lost at sea.

Samson, in his own inimitable style, discusses the attitude of the church and archaeologists to the burial of the Christian dead, and in doing so paves the way for a group of papers which reflect a growing concern with the ethical issues surrounding the recently dead, and the techniques involved in their excavation and recording. The main issues are articulated by Reeve and Cox, who express a concern that the potential of post-medieval funerary remains are not fully realised, a sentiment echoed by Richmond, who argues that analysis of coffin furniture can provide a valuable insight into Victorian attitudes to death. Personal insights into the excavation and analysis of human remains from post-medieval cemeteries are presented both by Boyle, who recounts her own experiences during the excavation of the church crypt at Sevenoaks, and Kirk and Start, who reflect on their memorable experiences during the excavation of the Quaker burial ground at Kingston upon Thames.

The concluding papers concentrate on forensics and palaeo-pathology. The increased involvement of archaeologists with police murder invest-igations is discussed by Hunter. Another contemporary issue is con-sidered by Roberts, who utilises the techniques of palaeo-pathology to explore the physical manifestation of certain fatal diseases, and the stigma attached to these diseases today. Beattie's work on the Franklin Expedition has become well known through his book 'Frozen in Time' (Beattie and Geiger 1987). In this contribution he discusses both his own experiences and the wider emotional impact of the well-preserved corpses of the nineteenth-century sailors.

Jane Downes and Tony Pollard

ACKNOWLEDGEMENTS

This book would not have been possible without the encouragement of the Scottish Archaeological Forum. The editors would like to thank a number of individuals who provided assistance and encouragement during the book's long gestation period, primarily Alan Leslie who helped start the whole thing rolling by chairing the Scottish Archaeological Forum conference and then provided support in seeing the publication through. Richard James and Louise Bashford assisted with the copy-editing. We would also like to thank both the contributors and those who shelled out their hard earned cash long before publication for their patience. There was a time when we too thought it would never happen!

NOTE

1. The first of these conferences, entitled 'Death and the Supernatural', was organised by Ross Samson and Alan Leslie for the Scottish Archaeological Forum and held at Glasgow University in 1993. The second, entitled 'The Archaeology of Death', was organised by the student Archaeology Society at the University of Sheffield and was held in 1994.

REFERENCES

Auden, W. H. and L. MacNeice 1967. *Letters from Iceland*. Faber and Faber, London.

Beattie, O. and J. Geiger 1987. *Frozen in Time: The Fate of the Franklin Expedition*. Bloomsbury, London.

Clarke, D. (ed.) 1993. *The Sociology of Death: Theory, Culture, Practice*. Blackwell, Oxford.

Connor, L. H. 1995. The action of the body on society: washing a corpse in Bali. *Journal of the Royal Anthropological Institute* 1, 537-559.

Davies, J. (ed.) 1994. *Ritual and Remembrance*. Sheffield.

Lynch, T. 1997. *The Undertaking – Life Studies from the Dismal Trade*. Jonathan Cape, London.

Palmer, G. 1993. *Death – the Trip of a Lifetime*. Harper, San Francisco.

Murray, T. 1993. The childhood of William Lane: contact archaeology in Aboriginal Tasmania. *Antiquity* 67, 504-519.

Shilling, C. 1993. *The Body and Social Theory*. Sage, London.

Death and after death

Shawn Haley

Death marks the end of life as we know it but few cultures see it as the end of everything. What happens after death depends on two aspects of the world's cultures – their perceptions of that part of the human that survives after death and their perceptions of where that surviving aspect goes. The 'soul' ranges from a poorly defined blob of energy to an incorporeal replica of the body that had once housed it. It seems that the more clearly the soul is envisioned by the living, the more complex the afterworld which, unlike the Judeo-Christian heaven, seems to be located in close proximity to the world of the living. In this paper, a brief overview of preliterate cultures will examine both aspects of life after death and attempt to offer some explanations for their existence with regard to a select number of cultures. Implications for archaeological research will also be considered.

It has often been argued *a priori* that religions were developed to enable people to explain death. Death, one of life's most enduring mysteries, has defied explanation since humans first began to speculate on it. Even modern medical science has so far failed to adequately deal with the subject. Medical doctors, even those specialising in palliative care, know no more about death than the average individual. A number of doctors, when asked for a definition of death, provided either a 'death-is-not-life' statement or a list of medical conditions that when met signified that the patient is dead.

Medical personnel, according to a recent survey, do not use a consistent definition of death. Many use the stoppage of the cardio-pulmonary system as the boundary between life and death while others consider patients who are in persistent vegetative states or irreversible comas to be dead (Gervais 1986, 137–41; Green and Wilker 1980;

Younger et al. 1989, 2205–10). Obviously, since even specialists cannot agree on the dividing line between life and death, there are many different and equally acceptable definitions of the phenomenon and they reflect the diversity of opinion in the Euroamerican community.1

In non-Euroamerican societies there is an even wider range of variation. For example, the Tapirapé of Brazil consider anyone too sick to fend for themselves as dead. There are accounts of Tapirapé individuals being buried (by our estimation) before their time (Wagley 1983, 257). The Dogon of Africa will perform funerary rites for someone presumed dead – perhaps an individual who fails to return from a trip. Should the unfortunate appear at some later date, he cannot be recognised or acknowledged since he is dead. Should he decide to remain among his own people, he will be a nameless beggar until the time of his 'real' death (Paulme 1940).

Just as people can die before they are technically dead in the Euroamerican sense, in some cultures one is not dead even when all physiological functioning has ceased. Among the Hindu, for example, the 'vital breath,' the essence that animates the body, enters the person through the suture in the top of the skull while he or she is still in his or her mother's womb. The vital breath remains in the body until it is able to exit through that same spot. This is facilitated by the chief mourner who cracks open the skull of the deceased midway during the body's cremation. Thus, according to Hindu tradition, a person does not die until the middle of his or her own funeral (Parry 1982, 79–81).

All peoples do agree however that death is the cessation of life as we know it and there is one other point of agreement: almost all cultures recognise that something, some part of that human, survives death. We can call it a 'soul' on the understanding that 'soul' is a term of convenience and does not carry with it all the Christian connotations implied by the word. We all know from the Christian tradition that the soul is roughly the same size and shape as the body it inhabits. Further, a Christian soul after death retains the personality, consciousness, and memory of the individual that once was. Most other cultures do not envisage a soul in the same terms. The way a soul is perceived depends on the attitude of the society towards death. For example, the Zapotec Maya of central Mexico view death from a negative point of view. For a Zapotecan, death does not relieve a person of the earthly sufferings and longings but it does take away the pleasures and security of life. So, a soul at death becomes a disembodied spirit trapped forever in a 'gaseous solitude' – alone and lonely forever. Zapotec fatalism goes one step further. They believe that the air is becoming more and more populated with these lonely (and therefore malevolent) spirits – an indication that the total environment is changing for the worse (this represents a kind of supernatural pollution that parallels the air pollution of central America) (Kearney 1986, 56–57, 84–85; Tannenbaum 1950, 16–17).

Fear is an emotion that often surrounds death. The Navajo of New Mexico will abandon a homestead when someone dies there (Downs 1984, 108–09). A house in Blanding, Utah, has remained vacant for over a decade despite the best efforts of the landlord because in the early 1980s an old Navajo woman died in her sleep in that house. A Hopi Indian of Arizona will run away as soon as death enters a conversation (Beaglehole and Beaglehole 1976, 11) whereas a Hutterite longs for death and the release it will bring from earthly temptation (Hostetler and Huntington 1980, 89–90).

With a broad range of attitudes toward death comes an equally broad range of types of souls available to us. The Hadza and the Baka (Pygmy) of Africa deny a soul's existence entirely. They say: 'One lives. One dies. One rots' (Woodburn 1982, 193). The Trobriand Islanders do not recognise perpetual individuality and instead have a fixed quantity of 'soul stuff'. When a Trobriander dies, his soul travels to *Tuma*, the Island of the Dead, and there lives one lifetime. It then returns to enter the womb of a woman and is reborn as another person (Malinowski 1948). The Tapirapé also have a fixed number of souls. They use this limit to explain why conception does not follow each and every act of sexual intercourse (Wagley 1983, 134).

Souls are often weak during the first few years of life. Among the Dani of New Guinea, parents must fend off ghost attacks upon their young children's souls. Fail to properly protect these weak, childish souls and the youngster dies (in most societies, separation of body and soul for any length of time equals death). I would suggest that the idea of 'weak souls' in children offers a rather neat and tidy explanation for the high infant mortality rates among preliterate and/or Third World cultures.

So far, I've only mentioned some groups that have one soul occupying each living body. That is not always the case. As the old men of the Tarahuamara of Mexico observe: 'women walk slower than men perhaps because men have three souls while women have four' (Kennedy 1978, 149).

Traditional Chinese have two souls: a *Po*, an animal or life soul, and a *Hun*, a spiritual soul. Both survive death but neither are truly immortal. The *Po*, the animal soul, remains until the corpse is completely decomposed. The *Hun* lasts as long as it is remembered with the appropriate sacrifices by its descendants (Morton 1980, 29–30).

The Zinacantecos Maya also have two souls. A personal soul lives in the body but it is broken into thirteen independent parts, all of which must be present in the body for a person to be healthy and happy (Vogt 1990, 24–25). Sorrow and illness are then merely the result of one or more of the thirteen parts of the soul gone missing. The other Zinacantecos soul is a kind of animal spirit alter-ego. It is housed in an animal that is kept in a corral inside a mountain and is, in effect, held hostage by the gods (Vogt 1990, 24–26). While in the corral, the spirit animal receives all the care it needs but should the human violate a taboo, the gods respond by tossing the animal spirit out into the forest to fend for itself. This exposes the animal and the human to a myriad of dangers and privations since anything that happens to one is felt by the other. Only a Shaman could, by performing the appropriate curing ceremony, convince the gods to readmit the animal spirit to its corral and therefore restore the natural order of things (Vogt 1990, 26–27).

The animal spirit alter-ego or double is common in Central and South America. The Yanomamo of Venezuela also have such an alter-ego, called *Noreshi*. The *Noreshi*, however, do not live corraled inside a mountain or anywhere in the spirit world. Instead, it is a real animal that lives in a forest and whose life parallels that of its human counterpart. When a man goes hunting, so does his *Noreshi*. When he sleeps, it sleeps. If one gets sick, the other ails as well (Chagnon 1983, 104).

This parallelism introduces an element of danger for the Yanomamo because, although the human and his *Noreshi* live far apart from one another, their lives are linked. The Yanomamo hunt for food and quite by accident could kill the *Noreshi* of another Yanomamo or even his own. Should the *Noreshi* die, the human also will die (Chagnon 1983, 104).

The *Noreshi* is only one of four souls each Yanomamo must have. A second, the *Möamo* lives near the liver and is the soul that can be stolen by sorcerers. Its loss brings death to the human. The other two souls are essentially inactive as long as the human lives but once he dies, his *No borebó* (a little man-like thing) runs up the hammock ropes into the afterworld. The fourth, the *No uhudi* remains with the body until its cremation. At that point, it escapes into the forest to become a malevolent jungle spirit (Chagnon 1983, 103–05).

The Lugbara of Uganda have at least three souls (Middleton 1966, 64–65) while the Huron of eastern Canada have as many souls as there are organs in the body (Vogt 1990, 24; Trigger 1990, 106–07). So, as we've seen, there are lots of different numbers of souls within and without the human body. Some look like the Christian soul but many do not. Both the Pacaa Nova of Brazil and the Netsilik Eskimo of Alaska have human-shaped souls but they are diminutive – about two inches tall (von Graeve 1989, 73; Balikci 1989, 198). To Mexican peasants, a soul is a foam-like figure vaguely resembling the deceased (Lewis 1960, 84) while the Japanese believe a soul resembles a ball of fire or a Medusa jellyfish (Stearman 1989, 129). In pre-Socratic Greece, a soul was thought to be like an ethereal vapour (James Cough, personal communication 1992).

No matter how many immortal bits an individual has or what they look like, they abandon the body at or near death. Having left the body, it must have somewhere to go. I'd like to take you on a tour of the afterworlds now: Many souls, like those of the Aztec, simply cease to exist after a time. Or they could remain on Earth but in an altered form (Sandstrom 1991, 298–99).

A Navajo who has led a wicked life becomes a coyote upon death (Simmons 1980, 137). This is the ultimate humiliation for a Navajo (Simmons 1980, 137; Hassell 1966, 5, 38–39). Incidentally, Navajo who live normal, acceptable lives, become evil ghosts at death. Aztec warriors are transformed into butterflies or hummingbirds (Berdan 1982, 95).

Ghosts are common in many societies. Among Australian Aborigines, in New Guinea, North, South, and Central America, people die and their souls become ghosts whose only interest is harming their still living relatives. Generally, they do not rest until a relative dies. The exceptions to this malevolent type are found in cultures with strong family political units. The ghosts then become ancestral spirits who continue to participate in the decision-making processes.

Another afterlife activity is reincarnation. The Makuna of south-east Columbia possess the simplest reincarnation belief possible. When a Makuna child is born, it obtains the soul of a deceased grandparent who has been waiting in an underwater longhouse. The Makuna are able to identify the soul as it enters the infants body and so the child receives the name of the soul-giving ancestor as well as the soul (Arhem 1992, 52).

Chinese buddhists have an extremely complex reincarnation cycle that involves a heaven, a hell with ten courts for judgement, and a wheel of transmigration spun by a god-king. Whatever is selected by the wheel becomes the next bodily destination for the soul (Guirand 1959, 408–10). Some afterworlds, like those of the Aztec and the Maya, are similar to the Christian versions – paradise for the good, hell for the evil. However, most are located close to the land of the living and are surprisingly similar to earthly villages. The Huron souls, for example, live in a longhouse village, farm, and otherwise live normal lives. The only difference is a lack of sexual intercourse in the Village of the Dead (Trigger 1990, 122).

It is interesting that many souls must go on a journey or submit to a test before being allowed entry into the relevant afterworld. For example, ancient Egyptians had their evil deeds weighed against a feather. If they outweighed the feather, Osiris denied the soul entry (Budge 1971).

Fijian souls had to get past a giant who hated bachelors and every Fijian male soul carries a lock of his wife's hair as proof of marriage and as a passport (Howells 1986, 153). Menomini Indians had to get past a huge dog who automatically barred any who had been mean to dogs (Howells 1986, 153; Skinner 1913).

The Mexica of central America must undertake a four-year journey into the underworld. It is a hazardous journey that gets more and more difficult as the soul approaches its destination (Berdan 1982, 95–96). Crossing rivers is a fairly common activity for the newly deceased. The most famous of the supernatural rivers was the River Styx of Greek mythology. Said to be like the menstrual blood of Mother Earth, Styx separated the natural world from the underworld. Even today, many Greeks, Irish, and others place money in the corpse's mouth to pay Charon for the ferry ride across the river (Walker 1983, 959–60).

The Lodagao of Africa also send their dead across a river. Each person must pay twenty cowrie shells to take the ferry across although there is no guarantee of a successful crossing. Only good people cross easily. Bad people fall through the ferry and must swim for it (Mbiti 1969, 159–60).

The Ga, also of Africa, believe that the soul must cross a river and have its nose broken on the other bank. This accounts for the nasal sound of the voices of the dead (Mbiti 1969, 160).

By now, you are wondering what a discussion of death and after death has to do with archaeology. Well, how a society perceives death and its aftermath as far as the deceased's soul is concerned is reflected in its treatment of its dead – how it disposes of the body, for example. Hindu bodies must be cremated and the soul cracked open to release the spirit. Orthodox Jewish people would on the other hand never consider cremation since the soul is believed to directly experience the pain of the burning as if it still resided in the body.

Many cultures send their deceased loved ones off with goods they will need in the afterworld. Greeks put coins in the mouth to pay the ferry master. Fijians travel with a lock of their wife's hair. Food, furniture, and all manner of stuff find their way into the graves. Death and a culture's attitude towards it also affects other aspects of life.

The Yanomamo spend hours every day taking psychedelic drugs to help fight off sorcerers' attempts to steal their souls. The Navajo abandon houses (and their contents) when someone dies within them. Promises of instant paradise turn ordinary people into fanatical martyrs and the knowledge that the afterlife will be worse or better than life forces people into resigned acceptance of their current life.

Whether we realise it or not, death, the end of life, affects almost everything people do in their lives. They cover their faces when they sneeze to keep their souls from being blown out of their bodies by the force of the sneeze. They engage in fitness activities to put off the inevitable. They develop elaborate funeral rituals and inheritance rules and they drive to achieve recognition in this life so they will be remembered after death. So death affects the ways all people live. By realising this, we can examine prehistoric and ancient cultures with new eyes. We can explain what appears to be irrational, odd, or strange. We can extend our knowledge of the ancestors far beyond what we now know by altering the perspective through which we view the world at large.

NOTES

* This paper was first presented at the Scottish Archaeological Forum Conference on Death and the Supernatural on 24 April 1993, Glasgow, Scotland.

1. Euroamerican or Euroamerican Community refer to the cultural complex typical of the Caucasian Judeo-Christian groups that form the majority populations of Europe and North America.

BIBLIOGRAPHY

Arhem, K. 1992. Dance of the Water People. *Natural History* 1/92, 46–53.

Balikci, A. 1989. *The Netsilik Eskimo.* Waveland Press, Inc. Prospect Heights.

Beaglehole, E. and P. Beaglehole 1976. *Hopi of the Second Mesa.* Kraus Reprint Co. (Memoirs of the American Anthropological Association), New York.

Berdan, F. F. 1982. *The Aztecs of Central Mexico: An Imperial Society.* Holt Rinehart and Winston, New York.

Budge, W. 1971. *Egyptian Magic.* Dover Publications, Inc., New York. [Originally published in 1901].

Chagnon, N. A. 1983. *Yanomamo: The Fierce People* (third edition). Holt, Rinehart and Winston, New York.

Downs, J. F. 1984. *The Navajo.* Waveland Press, Prospect Heights.

Gervais, K. G. 1986. *Redefining Death.* Yale University Press, New Haven.

Green, M. and W. Daniel 1980. Brain death and personal identity. *Philosophy and Public Affairs* 9 (2), 105–133.

Guirand, F. (ed.) 1959. *Larousse Encyclopedia of Mythology.* Batchworth Press Ltd, London.

Hassell, S. 1966. *Know the Navajo.* Estes Park, Colorado.

Hostetler, J. A. and E. H. Certrude 1980. *The Hutterites in North America.* Holt, Rinehart and Winston, New York.

Howells, W. 1986. *The Heathens Primitive Man and His Religions.* Sheffield Publishing Co., Salem. [originally published in 1948].

Kearney, M. 1986. *The Winds of Ixtepeji: World View and Society in a Zapotec Town.* Waveland Press, Prospect Heights.

Kennedy, J. G. AHM. 1978. *Tarahumara of the Sierra Madre: Beer, Ecology, and Social Organization.* Publishing Corporation, Chicago.

Lewis, O. 1960. *Tepoztlan Village in Mexico,* Holt, Rinehart and Winston, New York.

Malinowski, B. 1948. Baloma. The spirits of the dead. In *Magic, Science and Religion.* Faber and West, London.

Mbiti, J. S. 1969. *African Religions and Philosophy.* Frederick A. Praeger, New York.

Middleton, J. 1966. *The Lugbara of Uganda.* Holt, Rinehart and Winston, New York.

Morton, W. S. 1980. *China: Its History and Culture.* McGraw-Hill, New York.

Parry, J. 1982. Sacrificial death and the necrophagus ascetic. In M. Bloch and J. Parry (eds), *Death and The Regeneration of Life,* 74–110. Cambridge University Press, New York.

Paulme, D. 1940. *Organisation Sociale Des Dogons.* Institut de Droit Compare (Etudes de Sociologie et D'Ethnologie Juridique 32).

Sandstrom, A. R. 1991. *Corn is Our Blood: Culture and Ethnic Identity in a Contemporary Aztec Indian Village.* University of Oklahoma Press.

Simmons, M. 1980. *Witchcraft in the Southwest. Spanish and Indian Supernaturalism on the Rio Grande.* University of Nebraska Press, Lincoln, NE.

Skinner, A. 1913. *Social Life and Ceremonial Bundles of the Menomini Indians.* (Anthropological Papers of the American Museum of Natural History 13).

Stearman, A. M. 1989. *Yuqui Forest Nomads in a Changing World.* Holt, Rinehart and Winston, New York.

Tannenbaum, F. 1950. *Mexico: The Struggle for Peace and Bread.* Knopf, New York.

Trigger, B. G. 1990. *The Huron: Farmers of the North* (second edition). Holt, Rinehart and Winston, New York.

Yogt, E. Z. 1990. *The Zinacantecos of Mexico: A Modern Maya Way of Life.* Holt, Rinehart and Winston, New York.

von Graeve, B. 1989. *The Pacaa Nova Clash of Cultures on the Brazilian Frontier.* Broadview Press, Peterborough.

Wagiey, C. 1983. *Welcome of Tears The Tapirapé Indians of Central Brazil.* Waveland Press, Prospect Heights.

Walker, B. 1983. *The Woman's Encyclopedia of Myths and Secrets.* Harper Collins, New York.

Woodburn, J. 1982. Social dimensions of death in four African hunting and gathering societies. In M. Bloch and J. Parry (eds), *Death and The Regeneration of Life,* 187–210. Cambridge University Press, New York.

Youngner, S. J., C. S. Landefeld, C. J. Coulton, B. W. Juknialis, and M. Leary 1989. 'Brain death' and organ retrieval. A cross-sectional survey of knowledge and concepts among health professionals. *Journal of the American Medical Association* 261 (15), 2205–2210.

2

Fearing and celebrating the dead in southern Madagascar

Mike Parker Pearson

In the not-so-recent film, *The Addams Family*, there is a scene where Gomez and Morticia are standing in a cemetery. 'Do you remember when we met?' he asks her. 'It was my first funeral', she replies. 'A boy, a girl, an open grave.' The Addams family are presented as the morbid, dysfunctional negation of family life and yet, for millions of people outside the 'western way of death', funerals are precisely the situations when they will meet members of the opposite sex and even form sexual liaisons with them. Such celebrations of death, involving hundreds or even thousands of mourners in noisy and lengthy ceremonies, are common in many parts of the world (Huntington and Metcalf 1979; Bloch and Parry 1982). Madagascar is well known for its cults of ancestors and elaborate funerary rituals, such as the *famadihana* ('bone turning' or secondary funeral) amongst the Merina, when corpses are removed from the collective tomb, some years after their burial, and danced around before being returned in new wraps to their place of rest (Bloch 1971; Mack 1986).

Amongst the Tandroy ('people of the land of thorns') of the extreme south of Madagascar, funerals have a similarly festive quality but the dead remain undisturbed after the moment of burial. This is a tradition of single burial which is found amongst groups such as the Mahafaly, Karembola, and Sakalava in the south and west of Madagascar, differing from the collective rites so common elsewhere in this large country, the fourth largest island in the world. For the Tandroy the dead never return physically to the world of the living but, as is common throughout the country, individual spirits of the dead may possess particular people and guide their actions. The ancestors are also invoked at ceremonies and may bring good fortune or ill chance to their successors.

Tandroy mortuary practices have been written about since the eighteenth century (Drury 1729; Defoort 1913; Decary 1930, 1933; Heurtebize 1986) and there are also detailed studies of their neighbours, the Mahafaly (Schomerus-Gernböck 1981), the Karembola (Middleton 1987), the Bara (Huntington 1988), and the Sakalava (Feeley-Harnik 1991). A current project by the University of Sheffield and the Museum of Art and Archaeology in Antananarivo is investigating the long-term development of these practices, which have been given form in the shape of changing tomb styles, culminating in the monumental stone tombs that are constructed today. This project is attempting to place these changes within the context of human settlement and land use in the region over the last two thousand years, using archaeological survey, vegetational analysis, oral history, palaeo-ecology, and written history.

FUNERALS TODAY

The moment of death is normally marked by the blowing of a conch shell and the slaughter of a bull, steer, or cow. The traditional associations of a cow for a woman, a favourite bull for a man, and a calf for a child are not always followed. Cattle are the required animals for sacrifice during funerals, though sheep are the other species through whose sacrifice communications with the community of ancestors are initiatied. For the funerals of both women and men, steers are the preferred animals of sacrifice. Sometimes, in anticipation of the death of an ailing or very elderly person, preparations will be made prior to death, including the making of the tree-trunk coffin. The corpse is washed and remains in the house where the death took place. A shelter of green aloe leaves (called a *lapa* or 'palace') is built onto the south side of the house and a fire is lit and tended at one corner. From this moment until completion of ceremonies, the dead will be tended by a *tsimahaivelo* ('he who does not know the living' or funerary priest). The relationship of this man and his assistants to the family holding the funeral is one which is fixed by obligation. Whereas in some areas it is a task required of wife-taking lineages by wife-givers (Middleton 1987), in central Androy it appears to derive from century-old ties between free lineages and ex-slave lineages. The *tsimahaivelo* must take on the pollution and moral blame of death by organising the rites and protecting the living during this dangerous time. In the proceedings to come, he must ensure that the living are finally separated from the dead by cutting a thread which is attached at one end to the tomb and held at the other by the mourners. The possessions of the deceased and the house in which death occurred are also polluted; the house, with items inside, is burnt at the end of the funeral sequence.

The funeral may take place several weeks or months after death; elaborate arrangements must be made and long-distance invitations must be communicated. During that time the immediate kin will mourn the dead within the *lapa*. The funeral normally takes between one and three days, involving hundreds or even thousands of people. It is a costly undertaking, which requires the purchase of rice, home-made rum and other alcohol (such as wine), gun cartridges, the coffin, and funerary cloths, the provision of cattle, sheep, and goats as gifts and food for the mourners, and the hiring of praise-singers and gunmen. All of these expenses are set down on paper and are totalled against the income which the funeral brings: gifts of money, cattle, sheep, goats, and perhaps other smaller items. The main events take place in the village of the deceased; the men sit in a line or half-circle on the east side, shaded by umbrellas from the sun and facing the women who sit, stand, sing, or dance. The men will join in the dancing and, amongst the hubbub, shotguns are fired at irregular intervals. Before dawn the hosts will have slaughtered cattle, sheep, and goats which will be stewed in pots during the day. Each group of guests receives a sheep or goat for their own consumption during the celebrations. In return, they will each present a gift of paper money fixed to a bamboo pole and known as *basy mena* ('red gun'). In addition, those families who are wife-takers of the host lineage will provide a gift of cattle whilst a similar gift is demanded of the host by those who are his wife-givers. It is not uncommon for the wife-givers to belittle or humiliate the wife-taking group for the quality or number of cattle offered. This relationship based on marriage ties is at the heart of Tandroy exchange and is mobilised principally at funerals. The Tandroy enjoy a reputation throughout Madagascar as hard workers, moving to plantations and towns to work for money which will be saved for funerals and tomb construction. Attempts by the French administration prior to independence in 1960 to prevent what they saw as wasteful use of resources only stimulated Tandroy defiance, manifest in part by increasing consumption (Guérin 1977). This extensive channelling of wealth (animal and monetary) and resources (labour and foodstuffs) into mortuary rituals might be described as a funerary economy.

On the night prior to burial the participants sing and dance late into the night and the older children and younger adults indulge in covert sexual liaisons. The raucous and uncontrolled behaviour of people during the funeral is mirrored in the deliberate stampeding of the lineage's cattle, which are shown off during the day. On the day of burial, as the sun is setting, the corpse is brought out of the house and taken to the cemetery area. Traditionally the coffin was fitted together on the walk to the cemetery, with the male top (marked by its frontal prong) fitted onto the female base. It is now more usual that the corpse is coffined in its house. The house wall is broken down for its removal and the coffin, tressed and draped in folded funerary cloths, is carried either by hand or by hand-pulled bullock cart. At two recent funerals, one of a politician killed at a demonstration and the other of the mother of Retsihisatse (one of this project's members), a car was used as the hearse. The cattle lead the procession to the burial place, followed by the coffin with the mourners behind. Only a proportion of the funeral-goers will attend this part and many start for home at this point.

At the cemetery one or more cattle are selected, roped, and pulled down on their left side to the east of the place of burial. Male cattle slaughtered at the tomb must be castrates so as to avoid the interference of their sexual potency with the sacredness of the burial place. The animals are dispatched with a spear wound to the lungs or a knife cut to the throat and their blood spills onto the ground. The *tsimahaivelo* takes a leafy branch and dips it in the blood of the first sacrifice, then marks with the branch on the ground where the grave is to be cut on an east-west axis. The grave is dug with a spade which will be discarded once this task is completed. Where the ground is stony, the ground is broken but only as a token grave trench. The coffin is then placed in the grave cut, the top is taken off and the brown funerary cloths (*lamba mena* or 'red shawls') are placed inside the coffin, which is then closed. After the grave is back-filled, it is covered by an oval stone cairn, piled up by the immediate kin. The moment of burial is normally timed for sunset but the cattle killing may take place much earlier. Those animals killed at the grave are provided by close kin of the deceased and the meat is taken by non-kin, notably the *tsimahaivelo* and the 'children of women' (the wife-takers to the hosts). The large amount of meat from the slaughtered animals may go off quickly in the heat and is something of a double-edged gift but today it is speedily butchered, loaded onto bullock carts, and may be taken to the nearest market for sale. In recent years, those groups who act as semi-professional *tsimahaivelo* have profited from this and from the provision of increasingly rare and expensive tree trunks suitable for coffins.

BUILDING TOMBS

Tombs are built in a variety of locations, normally on east-facing hillsides or along roadsides where they form prominent monuments. They may be sited singly or in a loose cluster tthat could be called a cemetery. They must be placed on the 'outside', away from settlement and fields, in areas that arenot cultivated. Thereafter, the ground, trees, and pasture in their vicinity may not be cut, harvested, collected, or grazed.

The spatial organisation of tombs follows certain rules of orientation. The lineage cemeteries grow from south to north (from senior to junior) and women are buried to the west of men. This matches the principle of seniority in the south as found in settlements; the most senior family within a patriline will normally have their houses to the south of other junior members. Equally, the houses of multiple wives of a polygamous husband will be placed similarly according to their seniority. At the settlement level the distinction between the sacred east and the profane west is often marked in the location of the latrine area to the west.

During the months and years after burial, tomb building is organised on an informal and intermittent basis. A single tomb may take as many as six years to construct. The work party gathers perhaps for half a day's labour every two to three weeks; rum is drunk and afterwards an animal is slaughtered and its raw meat is shared out. Around the oval cairn a large rectangular stone wall is constructed in stones and mortar between 7 and 30 metres in length, slightly less in breadth, and to a height of about 1.5 metres. The space between wall and cairn is then filled up with loose rubble to the height of the wall top. Male graves are marked by two standing stones, *vatolahy* ('man stones'), which are erected at the east (front) end and at the west (rear) end of the tomb. These are always put up prior to the construction of the walls, held in place with wooden scaffolding, and may stand to a height of 4 or more metres though most are around 3 metres. The most popular source for these standing stones is in the west of Androy on the edge of Mahafaly country along the Menarandra River, and they are transported by bullock cart. Carts are also used for hauling the rubble to fill in the tomb. In the sandy areas of Androy the stone may have been brought many miles. Prior to the introduction of carts in the 1930s, stones were carried by hand but stone tomb construction was restricted to those localities with easy access to materials. The tomb can be finished off with a 'death house' or sarcophagus representation above the oval cairn (in the case of men's burials although it can also be a feature of women's tombs), paintings all over the walls, and small wooden sculpted posts (the latter are a feature of Mahafaly tombs and are found in the western part of Androy). On completion of the tomb, more cattle are slaughtered and their bucrania, along with the bucrania of all the cattle killed from the moment of death, during the funeral and during the tomb building, are carefully arranged on the tomb so as to face eastwards.

The social relationships engaged in the construction sequence revolve around the relationship of wife-givers and wife-takers. In the case of the death of a man, his children are required to build the tomb walls. Those of the first wife construct the front, east wall and those of the second and third build the north and south walls. The precise order varies through-out the region but the front wall is always constructed by kin of the first wife. The growing professionalism evident in praise-singing, coffin manufacture, and *vatolahy* production is also encroaching into tomb construction; wealthy lineages may fulfil their obligations as wife-takers by employing professional masons to construct the tombs. In northern Androy, the formal divisions of responsibilities for building each wall may be abandoned so that all contribute to the paying of a mason who may receive two cattle for each of the four walls. It may be that the earlier relationship was similar to that noted among the Karembola, where the *tsimahaivelo* and assistants are drawn from the wife-takers (Middleton 1987), although Decary (1936) recorded that *tsimahaivelo* were drawn from slave families in eastern Androy. The choices of where to place individual corpses within tombs and the nature of their positioning also serve to define social relationships. The primary burial may be that of an adult woman or man. Women may be buried in their own tomb when they die before their husband. Children who die before the age of about six are buried in a children's burial area, normally under small cairns. These cemeteries are often placed nearer the abodes of the living, close to the fields. Older boys and girls who are still dependants of their parents, without their own offspring, may be buried in 'secondary' or satellite graves dug into the tomb of a parent or grand-parent. Widows are also often incorporated into the tomb of their last husband. In many parts of Madagascar it is expected that the woman's body be returned for burial from her husband's village to that of her natal kin. There is no fixed rule in Androy and women's funerals are negotiated between affines. Those dependants buried secondarily in a tomb are placed always to the north (the junior direction) of the primary burial. Those of males will be marked by a second pair of standing stones; it is almost never the case that men are secondary burials to women. Women are always buried slightly to the west of men when they share the same tomb. Secondary interments may involve the exten-sion of an existing tomb by adding a new section to its north side or by enveloping it within a larger build. Standing stones may be erected for other reasons, such as the result of a dream about the dead by a family member. Single standing stones may be put up, often away from the tomb areas, as cenotaphs for men who have died away from home whose bodies have not been returned for burial.

THE ORIGINS OF STONE TOMB BUILDING

There are, today, a large number of disused or in-use burial places hidden in primary forest. The graves are dug into the sand and are surrounded by rectangular enclosures constructed not out of stone but with timber posts. These palisades, known as *tseke*, are adorned with cattle bucrania. These burial places are very different from the highly visible stone tomb cemeteries, although the same word, *lonake*, is used for both (curiously it means 'lineage head' in the neighbouring Tanosy dialect). This method of burial is still predominant in the sandy areas of central and southern Androy but is being replaced by stone tombs, wooden palisade tombs with stone infill, and small stone and concrete Christian graves (the latter particularly in the far south). Today the difference between stone tombs and forest burial is perceived as a matter of wealth, the former requiring a greater investment.

The Tandroy tradition of palisade burial in forest cemeteries is recorded in the first decade of the eighteenth century. Robert Drury, who spent about six years from 1703 as a slave in Androy, described practices that have no modern counterpart:

> The veneration they have for the memory of their forefathers, and the assurance they have of their spirits always existing, appears in every circumstance of the few religious duties they perform. . . . Every family has a peculiar burying-place, which no other person durst infringe upon. . . . This is enclosed and fenced round with sticks like palisades; when they come near the place, the corpse [in its tree-trunk coffin] is set down without it, and they proceed to the rest of the ceremony, which is to make four fires, one at each corner of the outside of the burying-place. On these fires they burn the ox or cow, which was before killed on purpose, dividing it into quarters, and consuming it wholly with the fire; then they sprinkle frankincense on the coals and spread them round about. . . . Two or three persons are sent in to dig the grave, which is commonly made seven or eight feet deep, and the corpse is placed in it and covered with the earth. . . . There are commonly a great number of people without, who are busied in cutting up and dividing amongst themselves the cattle which are given them for that purpose, if it is a great and rich family who can afford it. But the poorer sort cannot gratify their friends so bountifully.

Today there is no knowledge of the quartering of a cow and the burning of each quarter at the corners of the enclosure, although fire is an important aspect of burial today: a fire is maintained prior to burial at the corner of the house, and another is lit at the front of the tomb to burn the fatty hump of the first steer to be killed at the graveside. This is an offering for the ancestors. It is a token in comparison with the rite recorded by Drury. It has been suggested that he actually described Sakalava funerary rites (Molet-Sauvaget 1992) but this interpretation leaves no room for short-term changes in ritual over some ten generations.

The earliest stone tombs are found in western and northern Androy, in areas which had been uninhabited or depopulated until the nineteenth century. They are constructed of drystone masonry and have low walls. Any bucrania or other items placed on them have long since disintegrated (the bucrania last about thirty-five years). These early tombs, dating to between 1850 and 1880, are small house-sized rectangular cairns, which resemble broken-down houses in stone rather than in wood. By 1880, certain individuals were buried under larger tombs, more akin to those of today and known as *valavato* ('stone cattle pen'), metaphoric translations in stone and bone of the wooden corrals and their living herds. Buried under the earliest stone tombs of both types were men of the middle-ranking Afomarolahy clan (Heurtebize 1986), who moved into the uninhabited margins of the Tandroy kingdom's north-western frontier between 1780 and 1850. They were located in areas of cattle pasture near the transitory cattle camps, at some distance from the traditional *tseke* cemeteries and in an area of potential conflict with other pastoralists, notably the Bara. In one sense the stone tombs were permanent markers laying claim to grazing areas and in another they marked a break with tradition and with the central authority of the Andriamañare (the royal clan), whose power was on the wane under the kingship of Bahary. Those buried under these early stone tombs were men wealthy in cattle but without the marriage connections and social positions of certain other Afomarolahy. They are remembered today not as founding ancestors themselves but as the sons and grandsons of founding ancestors of various lineages and sub-lineages of the Afomarolahy. The Afomarolahy population was growing exponentially at this time and the appearance of stone tombs may have served to assert distinctive new identities at lineage level in the face of an increasingly large and amorphous clan structure. Many *valavato* are marked by the association of a particular tree, the *hazomalanga*, which has been planted at the corners and along the walls of these tombs. It was thought that such trees marked royal burials (Decary 1962, 291; Parker Pearson 1992) but this is not generally the case. It would seem that these tombs were often those of senior members of different clans, generally dating to the early to mid-twentieth century. The fashion of stone tomb construction was adopted by the royal dynasty, copying the Afomarolahy, when one of the last princes, Mahasese, a member of the Andriamanare clan, who died around 1905–1910, was buried in a large stone tomb. Thus the association of these tombs with the early successors of the royal dynasty, such as Mahasese, is only a secondary phenomenon (*contra* Parker Pearson 1992).

The tradition of royal burial amongst certain members of the Andria-mañare clan is very different from that of the normal rite. As with the Sakalava kings and queens, whose bodies are considered especially dangerous and polluting (Feeley-Harnik 1991, 39–43), the bodies of Tandroy royalty were traditionally buried so as not to come into contact with the earth. To this end, they were buried above ground. One such burial place is a cave in the hillside of Angavo, a mountain that was once the northern border of Androy. This rite seems largely to have ended with the kingship although above-ground burial is still accorded to certain successors of the old monarchy.

The context for the innovation of monumental stone tombs is that of the collapse of kingship and the break-up of the cohesive and nucleated nature of androy settlement and society. Prior to the 1880s it appears, from settlement archaeology, that the Tandroy were settled in a variety of large and small settlements, among which were a number of royal capitals and sub-capitals. The chief of these, known as Fenoarivo and located near the modern village of Ambaro, fragmented into a variety of smaller villages. According to oral traditions of the Andriamañare, the various clans split up and moved to new lands. The precise reasons remain to be investigated and future work will attempt to clarify this problem.

ACKNOWLEDGEMENTS

Particular thanks are due to the field team: Karen Godden, Ramilisonina, Victor Razanatovo, Retsihisatse, and Jean-Luc Schwenninger. Tsihan-datse, Mahatomba, and other Andriamañare in Ambaro, Retsihisatse's family in Analamahery, and the Fokontany of Antanimora are to be thanked for their permission and help. We have benefited from the help and advice of Sarah Fee, Georges Heurtebize, John Mack, Karen Middle-ton, Chantal Radimilahy, Jean-Aimé Rakotoarisoa, and Henry Wright. Fieldwork has been supported by the British Academy, The Nuffield Foundation, the N.E.R.C., the National Geographic Society, and the Society of Antiquaries.

BIBLIOGRAPHY

Bloch, M. 1971. *Placing the Dead: Tombs, Ancestral Villages and Kinship Organization in Madagascar*. Seminar Press, London.
Bloch, M. and J. Parry (eds) 1982. *Death and the Regeneration of Life*. Cambridge University Press, Cambridge.
Decary, R. 1930 and 1933. *L'Androy (Extrême-Sud Madagascar): Essai de Monographie Regionale*, vols 1 and 2. Société d'Editions Géographiques, Maritimes et Coloniales, Paris.

Decary, R. 1962. *Le Mort et les Coutumes Funéraires à Madagascar*. Maisonneuve et Larose, Paris.

Defoort, E. 1913. *L'Androy. Essai de Monographie*. (Bulletin Économique de Madagascar 2), Antananarivo.

Drury, R. 1729. *Madagascar: or Robert Drury's Journal during Fifteen Years' Captivity on that Island*. Meadows, London.

Feeley-Harnik, G. 1991. *A Green Estate: Restoring Independence in Madagascar*. Smithsonian Institution Press, Washington.

Guérin, M. 1977. *Le Defi: L'Androy et l'Appel à la Vie*. Ambozontany, Fianarantsoa.

Heurtebize, G. 1986. *Histoire des Afomarolahy (Extrême-Sud de Madagascar)*. CNRS, Paris.

Huntington, R. 1988. *Gender and Social Structure in Madagascar*. Indiana University Press, Bloomington, Illinois.

Huntington, R. and P. Metcalf 1979. *Celebrations of Death: the Anthropology of Mortuary Ritual*. Cambridge University Press, Cambridge.

Mack, J. 1986. *Madagascar: Island of the Ancestors*. British Museum, London.

Middleton, K. 1987. Marriages and Funerals: Some Aspects of Karembola Political Symbolism (Madagascar). Unpublished D.Phil. thesis, University of Oxford.

Molet-Sauvaget, A. 1992. *Madagascar ou le journal de Robert Drury par Daniel Defoe*. Harmattan, Paris.

Parker Pearson, M. 1992. Tombs and monumentality in southern Madagascar: preliminary results of the central Androy survey. *Antiquity* 66, 941–948.

Schomerus-Gernböck, L. 1981. *Die Mahafaly: Eine ethnisches Gruppe im südwesten Madagaskars*. Dietrich Reimer, Berlin.

3

Cremation: a spectacle and a journey

Jane Downes

My *desire to study cremation* in another culture was fuelled by something common to many archaeologists at present – a wish to gain a more informed interpretation of past societies through a better knowledge of the beliefs of traditional societies. The Hindu religion is much famed for cremation rites, and has been the subject of much anthropological work (cf. Parry 1994), particularly Balinese Hindu cremation (cf. Covarrubias 1986; Hobart 1978). I wished to witness a Hindu cremation from an ethno-archaeological point of view, for the details of the technologies of cremation and the residues of the rites in relation to the architecture are not of prime concern in most anthropological studies.

A BALINESE CREMATION

I will describe here the cremation ceremony itself, although the word cremation in the context of the Hindu Balinese is generally used by anthropologists and other commentators as an umbrella term to encapsulate the lengthy series of events staged often over a long period and in a different locales. The burning of the body is only one short event within this sequence but it is the most public of the events, a spectacle and lavish celebratory ceremony entailing conspicuous consumption.

To better understand the significance of a very prescriptive series of rituals it is necessary to outline briefly the complex and derivative cosmological scheme which the Balinese employ. Space is ordered horizontally on two principal axes. The main directional axis is associated with ritual purity and given physical form in the topography of Bali, with the downhill flow of water from the central mountainous area where the gods reside, to the sea, home of demons. To the majority of Balinese, living on the southern tip of Bali, this axis runs north-south. The axis bisecting this follows the course of the sun from east to west. Each of the four major cardinal directions are associated with a particular deity, element, colour, part of the body, and other properties. The four major cardinal directions, the lesser four that lie between, and the centre form a nine-part ritual grid with wide applications. Space is also divided vertically into the ranked worlds of the universe: the heavens, the world of people, and the underworld. All aspects of daily life involve a conscious working knowledge of orientation and classification; a constant sense of place and awareness of direction. Nowhere is this better illustrated than through mortuary rites. Although these include cremation, the individual is transformed from a physical being to an ancestral spirit through an extremely lengthy and complex process during which the soul takes a journey from the house compound, through a series of purifications, to eventually return to the house and reside in the house temple.

To the Hindu Balinese, cremation of a deceased relative is the most pressing obligation a person carries, for it is only by this route that the soul can journey to heaven and finally achieve the status of a deified ancestor to be worshipped in the family temple. The ideal is not always realised, and many of the deceased remain interred in the graveyard and are never accorded a cremation ceremony, the most commonly stated reason being that the costs of the lavish ceremonies are prohibitively high. However, this was not the case with the cremation ceremony that took place during my stay which involved the immolation of a *pemangku*, or low caste priest, who had died approximately a week before and had not been interred. This was said by the family, with whom I both lived and attended the cremation, to be because Galungan, one of the major religious calendrical events when the deified ancestors descend to their former homes, was just over a week away. The presence of a corpse in the house compound at such a time was said to be unacceptable. It was also considered inappropriate to bury a *pemangku* as contact with the earth can pollute. The cost of the cremation was borne by the congregation of the temple of which the *pemangku* had been the keeper.

On the afternoon of the cremation we waited in the street that ran downhill to the 'death temple' (*pura dalem*) and cemetery, which lay at the south-western edge of the village (Fig. 1), not knowing quite what to expect. I felt excited that I was to see the cremation, but apprehensive at what felt like an intrusion into a private ceremony. Coming down the hill towards us we suddenly saw people running, and behind them, carried on a wooden frame by about fifty men, was a huge wooden bull

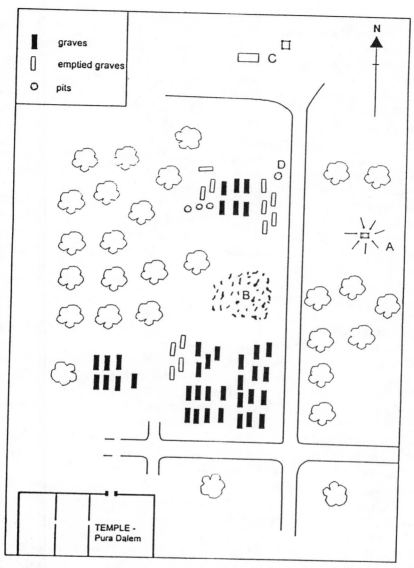

Figure 1. A Balinese cemetery showing A - cremation mound, B - burnt debris midden, C - site of further ceremonies, and D - refuse pit.

coloured white and decorated with yellow and gold. Straddling the back of the bull was a young man. Following the bull was a group of women all carrying offerings (*bantens*) decorated with deep yellow flowers. After the women came a very tall tower also carried on a frame.

This tower was also white and decorated with yellow and gold, and to its side clung a *pedanda*, or high caste priest, dressed in black in sharp contrast to the tower. The tower was decorated on the rear with a large swan with wings outstretched. An orchestra followed the tower, playing loud percussion music. Women carrying trays of pots of holy water came next, and finally a throng of villagers and some tourists. The procession rushed down the street noisily, with the bull and the tower swaying. At the junction with the lane leading west into the graveyard the tower containing the corpse was turned around three times, which I was aware was to confuse the spirit of the deceased should it try to find its way back to the house. Finally, the procession stopped at the foot of a small artificial earthen mound (Fig. 1, A) upon which was situated a tall four-posted open bamboo tower, suspended from the roof of which was a white cloth. This mound was at the end of a narrow path which skirted the graveyard. We stood close to the open graves from which bodies had been disinterred for cremation, craning to see. The whole area was heavily wooded and a large canopy of trees overhung the cremation mound giving the place an enclosed atmosphere after the bright street.

A white, cloth-wrapped bundle of effigies was removed from the *wadah* tower while the bull was placed on a platform under the bamboo structure. The back of the bull was removed and the white covered coffin lifted down from the *wadah* tower and brought over to the bull, after which the body was removed from the coffin and placed in the bull. Close family crowded around the sarcophagus and placed offerings on the body, and then a lengthy period elapsed while the final lustrations took place. Tray after tray of small earthenware vessels of different shapes containing holy water were passed up to the officiating *pedanda* who stood up high to the north of the corpse. After each pot was emptied of holy water it was thrown to the ground and smashed as items connected with the ceremony were polluted and could not be retained or removed from the cemetery. While these ablutions took place, the women of the family stood to the west at the foot of the mound, holding the effigies at shoulder height. At the conclusion of the cleansing of the corpse with holy water these were passed up, placed on top of the corpse and the lid of the bull replaced. The *bantens* and other food offerings were put on the platform underneath the bull on top of a pile of split palm and bamboo, as were large congratulatory wreaths from other sectors of the community. The pyre was ignited by a male relative, by means of lighting two gas jets one at each end of the wood pile. The *wadah* tower was also ignited at a site not far from the pyre (Fig. 1, B). During the burning the men and small boys sat on the ground at the foot of the mound. The women and the widow stood to the north of the pyre. A *pemangku* herself, the widow was dressed in a white blouse while the rest of the women wore black blouses.

The pyre blazed through the bottom of the wooden bull while the sides and legs remained intact. After the body had fallen through the bottom of the bull onto the pyre, one or two men assisted the body to burn more quickly by poking it with long sticks and lifting it up to help the air circulate. The manipulation and fragmentation of the body during burning also serves to aid the spirit to escape the body. When the flesh had burnt off and the bones had been reduced through agitation to fairly small fragments, the pyre was quickly quenched with water brought up in large buckets by the women. The widow took a small pot of holy water and sprinkled it over the remains, immediately after which the bone fragments were rapidly picked out of the ashes by the women and put in a two clay bowls, while the children searched the pyre for coins which had formed part of the effigies and offerings. The bowls were carried to the base of the mound where the bones were washed and transferred to another bowl; the first bowls were then smashed on the ground. The cremation had taken two and a half hours, the use of the gas jets having shortened the length of time greatly from the whole day that used to be set aside for cremations. The cremation ceremony takes place within a day; the cremated bones are required to be in the river or sea by sunset.

The focus of activity then shifted over to a clearing just north of the cemetery (Fig. 1, C), where another bamboo tower had been erected, underneath which stood large pots of holy water. The pot containing the burnt bone was taken to a long table situated near this tower, and a screen was drawn around the table. It was said that the bones were re-assembled in human form. Prayers were chanted, predominantly by the women, with the widow presiding. As darkness drew in, the bone fragments were wrapped in white cloth and placed in a large silver vessel which sat under a small bamboo tower in the back of a van. The family then proceeded to the river where the bones, offerings, and the tower were thrown in to be swept downstream and out to sea.

The coincidence that occurs between the spiritual journey of the soul from life to death and the physical journey of the corpse through space and time should be stressed. Both paths are defined through classifications derived from cosmological interpretation and their coincidence in ritual performance provides essential metaphorical links between religious experience and daily life (Richards 1996). The deceased makes a journey, the movement of which is on two planes which is detailed in a paper by Hobart (1978) in which he describes the movement of the body from the house, downhill in a southerly, inauspicious direction, finally to the sea as cremated bones, and the return of the soul northwards and uphill back to the house to reside in the family temple.

CREMATION RESIDUES

A visit to the cemetery was made the day after the cremation had taken place, and a careful record made of the location of the debris. Upon the cremation mound itself (Fig. 1, A) two sets of post-holes were visible, of which the inner, slighter, four had held the fuel in place, and the larger four had held the posts of the tall superstructure. To the south side of the structure was a large spread of c. 200 small trampled abraded sherds of pottery, which remained from a previous cremation ceremony on the mound. The spread of pottery sherds to the north of the structure comprised c. 85 sherds from 8–10 vessels – these sherds were the result of throwing down vessels during the lustration, and had subsequently been fairly well trampled. Complete small vessels were also present that had failed to break when thrown to the ground. On the north-west of the mound and out beyond the mound were discrete groups of pottery of larger sherds; these had resulted from the breaking of the vessel used to wash the bones late on in the ceremony, and as a consequence had not been so heavily trampled.

A return visit was made to the site of the cremation after one month had elapsed. Although the broken vessels were still situated on the mound, the groups of larger sherds that lay on the ground to the north west had been removed and placed on the burnt debris remains of the *wadah* tower (Fig. 1, B), as had the remains of the bamboo four-posted cremation tower. A pit had been dug (Fig. 1, D), into which had been placed the burnt remains of the ceremonial structures that had stood in the clearing to the north of the cemetery and the larger sherds of vessels used in this part of the ceremonies. This pit was not filled in, neither were similar pits amongst the graves which contained the remains of previous cremation ceremonies. It is clear that the material remains were sorted and disposed swiftly and in a proscribed manner. The smashing of the pots and the burning of the structures had been undertaken out of a desire to destroy those artefacts which had been polluted by their contact with the dead and to ensure they did not leave the graveyard. Although an architecture had been created through the rites, it was ephemeral in nature; few traces survived in situ, and the traces evoked little of the spectacle of the event. Conversely, the family temples, which comprise a series of stone-built shrines and are located within the northern part of each family compound, are more permanent structures and, although removed in space from these events, are the resting place of the ancestor.

The Balinese cemetery is the site of some of the purificatory and trans-formatory rites accorded the dead. The cemetery is a place where the dead are interred, but it is not a resting place for the dead; the inhumed dead have to be placated with offerings until they can be cremated.

Although Balinese cemeteries can undergo continuous use for generations, if considered archaeologically, it would not be apparent that cremation is the preferred rite, neither would the complexity of secondary rites be obvious. The mound upon which the bodies are burnt retained no visible indications, even a short time after the ceremony, that a body had been burnt. Rather than filling us with dismay about the limitations of archaeology, the cremation in Bali highlights the importance of considering cremation within the context not only of funerary rituals but in the wider context of social practices.

ARCHAEOLOGICAL INTERPRETATION

The archaeology of death has changed dramatically over the last fifteen years and this research, particularly in the Neolithic and Bronze Age, has been a central arena for the development of a post-processual approach to archaeology. Instead of attempting to assess the quantity and quality of grave goods and the juxtaposition of one body in relation to another as an indication of rank or status, the burial assemblage is considered in the context of mortuary rites (cf. Barrett 1988, 1994; Garwood 1989). This approach allows an exploration of the role of ritual in social reproduction. Until relatively recently, due to a paucity of settlement evidence, studies of the Bronze Age have been heavily reliant on the burial evidence. The focus of this research has been inhumation rites even though cremation was prevalent through the Bronze Age in many parts of Britain. As a consequence there is an enormous discrepancy between the amount of synthetic and interpretative work that has been produced concerning cremations on the one hand and inhumations on the other. As McKinley (1994, 132) notes, 'cremation burials have been the "poor relation" of British cemetery studies', and cremated bone was often discarded upon excavation. This was because cremated bone was perceived as having little potential in the analysis of the sex and age of the individual. Indeed it often appeared difficult to distinguish between cremated human and animal bone deposits. The procedures followed now for the analysis of cremated bone derive from two papers, one by Wells (1960) and the other by Gejvall (1963). These papers were without doubt important in establishing a method of analysing cremated bones, and from that time cremated bones have routinely been analysed and included within excavation reports. However, these papers mark the time at which the study of cremated bone entered the domain of a self-contained 'scientific' approach. Although brief reference is made to ritual and the need to investigate that aspect of cremation, what is meant by the term 'ritual' is the simple comment on the presence or absence of grave goods.

[25]

Bronze-Age cremations were not as commonly accompanied by grave goods as were inhumations, and the range of goods present have been deemed by archaeologists to be 'poorer' than those from inhumations. This is one factor that has led archaeologists to conclude that those who were cremated were of lower status than those who were accorded inhumation. An inhumation often survives as a skeleton with grave goods adorning it or positioned around it; the position of the skeleton within the grave, the direction and orientation, the nature and location of artefacts all give rich scope for discussion of 'the body' and provide many sets of data for looking at patterning and variation. When similar analysis is attempted with interments of cremated bone, it is generally found to be unrewarding for the data is not of the same nature.

Cremations often occur as later insertions into existing burial mounds – these deposits are frequently referred to as secondary burials. The use of the term 'secondary' is misleading for it can be confused with secondary burial, employed in describing a set of rites in a double funeral; moreover it is divisive because the cremation burials have been considered to be of secondary importance to those 'primary' inhumations buried under the mound. That cremated burials were frequently inserted into an existing burial mound or lie within flat cemeteries, in combination with the poverty of grave goods, has been taken to indicate that less effort was expended on the interment of the deceased (cf. Burgess 1980; Megaw and Simpson 1979).

CREMATION RITUAL

There exists great potential for investigating the rites surrounding cremation archaeologically. However, archaeologists have failed to adopt an approach to fieldwork that enables this potential to be realised. I will describe here what I consider the possibilities with regard to Bronze-Age cremation, relating to, but not drawing an analogy between, the Balinese cremation. In Bali, different domains of social experience operate through shared references to a single cosmological structure. It could be asserted that the practices of daily life will always be orientated by such principles: the way in which people order and classify the world to understand their place within it. Interpretations of the role of architecture and material culture within such schemes have been undertaken in the Neolithic and Iron-Age periods and have been useful in breaking down the divides we have created between 'domestic' and 'ritual' (cf. Parker Pearson and Richards 1994). Architectural form and the use of materials can be considered in the context of Bronze-Age cremation ritual as expressive of a classificatory scheme. For instance, grave goods, and artefacts that accompany the body on the pyre, are more profitably interpreted as symbols used in ritual rather than being representative of the possessions of the deceased. The use of materials in artefacts, the construction of a container for the remains, and the position of the remains seem to us to have been subject to many variables which we find confusing to interpret. In the instances of cremation burials, there are traces of rites which can allow a different type of analysis compared with remains from inhumation burial. The recovery of the pyre site is of great significance and is a feature which is seldom found, perhaps because it is rarely looked for. The pyre site can provide evidence of pyre technology, which as McKinley (cf. McKinley 1989) has stressed is a crucial source of information as to how the body was positioned and tended, how the pyre was built, and what fuels were utilised. Ritual labour demands a practical knowledge of resources and a control of technology. Burial rites create an architecture and change the topography (Barrett 1994). Part of this architecture can be the place where the body was stored prior to being cremated, the place where the body was burnt, and the place(s) where the remains were deposited. The journey taken through these rites made careful and particular use of topography (Downes forthcoming), and the location of the pyre itself can be carefully positioned as to be visible from a distance, imposing at close range.

The structuring principles of the funerary ritual are built around a journey. The burial ritual exposes, in explicit terms, principles which find metaphorical re-application in the day-to-day practice of people; they express a practical knowledge rather than a static cosmological scheme. There is not space here to cover the current discussions of structure (or culture) and agency, except to acknowledge the dynamics between the two. The dislocation or congruence of different rites in space may be an indication of beliefs about pollution or the dangerous nature of the dead. However, the location of the events surrounding death in time is (although harder to recover archaeologically) perhaps more significant. The staging of funerary rituals over time can bring a measure of control back to a bad death, can help restore 'ontological security'. As Parry (1994, 6) has said of death and contingency in the context of Hindu funerary rites, 'at the most general level the overall thrust of the whole sequence is to make death appear subject to human control.' A good death is in the right place and at the right time (ibid., 160); the manipulation of both dimensions of time and place can help to restore order in the case of a bad death.

It has often been asserted that two-phase mortuary rites are common to almost all traditional societies. These rites permit a period of separation, or disaggregation, to be followed, after a period of transition, by reintegration or reinstallation. By this process the dangerous nature of the departed soul is made safe by its incorporation into the society of the dead, and the mourners rejoin everyday life. But what if funerary rites are not effective and the dead do not rest, if the ancestors are not benign? There can be no end to mortuary rituals. The tending of the cemetery, the restructuring of burial monuments, and addition of further deposits during the Bronze Age may reflect actions that had to be carried out to contain the dead as a whole, to maintain the equanimity of the spirit world.

In this context, the use of fire as a transformatory agent may be particularly significant. Other elements transform and purify, but fire is powerful, highly visible, uncontrolled/controllable and demands a knowledge of technology and resources. Fire may be more effective in dealing with the polluting nature of the dead, or their dangerous nature, than other agents. The well being of the living can be threatened, not by death but by a bad death or by a failure in the proceedings surrounding death. As a way of making the dead work or rest, cremation may have been more effective than inhumation, or have been deployed in different types of deaths. We must surely consider more than what rituals were enacted, but what the rituals did and how effective they were. If we do not think beyond the small grey fragments of bone we encounter as residues, we cannot do justice to the intentions and beliefs of those we study.

ACKNOWLEDGEMENTS

The field study in Bali was undertaken together with Colin Richards, and with the guidance of the people of Peliatan, Bali. This paper has benefitted from comments by John Barrett and Colin Richards.

BIBLIOGRAPHY

Barrett, J. C. 1988. The living, the dead and the ancestors: Neolithic and Early Bronze Age mortuary practices. In J. C. Barrett and I. A. Kinnes (eds), *The Archaeology of Context in the Neolithic and Bronze Age: recent trends*, 30-41. J. R. Collis, Sheffield.

Barrett, J. C. 1994. *Fragments from Antiquity*. Blackwell, Oxford.

Burgess, C. 1980. *The Age of Stonehenge*. Dent, London.

Connor, L. H. 1995. The action of the body on society: washing a corpse in Bali. *Journal of the Royal Anthropological Institute* 1 (3), 537–559.

Covarrubias, M. 1986. *Island of Bali*. KPI, London.

Downes J. forthcoming. Linga Fiold: The Excavation of a Bronze Age Cemetery on Mainland, Orkney.

Garwood, P. 1991. Ritual tradition and the reconstitution of society. In P. Garwood, D. Jennings, R. Steates, and J. Toms (eds), *Sacred and Profane*, 10-32. Oxford University Committee for Archaeology (Monograph 32), Oxford.

Gejvall, N. G. 1969. Determination of burnt bones from prehistoric graves. *OSSA Letters* 2, 1-13.

Hobart, M. 1978. The path of the soul. In G. B. Milner (ed.), *Natural Symbols in South East Asia*. Soas, London.

McKinley, J. I. 1989. Cremations: expectations, methodologies and realities. In C. A. Roberts, F. Lee, and J. Bintliff (eds), *Burial Archaeology. Current research, methods and developments*, 65-76. British Archaeological Reports (British Series 211), Oxford.

McKinley, J. I. 1994. Pyre and grave goods in British cremations: have we missed something? *Antiquity* 68, 132–134.

Megaw, J. V. S. and D. D. A. Simpson 1979. *Introduction to British Prehistory*. Leicester University Press, Leicester.

Parker Pearson, M. and C. Richards 1994. *Architecture and Order: approaches to social space*. Routledge, London.

Parry, J. P. 1994. *Death in Banares*. Cambridge University Press, Cambridge.

Richards, C. 1996. Life is not that simple: architecture and cosmology in the Balinese house. In T. Darvill and J. Thomas (eds), *Neolithic Houses in North West Europe and beyond*, 171-184. Oxbow (Monograph 57), Oxford.

Wells, C. 1960. A study of cremation. *Antiquity* 34, 29-37.

4

The drowned and the saved: archaeological perspectives on the sea as grave

Tony Pollard

While in Nantucket he had chance to see certain little canoes of dark wood, like the war wood of his native isle; and upon inquiry, he had learned that all whalemen who died in Nantucket were laid in these dark canoes, and that the fancy of being so laid had much pleased him; for it was not unlike the custom of his own race, who, after embalming a dead warrior, stretched him out in his canoe and so left him to be floated away to the starry archipelagos; for not only do they believe that the stars are isles, but that far beyond all visible horizons, their own mild uncontinented seas interflow with the blue heavens; and so form the white breakers of the milky way. He added, that he shuddered at the thought of being buried in his hammock, according to the usual sea-custom, tossed like something vile to the death-devouring sharks.

– Herman Melville, *Moby Dick* (1851, 589)

Parts of this paper were written in the comfort of a small cottage in the village of Melness, on the northern coast of Sutherland. The house has long been associated with the sea, having once been the home of a fisherman who rebuilt the place so that the windows overlooked the water rather than the nearby church as they had done originally. Looking out from the living room window it is not hard to understand why such a dramatic modification was undertaken. To the left you can see the single-walled harbour, which at this time of the year (Christmas) shelters just two small lobster boats. In contrast the right-hand side of the window is dominated by an archipelago of small islands. Just breaking the surface of the water between the harbour and the islands is a ribbon of black rock, which stirs up a flurry of white waves. Out beyond these rocks the waters of the Atlantic stretch out grey and unbroken to the distant horizon.

As I write this paragraph the water is relatively calm, but the scene is not always so peaceful. On a dark winter's night in 1945 the S.S. *Ashberry*, a 4,000–ton armed merchant vessel, fell victim to one of the many storms for which these waters are notorious. In heavy seas the ship's steering gear snapped and despite an attempt to tow her to safety she foundered on the rocks now framed by the cottage window. The violence of the collision snapped the hull in two and spilled her contents, both cargo and crew, into the sea. The wind carried the drowning men's screams to the land, where the villagers spread themselves out along the beach, waving torches in the hope that these guiding lights would be of some help. Alas, all efforts were in vain and over the next few days the bodies of the entire crew, 42 officers and men, were washed ashore.

The bodies were laid out in the same church which the cottage had overlooked prior to its rebuilding. Coffins were brought in from Thurso and the bodies removed, possibly for burial in Newcastle, which had been the ship's destination, as none of the drowned appear to have been interred in the local cemetery, which sits on the shore about two miles further down the loch.

Before arriving at the cottage in Melness I was totally unaware of the tragedy which had taken place in view of its windows. Many of the details were provided by a newspaper clipping which now hangs on the wall just inside the front door of the cottage. The short article, somewhat prosaically entitled 'Village that can't forget the night 42 men died' (*Sunday Express* reporter), noted that a diver had offered to recover the ship's deck gun from the seabed and present it to the village for use as a memorial. Although the gun was recovered it has yet to be installed as a memorial and I was later informed that it is presently rusting behind the local hotel.

The shipwreck described above is typical of many which have occurred in the coastal waters of northern Scotland. Indeed, Melness itself was no stranger to tragedy before this wartime incident. On June 25th 1890 a total of 51 people are recorded to have died as the result of a severe summer storm which swept over much of Scotland, with most of these drowned at sea. The victims included the seven-strong crew of the open fishing boat *Excelsior*; a tragedy which at a stroke wiped out most of the able bodied men of Port Vasco, a small hamlet or clachan in Melness (Temperley 1988).

It is not known whether the bodies of all or some of these unfortunate fishermen were washed ashore, whereas the bodies of the *Ashberry's* crew are reported to have ended up on the beach. Although the sea does not always give up its dead, the shore has long been associated with the dead and the first part of this paper will provide a brief examination of the ways in which this close relationship has manifested itself.

THE SHORE AS GRAVE

One notable feature of the Scottish coastline is the presence of raised beaches. These areas of relatively flat land fringe the shore, appearing as terraces sitting at various heights above present sea level. In the north-west in particular they represent small, but valuable, parcels of exploit-able land in areas otherwise dominated by less forgiving uplands, and today they are often occupied by arable fields or towns and villages.

As the term suggests 'raised beaches' are dry land which had once been submerged beneath the sea, their inland boundaries previously washed by waves as they broke against the shore. In Scotland, fluctua-tions in sea level occurred as a direct result of the end of the most recent (Devension) glaciation when the release of water from the melting ice sheet caused a eustatic rise in sea level. The raised beaches were formed with the recession of these high sea levels and by the upward isostatic rebound of the land, a delayed response to the removal of the down-ward pressure of the massively weighty ice. At the onset of the Holo-cene (post-glacial period), eustatic rise in sea level and isostatic recovery of the land overtook one another several times, with the most important of these events in the present context being the so-called 'main post-glacial transgression' (ca 6,500 BC to 4,000/3,500 BC), which cor-responded in human terms with the Mesolithic period. Evidence for marine exploitation during that time now takes the form of numerous shell middens, which although once situated on the immediate shore are now to be found further inland, removed from their original context by the isostatic recovery of the land.

Past approaches to shell middens have generally been geared toward their role as economic indicators, with the analysis of shells and fish bones providing a useful insight into the nature of prehistoric diet and subsistence. This tightly focused interest has led to the neglect of other aspects of shell middens, including the relatively common occurrence of human remains, usually in the form of disarticulated bones.

The small coastal town of Oban, Argyll boasts perhaps the most famous series of Mesolithic shell middens in Scotland, with the place giving its name to the 'Obanian' culture. The majority of these sites are located in caves discovered in the later part of the nineteenth century. Human remains are recorded from a number of these sites, and the recent radiocarbon dating of human bones from the upper levels of the MacArthur Cave shell midden has established them to be of Iron-Age rather than Mesolithic date as appears to be the case for the shell midden deposits beneath (Saville and Hallen 1995). Although these deposits may indicate the not unusual use of a cave for human burial, which in this case just happens to have been occupied by deposits representing much earlier human activity, I prefer to see the deposition of these bones as a continuation of a long-term identification of the shore with the disposal of the dead.

Evidence for the placement of human remains within shell middens during the Mesolithic has been established by the excavation of several shell middens in the open (as opposed to those in caves) on the island of Oronsay, some 65 km to the south-west of Oban. Within these dense deposits of marine shells a number of disarticulated human bones have been identified. In the nineteenth century it was thought that the deposition of human bones along with the food waste represented by marine shells, at Kiess, Caithness (Laing 1866, 28) and Ardrossan, Ayrshire (Smith 1892), was indicative of cannibalism, and even today there may be a temptation to regard these human remains as just another form of refuse (cf. Smith 1992). However, if we pause to consider the wider cosmological implications of these sites and the environments within which they are located the association between human remains and shell middens can be seen to be more complex.

There is a considerable amount of evidence for excarnation during the Neolithic period in Britain, with disarticulated skeletons in chambered tombs and possible excarnation structures recorded in Scotland (eg. Barclay and Russell-White 1993; Pollard in press). Excarnation is the process, still practised today in places like Tibet and India, where the corpse is left to decay, perhaps on a raised platform. The corpse is commonly associated with strong taboos, occupying the dangerous liminal phase between life and death, inhabiting neither one domain or the other (Van Gennep 1909; Douglas 1966; Huntington and Metcalf 1979). Excarnation ensured the successful passage between life and death with the corpse reduced to clean bones, which could then be disposed of safely and perhaps at times even utilised as a form of material culture in rituals related to the worship of the ancestors.

The discovery of scattered human bones in the Oronsay shell mounds, as well as in several of the middens in Oban, may suggest selective deposition, with the small bones of the hands and feet occuring most frequently (Meiklejohn and Denston 1987; Lorimer 1992). Alterna-

[33]

tively, the presence of these bones may suggest a different depositional process altogether, with the small bones of hands and feet being those one would expect to find left behind once the bones from an excarnated corpse have been collected up and taken elsewhere. Shell middens may therefore have represented places of excarnation, perhaps at times when the shell middens, which at least on Oronsay appear to have accumulated seasonally (Mellars 1987), were not being used as sites for food processing and consumption. Here the world of the living, especially that part of it concerned with the procurement and processing of food, meshed with the world of the dead. This juxtaposition becomes more logical if one considers the context within which the shell middens were situated, straddling the interface between land and sea. The shore is a liminal zone, being neither land nor sea, with the tide suggesting the dominance of one and then the other as it rises and falls.[1] The shore may therefore have been regarded as a safe place within which to deposit corpses, which themselves were passing through the liminal phase between life and death. The various transformations which take place on shell middens, marine animals into food and animal bones into artefacts (antler harpoon heads etc.), are mirrored by the powerful transformation which affected the excarnated corpse (Pollard 1996).

Once the exposure of corpses had done its work, the clean bones were collected together and taken away from the shell midden, perhaps to be buried on the mainland or perhaps even to be buried at sea, with the latter completing the passage from one world to another, life to death, land to sea. Thereafter, the shell midden, which in the case of the Oronsay sites represent quite impressive mounds, may have served as a powerful memorial to the dead. Indeed, there are several instances on the west coast of Scotland of Neolithic chambered tombs being built directly over earlier shell middens (ibid.).

ISLANDS OF THE DEAD

The importance of the shore as a focus for the disposal of the dead is not limited to prehistory. One only needs to visit the northern coast of Scotland to realise that a high proportion of medieval and post-medieval cemeteries are located very close to the shoreline (Fig. 1). Of course, it can be argued that there is a very straightforward reason for this, as in many places the shore represents the only suitable land for settlement and burial. However, in a number of instances these sites are found in places which provide clear views of the sea (on promontories, cliff tops, knolls, etc.) and are located away from settlements; their bastion-like walls isolating the domain of the dead within from that of the living

Figure 1. Walled coastal cemetery at Balnakeil, near Durness, Sutherland.

without. It is in this physical separation that these coastal graveyards bear a similarity to the numerous islands, in sea and freshwater lochs, which have themselves served as burial grounds for many generations. As with some of the graveyards, the majority of these islands of the dead also accommodate small churches or chapels, and include St Mungo's Isle in Loch Leven (Stewart 1883) and Isle Maree in Loch Maree, while the souls of all the dead of Ireland were thought to inhabit the three islands known as 'Tech Duinn' or 'the house of the dead', in Ballinskellings Bay, south-west Kerry (Thomson 1954, 41).

This deliberate isolation of Highland burial grounds, which is not limited to coastal cemeteries, obviously has important implications for the nature of funerary rituals centred upon them. Burial within one of these cemeteries will require the coffined corpse to be transported over some considerable distance from the settlement, with the closest hamlet or village not necessarily being the point of origin of the corpse. Movement of the coffin with its attendants would take the form of a progression through the landscape, necessitating a passage through places which would have been familiar to the deceased in life. These routes were often formalised and became known as 'coffin tracks'. One example, which runs from Oldshoremore to Durness parish church, covers a distance of over twenty kilometres. Cairns are spaced along the course of the track, marking places where the funerary procession stopped to rest and change coffin-bearers (Dorothy Low pers. comm.).

Inscriptions on the majority of gravestones in these cemeteries make explicit the place of death, this often appearing in preference to other details such as profession, family details, cause of death, etc. A sense of place is important to most of us; we make constant reference to where we live and where we come from in our dealings with other people, often asking these questions of people we meet for the first time. In the Highlands this sense of place and belonging is so strong that people will often say, for example, 'Hugh belonged to Melness', rather than 'Hugh came from Melness'. What a gravestone inscription giving the place of death serves to do is provide a starting point for that final journey through the landscape to the last resting place, the cemetery being journey's end (the importance of the journey as a metaphor in death rituals is touched upon again later).

Perhaps not surprisingly, coastal burial grounds often include the graves of those drowned at sea. The inscriptions on the gravestones of the drowned usually make explicit the cause of death, and in this they stand in marked contrast to the gravestones of those who died on land. In the case of terrestrial demise it is usually the place of death, which not too long ago would more than likely also have been the place of birth, rather than cause of death which is inscribed on the stone. Although the final journey alluded to may have an end for the buried victim of drowning (the burial ground) it does not have a beginning, a place where that person can be said to have died. The sea cannot be regarded as a place, or point of origin, in the same way as a village or a town; it is an alien environment which exists beyond or between the places where people live and die, hence the term 'all at sea' to express a sense of confusion and uncertainty. An interesting exception to this is the stone dedicated to Captain John Stewart, which sits in the seaward corner of the burial ground at Autl-a-chrinn, Wester Ross (Fig. 2). The inscription reads:

> *To the Memory of*
> *Capt. John Stewart*
> *of the Sloop the hawke of Rothesay*
> *Aged 44 Years*
> *Who was unfortunately drowned*
> *on Saturday . . . of October 1808*
> *This Stone is Erected by*
> *his widow CHRISTIAN CLARK*

The phrases 'To the Memory of' and 'This stone is Erected by' may suggest that Stewart is not actually buried here and that the stone simply stands in memorial to someone lost forever to the sea. However, most telling is the phrase: 'Capt. John Stewart of the Sloop hawke of *Rothesey'*. There is obviously a place-name given, Rothesay (Bute), but this is prefixed by the name of the drowned mariner's ship, *the hawke*. The ship provides a point of origin, a place at sea. The fact that the ship, and possibly the captain, came from Rothesay is seen as a secondary biographical detail.

The burial of corpses washed ashore in consecrated graveyards only became common practice after 1808 (coincidentally the year of John Stewart's death), when a bill was passed which made the Christian burial of those washed up from the sea a legal right (E. and M. Radford 1961). Before then it was usual for them to be buried outside consecrated graveyards, on the immediate shore, within the tidal range or close to its upper limit. The reasons for this exclusion may have something to do with the idea that the sea is an abstract entity which does not fit within straightforward categories of place and as such makes the drowned different and more *dangerous* than the average corpse. However, this exclusion may have applied only to those who were strangers, as opposed to local people who may have drowned on fishing trips and eventually washed ashore close to their homes.[2] The burial of two fishermen from Fleetwood outside the burial ground located on the raised beach at Camas Nan Geall, in Ardnamurchan, in 1905 (Moffat et. al. 1990) appears to demonstrate that the tradition of exclusion from burial grounds continued well after 1808. However, this may have had more to do with the fact that the burial ground was reserved for members of the Roman Catholic Campbell family than any deep rooted belief that the drowned were dangerous. Although the identity of these men was known – they had been swept out to sea in a dinghy while rowing from Tobermory pier to their vessel – this was not always the case. Those from outside the local community may well have sailed from foreign lands before meeting their fate, thus interment in a Christian burial ground may not have been appropriate. Following on

[37]

Figure 2. The 'grave' of Capt. Stewart in the burial ground at Autl-a-chrinn, near Sheil Bridge, Wester Ross (Loch Duich in background).

from this the immediate shore may also have represented the point closest to the stranger's homeland.

In northern Scotland, including Orkney and the Outer Hebrides, there is a tradition that the drowned belong to the sea which will 'search the four russet divisions of the universe to find the grave's of her children' (E. and M. Radford 1961). Burying the drowned on the shore would therefore make the sea's search easier and thus avoid her wrath. On a more pragmatic level it is probable that a body washed ashore will have suffered serious decomposition while in the water, and little time would therefore be wasted in getting putrefied remains below ground.

Somewhat ironically, fishermen, who obviously spend a good deal of their lives at sea, are renowned for their inability to swim. In northern waters this may reflect a fatalistic acceptance that once tipped from a boat into the water there was little point in delaying the inevitable, but more than anything it demonstrates an understanding of the sea as an alien environment in which only fish and their ilk are permitted to exist. However, in some places the absence of aquatic skills was compensated for by the execution of rituals which served to protect a fisherman from drowning. A lucky few were protected from birth; those born with a caul (a thin membrane) covering their face never had to fear drowning in later life (Munro and Compton 1983).

Others had to make do with lucky charms, and the caul itself was highly regarded, with some fisherman never leaving port without one in their pocket (ibid.). On the west coast of Scotland, the Molucca bean, which if picked up from the beach after drifting from South America on the Gulf stream, would serve as a powerful charm against drowning (Thomson 1954). Similarly, beach pebbles of the green stone known as Iona marble also guard against mishap at sea if carried on the person (O. Lelong pers. comm.). Supposedly even more effective was a piece of hide cut from the mythical King Otter, reputedly as white as Moby Dick (Thomson 1954).

It was not only through the carrying of charms that good fortune at sea was ensured. In Shetland, for instance, much faith was placed in the examination of wood knots in the timber imported from Norway for use in boat construction. Depending on their position and shape, wood knots could be interpreted either as 'fishy knots', which promised full nets, or 'watery swirls' which foretold misfortune at sea (Marwick 1975, 72). The former were gladly incorporated within a new boat, while the latter were kept well away from any boat, old or new.

Just as these and other superstitions served, and in some cases still serve, to protect a fisherman from drowning so could others serve to seal their doom. In the Northern Isles there is a tradition that the sea chooses its victims, the corollary being that rescue of a chosen victim would simply cause the sea to select the saver in replacement. It was therefore considered bad luck to save a person from drowning, even to the extent of standing by and doing nothing while the poor unfortunate struggled in the water (McPherson 1929; E. and M. Radford 1961).

THE SEA AS GRAVE

For as long as people have been taking to sea in boats they have been dying at sea. At first it was the sea itself which brought death, drowning its victims in squalls and storms, but later, as voyages became longer and ships larger, people began to die without ever touching the water. Diseases were carried on board following spells ashore in tropical regions, while bad nutrition or poor hygiene represented a serious threat to life on board ship well into the nineteenth century. Ships could also bring death to their ports of call, with the ship or black rat thought to be responsible for bringing bubonic plague to Europe in the wake of the Crusades (Zeigler 1969). Similarly, there is a strong tradition from Kintyre that a ship carrying infected sailors brought, along with its cargo, an outbreak of cholera which devastated the population of Tarbet in 1647 (Martin 1984).

When death occurred on board ship, especially on voyages which had weeks or even months between land-falls, burial at sea was the only option. Aside from the technical difficulties related to embalming a corpse[3] the spread of disease on board a ship would be a constant threat.

Dropping the corpse overboard would therefore be an obvious means of disposing of the dead, and like all of burial it has developed into an act imbued with its own form of ritual and symbolism. Among western sailors burial or loss at sea is traditionally referred to as being consigned to 'Davy Jones' Locker'. Davy Jones is a spirit of the sea, and although the origin of the name is uncertain it may be a corruption of Jonah, with the Davy prefix perhaps suggesting a Welsh origin (Weekley 1921). The book of common prayer, traditionally carried on all British ships, merchant and military, has a section devoted to forms of prayer to be used at sea. These include prayers to provide protection from storms and thanksgiving after victory or deliverance from an enemy. Most relevant here though is the prayer to be used during the burial of the dead at sea. The instructions laid out recommend the maintenance of the standard terrestrial funeral prayer but with the deletion of 'commit his body to the earth' and the insertion of the following: 'We therefore commit his body to the deep, to be turned into corruption, looking for the resurrection of the body (when the sea shall give up her dead,) and the life of the world to come . . . ' (n.d. 356).

The traditional treatment of a corpse prior to burial at sea involves sewing it tightly into a shroud of sail cloth. Hammocks were usually made of sail cloth and their use as shrouds would obviously carry with it a strong memory of their former use, with sleep being a metaphor for death. It was normal in some parts to put the last stitch through the nose of the deceased, supposedly to prevent the ghost of the dead man from returning to haunt the ship (Melville 1850), but perhaps on a more pragmatic level this practice also ensured that the person really was dead before committing them to the deep. The importance of this latter point is made clear in a manual on first aid at sea published by the United States government, which states: 'It must be realized – and this fact should never be forgotten – that a person may appear to be dead when he is still alive' (United States Public Health Service and the War Shipping Administration 1947). In Melville's semi-autobiographical work 'White Jacket' (1850) the main character expresses shock at this practice and pursuades the sailmakers responsible for sewing his deceased friend into a shroud not to pierce his flesh with their last stitch.

During the funeral service on board ship the corpse was placed on a 'death-board', which on military vessels at least were usually kept for this particular purpose (Melville 1850; 346), although the more recent (1947) merchant mariner's first aid manual previously cited suggests the use of: 'two saw horses or similar supports about the height of the ship's railing, are placed. . . . The flag-draped body of the deceased is then brought forth on a stretcher (or similar flat surface)' (op. cit., 443). Upon completion of the service the death-board or stretcher was then tipped to allow the corpse to slide, feet first, over the side of the ship.

Shrouded corpses required weighting to ensure that they sank and on military vessels of the nineteenth century it was traditional to use cannon balls. The natural tendency of wooden coffins to float has generally precluded their widespread use in burials at sea. It was, after all, Queequeg's coffin which saved Ishmael from drowning at the end of Moby Dick (the 'dark canoes' which Queequeg observes in Nantucket are, of course, regular wooden coffins). Necessity, however, is the mother of invention and at least once during the Second World War the buoyancy problem was overcome by perforating a wooden coffin made on board ship with machine gun fire, presumably before the corpse was placed inside it (Mhokana 1995). As recently as 1984 a fire axe was taken to an aluminium casket prior to dropping it over the side of the USS *Paul* (ibid.). There was no need to revert to such drastic means during the funeral of Sir Francis Drake, who in 1596 was committed to the deep off the coast of Central America in a lead coffin.

Burial at sea has enjoyed an increased popularity outside the mariner's community in the recent past, especially in the United States. However, it is not the traditional mariner's funeral, involving the burial of a shrouded corpse, but the scattering of cremated ashes on to the sea which is the preferred rite among these late-twentieth-century 'land-lubbers'. The reasons for this upsurge are uncertain but may be related to an increase in humanistic, secular attitudes to death. These motives are perhaps not unrelated to Mitford's (1963, 21) assertion that 'the American public is becoming sickened by ever more ornate and costly funerals, and that a status symbol of the future may indeed be the simplest kind of "funeral without fins"?' It is, of course, the fins of gas-guzzling hearses to which she refers here and not those of the fish which are more appropriate in the present context.

THE LAST VOYAGE

Just as the sea can be the cause of death, through drowning, and represent the grave itself, it can also represent something else, the means of access to the afterworld. It has already been established that boats were used as a means of ocean-going transport early in Scotland's prehistory. The shell middens on Oronsay, which, it has been argued, represented not only sites where marine foods were processed but also a place where corpses were excarnated, were reached only after a voyage across the sea, probably from Jura or Islay to the east, although the closer island of Colonsay may have carried a semi-permanent population at this time. It is possible that the dead were carried on this voyage with the explicit purpose of placing them on the shell middens, rather than the bones from the shell deposits representing the remains of people who actually died on Oronsay.

This voyage of the dead may have played an important role in the lives of the living and, if this were the case, the voyage may have been regarded as a metaphor for life itself, having a beginning, a middle, and an end,[4] with all of these points occupying different times and places. The island of Oronsay may have become as closely associated with the dead as it surely was with the seasonal exploitation of marine food resources (the continued use of small islands as burial grounds well into the post-medieval period has already been touched upon). The use of boats to transport the dead from the world of the living to the world of the dead figures strongly in various myths and legends, the best known of which include the passage of the dead across the River Styx to Hades, in the care of Charon the ferry man, and similarly the transfer of Arthur's body to Avalon, another isle of the dead.

Although it has been suggested that the belief that the afterworld lay across the sea may have had its origins in the Mesolithic period, in north-western Europe it is the Norse who are most strongly identified with the belief that this passage involved a sea voyage. Its currency elsewhere, up until more recent times, is suggested by the use of canoes to transport the dead to the islands of the dead in Aboriginal Australia, New Zealand, and North America has been noted by Shetelig (1905, 329).

The Norse in Scotland are known to have buried at least some of their dead in boats or ships.[5] The most recently discovered example of this rite, and certainly the best documented, comes from Scar on Sanday in the Northern Isles (Dalland 1992). Here, the partial remains of a small boat were discovered eroding from sandy soil by the shore. Excavation revealed that the boat had been buried with the corpses of a man, a woman, and a child lying in its hull, along with numerous grave goods. Less clear evidence for this practice comes from Kiloran Bay on Colonsay, where a rectangular enclosure of stone was found to contain numerous rivets and nails, some of which still had wood adhering to them (Shetelig 1906). The presence of a human burial and grave goods, including a sword, shield, and Norse coins, also within the enclosure may suggest a ship burial.

The dead also set sail for the afterlife in symbolic vessels, with boat-shaped settings of stone taking the place of the wood and iron of real ships. In Scandinavia these monumental arrangements of stone are known to have been constructed from as early as the Neolithic (Andrén 1992), although they are most commonly cited with reference to Norse funerary ritual.

It was a very real boat in which the author set sail for the group of small islands known as St Kilda, possibly for the last time, in the summer of 1994. What lay at the end of this forty-mile voyage into the open Atlantic was the island of Hirta and the second season of excavations by the Departments of Archaeology at Glasgow and Durham Universities. Although best known for the village abandoned in 1930 when the island's population was evacuated, and which has its own walled burial ground, recent excavation by the author (Pollard 1996; Morrison and Pollard forthcoming) and others (Cottam 1979; Emery and Morrison 1995; Turner 1996) strongly suggests that people were at least visiting the island as far back as the Bronze Age.

Among the many archaeological features on the island are the enigmatic stone arrangements which have been termed 'boat-shaped' settings (Cottam 1979; Stell and Harman 1988). The stones from which these features are constructed sit low on the ground and from a distance appear little different from the other rocks and small stones which litter the lower slopes of the corrie-like hollow known as An Lag upon which a number of these features are scattered. Only when walking over this

Figure 3. A boat-shaped setting during excavation, An Lag, Hirta (Village Bay in background).

ground does it become obvious that there is more here than first meets the eye. The clearest examples are curved arrangements of small grano-phyre boulders, their sides coming to a point at least at one end, fairly much like the prow or the stern of a small boat. With the best of them the term 'boat shaped' needs no further explanation, but others are less clear and may even represent different types of structure (Turner 1996). Although one would think it tempting to view these as Norse features, especially with the probable presence of the Norse on St Kilda and the possible Norse origin of the name Hirta (Crawford 1987), this idea has never really gained much support (Stell and Harman 1988).

A Norse origin was certainly not evident when the results of the first excavation of one of these structures, set into the hill side overlooking Village Bay, became known (Cottam 1979). A trench cut across the setting demonstrated that the stones were set into a shallow scoop which contained an organic peat-like deposit. This provided a radio-carbon date of 1833±47 bc (SRR-316), which may suggest a Bronze-Age date for the structure, although the relationship between the peat and the structure is, to say the least, somewhat uncertain.

I supervised the more extensive excavation of similar features in 1993 and 1994. Two closely spaced settings were selected for excavation in an attempt to clarify their age and function. The removal of the thin turf revealed that the 'boat shapes' represented the central settings of low oval cairns with roughly constructed concentric kerbs. The presence of the cairns immediately strengthened the suggestion that the features were Bronze Age, bearing some similarity to platform cairns on the west coast of mainland Scotland and on the Outer Hebridean islands to the east of St Kilda. These include those in Morvern, where central stone cists contained cremated remains along with grave goods (Ritchie and Thornber 1975).

The presence of cairns on Hirta strongly suggests that these features were related to burial, with the central settings representing an obvious focus for the ensuing attempt to locate burial evidence. However, other than a number of enigmatic scoops and pits no evidence for burials was identified within the settings or elsewhere on the site. To my mind, excavation, although a frustrating exercise, had succeeding in establishing that these features represented ritual monuments of some sort, even though it had failed to explain why they had been constructed.

When first confronted with these features, during a survey of An Lag, I regarded the term 'boat shaped' with some suspicion, shying away from the use of loaded terms applied to structures we knew next to nothing about. However, my belief that excavation would quickly resolve this uncertainty gradually dissolved as two seasons of work failed to provide anything in the way of conclusive evidence. It is suggested here that the experience of being on the island and travelling to and from it has played as important a role as excavation in contributing to an understanding of these features.

To the west of shelter-belt provided by the Long Island – Lewis, the Uists, and Harris – the open Atlantic becomes increasingly treacherous, showing little mercy to boats which run into heavy weather. Vessels en route to St Kilda will often have to moor in a Hebridean bay waiting for a window in the weather (I spent several days 'marooned' on North Uist during my first trip to the islands). Likewise, boats will often be stranded for some time in the shelter of Village bay, Hirta, before their crews make a dash for the Hebrides and the main land beyond (my voyage home was delayed for a couple of days by heavy seas, until eventually an army range launch braved a force 8 to take us off the island). Over the years these dangerous waters have taken their toll on those who have failed to respect them. Even the natives of St Kilda, who rarely risked the passage between St Kilda and the Long Island, periodically suffered loss of life at sea. In April 1863 the island's boat, the *Dargavel*, set out for Harris with eight passengers on board, only to be lost in what must have been heavy seas. The bodies of the seven men and one woman who had been on board were never recovered, although some items of clothing were reported to have been washed up on the island of Mealista off the west coast of Lewis (Quine 1982, 213).

When the sea refuses to give up its dead bereaved relatives are denied the public expression of grief during a funeral.[6] This denial can be at least partially overcome by providing a monumental focus for that grief and mourning. It will be suggested that such a response may lie behind the construction of the boat-shaped monuments on Hirta.

The idea of the cenotaph (from the Greek 'empty tomb') finds its most obvious expression in the multitude of monuments erected in British towns and villages in the immediate aftermath of the First World War, during which a large proportion of the male population was killed over-seas, where many of them were buried. Many simply went missing in action and their bodies were never recovered; over 73,000 British soldiers killed during the battle of the Somme alone have no known grave (Dyer 1994). Thousands of sailors were lost at sea during both world wars, the majority during the second. Many of them went down with their ships (trapped inside their hulls), with crews of several hundred men regularly lost in a single sinking. Although the wrecks of these ships, the location of the many of which are known, have been designated war graves they are not sites which can be visited by be-reaved relatives, although Pearl Harbour is a notable exception.

Memorials to those lost at sea take a variety of forms and mention has already been made of the intention to erect the recovered deck gun as a memorial to the dead of the S.S. Ashberry in Melness. Somewhat less militaristic is the chapel in New Street, Buckie, which was built to com-memorate those who have lost their lives at sea since 1945 (Smith 1991). Sculpted mother and child memorials to fishermen are quite common, with the monuments portraying the grieving dependants gazing mourn-fully out over the water, examples can be seen in Kirkudbright and Cul-livoe, North Yell, Shetland (the latter erected to commemorate the loss of 58 men during the great storm of 1881). More personal losses are also commemorated, with numerous 'grave' stones standing in memorial to those who may or may not be buried beneath them (Fig. 2). Notable here is a small stone memorial in a cemetery in King's Lynne, Norfolk, which takes the form of a replica fishing boat commemorating the loss of the eight-man crew of the 'Beautiful Star' from St Monans, Fife, which went down in a gale off the Norfolk coast in 1875 (Tanner 1996).

The dangers experienced by those journeying to St Kilda in pre-historic times must surely have been greater than those suffered by mariners benefitting from advances in technology in more recent times. Indeed, the challenge of reaching the island may have served to attract seafarers, much in the same way as it represents something of a Mount Everest to sea canoeists in the present day. It has been observed elsewhere that explorers venturing to foreign lands across the sea returned home in possession not only of new and exotic goods, be they bloodstone or breadfruit, but also arcane knowledge of a secret world which could then be exploited in order to enhance their standing at home (Helms 1988). It is probable that the islands figured in the imagination of those living in the Outer Hebrides, from where they were visible on the distant horizon, long before they were permanently occupied.

It is possible that the boat-shaped monuments commemorated a successful voyage to St Kilda. However, they may equally have marked failure, representing monuments to those lost at sea, either in trying to reach the island or returning to the east (Pollard 1996). If they do relate to a time when people were living on the island, rather than making a brief visit, they may represent those lost at sea during fishing trips. Similar structures in the Outer Hebrides, notably on Vatersay, a small island to the south of Barra, may also reflect this desire for commemoration. Although it might be argued that the larger size of these structures suggest a different function to those on Hirta, the temptation to label them as Norse burials should perhaps be avoided (Brannigan 1997, 285).

As I spent more time on the island, and more time than is comfortable taking a boat to and from it, my doubts began to fall away and I became more comfortable with the idea that these enigmatic monuments did in some way refer to boats and the sea. It was rare that I would look up from the trench, something which archaeologists should make more of a habit of doing, to see a boat or two bobbing gently in the bay below (Fig. 3). Having made this leap, not quite of faith, and come to terms with the term 'boat shaped' having validity on Hirta it was a relatively small step to taking seriously the idea that they were in fact memorials to those lost, or even perhaps buried at sea. Borrowing elements from recognised funerary structures of their time, in the form of platform cairns, they provided a focus for memory and grief through reference to both the sea (in the form of the boat-shaped setting) and death (in the form of the cairn). This coupling has continued into recent times with a carved stone referring to a vessel by name (Fig. 2) or a replica boat in a Christian burial ground serving the same purpose.

Obviously this idea remains highly speculative, as there is little in the way of hard evidence to prove that these features do represent cenotaphs. However, we have something of a Catch 22 situation here, as this interpretation is dependent on an absence of evidence, at least in the form of burials. Further excavation, both on St Kilda and elsewehere may well provide other explanations but until then it is hoped that if nothing else this discussion has made clear that the archaeologist can harness their own experience of place and give room to their imagination if they are to advance their understanding of excavated sites, and this does not just apply to those which, like the 'boat-shaped' settings on St Kilda, may defy ready interpretation.

CONCLUSION

This paper has suggested that the sea and its shores have played an important role in the various belief systems which have enabled people to deal with the dead and the passage from life to death.

The central aim of this volume has been to examine the relationship between archaeologists and an important aspect of their study: death. In doing so many of the contributions have centred upon physical contact with human remains, which can manifest themselves in a variety of forms: as cremated ashes, as disarticulated bones, articulated skeletons, or relatively well-preserved corpses. However, this paper has differed in that it has considered some of the circumstances which deny us contact with these remains. Loss at sea and burial at sea represent an obvious but rarely considered means by which the dead are removed physically not just from the realm of the living but also from the scrutiny of the archaeologist.

It is hoped that this paper has not only provided an impression of how people in the past expressed and came to terms with this sense of loss, through the creation of various monuments, but has also, on a different level, made some suggestion as to how archaeologists can begin to overcome this loss where it touches on their understanding of the past.

ACKNOWLEDGEMENTS

Glasgow University's work on St Kilda is carried out under the auspices of the National Trust for Scotland, and would not have been possible without the efforts of the various members of the National Trust for Scotland's archaeological work parties. Lorna Johnstone shared the experience of excavating the St Kilda 'boat shapes' and did much to shape the ideas about them presented here. Ian Oxley provided information through that now indispensable friend of the paper writer: e-mail. I would like to thank Luke Barber and Sheila Maltby for reading and commenting on earlier versions of this text.

NOTES

1. I would like to take this opportunity to put right an error made in an earlier paper concerning the sea (Pollard 1996, 203). There it was wrongly stated that the 'full moon coincides with the lowest or ebb tide, while the waning moon equates with the highest, or spring tide'. Of course, the ebb

tide is actually the receding tide rather than the lowest (neap) tide, while the new moon and full moon actually equate with the highest (spring) tide and the first and last quarters of the moon with the lowest (neap) tide. The book's few reviewers, like the author, appear to have been 'land-lubbers' and failed to notice this clumsy error.

2. Those drowned even relatively close to the coast can take a considerable time, if they ever are, to be washed ashore. In the Scilly Isles, off southern England, the body of a fisherman drowned in a storm not too far from the coast can take up to six weeks to be washed ashore (Wynne-Jones 1997).

3. Embalming did not become widely practised until the American Civil War (1861–65), where soldiers killed on the battlefield were quite often transported home for burial. This practice made its most profound expression during the Vietnam War where the return of bodies to the United States played an important role in transforming the popular perception of the war. This practice is in contrast to the British military tradition of burying the war dead in the place where they fell. American Civil War battlefield graveyards, such as those at Antietam and Gettysburg, do exist, but these cannot be described as 'foreign fields'.

4. Although it has been suggested that the fluid sea is an abstract entity rather than a physical place, this is of course not to say that those who are skilled in navigation are unaware of their position upon it, a factor re-inforced in the twentieth century by the arbitrary division of coastal waters into sectors with 'place names' such as Dogger, Fisher and German Bight. In coastal waters it is reference to known landmarks which often informs those at sea about their position (Lelong forth-coming). But it is important to note that it is their position in relation to the land which is calculated here, as opposed to astronomical navigation which fixes a point within a much wider and more abstract framework. Thus, the mid-point of a voyage to most Scottish islands would be known, as both the point of origin (mainland or other island) and destination (island) would both be visible.

5. The image of the Viking burial at sea, which involved the casting adrift of a burning ship carrying the corpse of a dead warrior is a popular image which appears to have some historical foundation. The cremation of corpses in ships on land was documented by an Arab emissary to the king of the Slavonians where he witnessed the funeral of Scandinavian trader chieftain on the shores of the river Volga (Shetelig 1905).

6. The trauma suffered by those who have experienced the loss of loved ones at sea has been emphasised in recent times with incidents such as the loss of the bulk carrier M.V. Derbyshire and all 44 crew members in a typhoon off Japan in 1980. She is the largest British merchant ship ever to be lost at sea and her 'mysterious' disappearance in the later part of the twentieth century, for all its advanced marine engineering skills and communication systems, caused surviving relatives great trauma and stress. With the uncertainty of the loss of the ship and without the re-covery of a body it is difficult to grieve. Submarine detection equipment has since located the wreck on the sea bed and it has been suggested that faults in the construction of the ship may have been responsible for her loss. When interviewed on television news some of the bereaved relatives admitted that they had expected to feel relief that they knew at last what their loved one's fate had been, but almost to their surprise they felt even more distraught than before. What they were experiencing was the onset of their true grief, which at last was free to run its course.

[49]

A similar case is the loss of the trawler 'Gaul' and all 36 crew in the Barents Sea in 1974. In the absence of irrefutable proof of the ship sinking, a small number of relatives until recently prefered to believe that she was boarded by the KGB and her crew consigned to Siberian salt mines as spies (Bosely 1997). As this paper was going to press it was reported in the Fishing News (29th Aug. 1997, 1–2) that divers from a TV documentary project had actually located the wreck of the Gaul in 150 fathoms of water 70 miles off the Norwegian coast. Relatives were reported to have 'expressed relief that the wreck had been found after 23 years of uncertainty, rumour and speculation.'

BIBLIOGRAPHY

Andrén, A. 1992. Doors to other worlds: Scandinavian death rituals in Gotlandic perspectives. *Journal of European Archaeology* 1, 33–56.

Anonymous. No Date. *The Book of Common Prayer*. Collins, London.

Barclay, G. J. and C. J. Russell-White 1993. Excavations in the ceremonial complex of the fourth to second millenium at Balfarg/Balbirnie, Glenrothes, Fife. *Proceedings of the Society of Antiquaries of Scotland* 123 (1993), 43–210.

Brannigan, K. 1997. Barra. *Current Archaeology* 152, 284–289.

Borwick, G., C. MacMillan, E. MacPhail, and T. Moffat (eds) 1990. *Ardnamurchan: Annals of a Parish* (second edition). Summerhall Press, Edinburgh.

Bosely, S. 1997. Deep secret. *The Guardian Weekend Magazine*. June 14, 1997, 30–42.

Connock, K. D., B. Finlayson, and A. C. M. Mills 1992. The excavation of a shell midden site at Carding Mill Bay, near Oban, Argyll, Scotland. *Glasgow Archaeological Journal* 17 (1991–92), 25–39.

Cottam, M. B. 1979. Archaeology. In *A St Kilda Handbook*, 36–61. National Trust for Scotland, Edinburgh.

Crawford, B. E. 1987. *Scandinavian Scotland*. Leicester University Press, Leicester.

Dalland, M. 1992. Scar: excavation of a Viking boat burial on Orkney. *Current Archaeology* 131, 475–478.

Douglas, M. 1966. *Purity and Danger*. Ark paperbacks, London. (Reprinted 1989.)

Dyer, G. 1994. *The Missing of the Somme*. Hamish Hamilton, London.

Emery, N. and A. Morrison 1995. The archaeology of St Kilda. In: *St Kilda: the Continuing Story of the Islands*, 39–60. HMSO, Edinburgh.

Helms, M. W. 1988. *Ulysses' Sail: an ethnographic odyssey of power, knowledge and geographical distance*. Princeton University Press, Princeton.

Hokana, M. 1975. E-mail communication. Mhokana@Mailstorm.Dot.Gov.

Huntington, R. and P. Metcalf 1979. *Celebrations of Death*. Cambridge University Press, Cambridge.

Lelong, O. forthcoming. A prospect of the sea: coastal relocation during the Highland Clearances. MOLRS conference proceedings.

Lorimer, D. H. 1992. Carding Mill Bay: report on the human bones. In: Connock et al. 1992.

Martin, A. 1984. *Kintyre: the Hidden Past*.

Marwick, E. W. 1975. *The Folklore of Orkney and Shetland*. Batsford, London.

Meiklejohn, C. and C. B. Denston 1987. The human skeletal material: inventory and initial interpretation. In Mellars 1987, 290–301.

Mellars, P. 1987. *Excavations on Oronsay*. Edinburgh University Press, Edinburgh.

Melville, H. 1850. *White Jacket* (Signet Classic reprint, 1979). New American Library, Times Mirror, New York.

Melville, H. 1851. *Moby Dick* (reprint 1982). Penguin, Harmondsworth.

Mitford, J. 1963. *The American Way of Death*. Simon and Schuster, New York.

Morrison, A. and T. Pollard forthcoming. Excavation of 'boat-shaped' settings in An Lag, Hirta.

Pollard, T. 1996. All at Sea: the excavation of boat-shaped settings on Hirta. *St Kilda Mail* 20 (April 1996), 26–31.

Pollard, T. 1996. Time and tide: coastal environments, cosmology and ritual practice in prehistoric Scotland. In T. Pollard and A. Morrison (eds), *The Early Prehistory of Scotland*, 198–213. Edinburgh University Press, Edinburgh.

Pollard, T. in press. A Neolithic settlement and ritual complex at Beckton Farm, Lockerbie. *Proceedings of the Society of Antiquaries of Scotland* 126.

Quine, D. A. 1982. *St Kilda Revisited*. Downland Press, Frome.

Radford, E. and M. A. Radford 1948. *Encyclopedia of Superstitions* (revised and edited by C. Hole in 1961). Hutchinson, London.

Ritchie, J. N. G. and I. Thornber 1975. Cairns in the Aline valley, Morvern, Argyll. *Proceedings of the Society of Antiquaries of Scotland* 106 (1974–75), 15–39.

Saville, A. and Y. Hallen 1995. The 'Obanian Iron Age': human remains from the Oban cave sites, Argyll, Scotland. *Antiquity* 68, 715–723.

Shetelig, H. 1905. Ship burials. *Saga Book of the Viking Club* 4 (part 2), 326–363.

Shetelig, H. 1906. Ship-burial at Kiloran Bay, Colonsay, Scotland. *Saga Book of the Viking Club* 5, 182–237.

Smith, C. 1992. *Late Stone Age Hunters of the British Isles*. Routledge, London.

Smith, J. 1892. The investigation of a shell-mound at Ardrossan. *Glasgow Geological Society Transactions* 9 (1891–1892).

Smith, R. 1991. *One Foot in the Sea*. John Donald, Edinburgh.

Steel, T. 1975. *The Life and Death of St Kilda*. Fontana/Collins, Glasgow.

Stell, G. P. and M. Harman 1988. *Buildings of St Kilda*. RCAHMS, Edinburgh.

Stewart, A. 1883. *Nether Lochaber: the natural history, legends and folk-lore of the West Highlands*. William Paterson, Edinburgh.

Tanner, M. 1996. *Scottish Fishing Boats*. Shire publications, Princes Risborough, Buckinghamshire (Shire Album 326).

Temperley, A. (ed.) 1988. *Tales of the North Coast*. Luath Press, Barr, Ayrshire.

Thomson, D. 1954. *The People of the Sea*. Canongate, Edinburgh.

Turner, R. 1996. Excavations at the Gap, St Kilda. *St Kilda Mail* 20, 2–3.

United States Public Health Office and the War Shipping Administration. 1947. *The Ship's Medicine Chest and First Aid at Sea*. United States Government Printing Office, Washington.

Van Gennep, A. 1909. *Les Rites de Passage*. Emile Nourr, Paris.

Weekley, E. 1921. *Etymological Dictionary of Modern English*. John Murray.

Wynne-Jones, R. 1997. A Scilly offer. *Independent on Sunday* 6 April 1997.

Zeigler, P. 1969. *The Black Death*. Harper Torch Books, Harper and Row, New York.

5

Sleep by the shores of those icy seas:[1] death and resurrection in the last Franklin expedition

Owen Beattie

In 1845, 129 British sailors began a journey of arctic discovery only to perish over the following three years in a mass disaster unprecedented in European arctic exploration. Such an event can traumatise a nation, and a leader's words – in a speech to that nation – can signal the beginning of the healing process:

> we've never had a tragedy like this. . . . We mourn [these] heroes. . . . We mourn their loss as a nation together . . . painful things like this happen. It's all part of the process of exploration and discovery. It's all part of taking a chance and expanding man's horizons. The future . . . belongs to the brave. . . . In [the lifetime of an explorer] the great frontiers [are] the oceans. . . . We will never forget them, nor the last time we saw them . . . as they prepared for the journey and waved good-bye. . . .

These words, however, were not spoken in memory of those nineteenth-century British sailors. They were spoken by American President Ronald Reagan on the day of the loss of the space shuttle *Challenger* and its seven astronauts, 28 January 1986 (see Kottmann 1995). Their applicability to an event of 140 years earlier, though, is direct and relevant, and represents the underlying theme of the following paper.

INTRODUCTION

The deaths of individuals attempting what is perceived as an heroic and worthy quest can have a powerful and lasting effect on a people and a nation. The endurance of adversity, acceptance of suffering, and apparent fearless welcoming of awesome risk and death are attributes that evoke emotion and admiration from most of us. These feelings can be so strong that they drive people to relive the heroes' experiences through actual or fictitious recreation of the quest. In part because of the tremendous emotional investment that is made to support and champion the status of the heroes, these same feelings can also prove to be formidable barriers to any objective reassessment of the quest.

Many of our heroes are those of our kin group, tribe, faith, nation, or state that have directed their lives to the discovery of new lands and peoples. They are usually referred to as explorers. One arena of European exploration has spawned more than its share of heroes: the search for the Northwest Passage; and no name conjures up the stereotype of the reluctant hero more than British explorer Sir John Franklin. During his quest for the Northwest Passage from 1845 to 1848, Franklin and his crews – totalling 129 men – perished to a man, deep in the arctic regions. Here, I will attempt to describe some of the various public and professional issues, circumstances, and responses regarding the examination of human remains that our research team dealt with in its recent investigations of the nineteenth-century mass disaster usually referred to as the third Franklin expedition. These issues – often pitting objective scientific enquiry against subjective emotional response – were particularly pertinent to our project because three of the subjects of our investigation were sailors of known identity whose bodies had been preserved in arctic permafrost since 1846.

BACKGROUND

By 1845 the British had experienced a number of centuries of searches for land and/or sea-based trade routes to the lucrative and desirable markets of the western Pacific rim (see Neatby 1958; 1970). The impediment to this route was the vast size of the North American continent. Dozens of expeditions attempted to cross this formidable barrier by land, or sail around by ship or canoe. The search for the Northwest Passage across the northern limit of the continent was linked to this desire to discover a relatively safe, swift, and economically viable water passage to the Pacific.

The Northwest Passage expeditions, as well as other polar expeditions, generated many heroes, though by 1845 none had yet succeeded in completing a voyage from either Atlantic to Pacific or Pacific to Atlantic. It is fascinating to study a map of the Arctic that combines all of the exploratory accomplishments of these European explorers. Like a

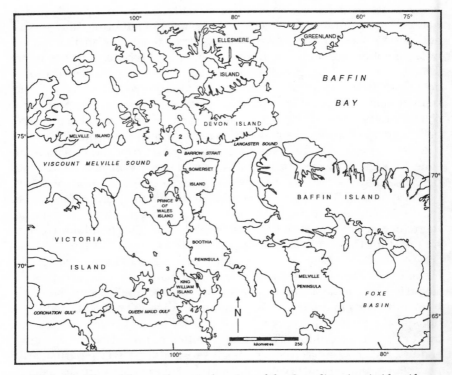

Figure 1. *Map of the north-central region of the Canadian Arctic identifying (by number) important locations relating to the third Franklin expedition: 1. Beechey Island, where three of the expedition's sailors are buried in permafrost; 2. Cornwallis Island, circumnavigated by the expedition in the late summer of 1846; 3. The location where the Franklin expedition ships were beset in September 1846 and deserted in April 1848; 4. Starvation Cove; 5. The mouth of the Back River, referred to as 'Back's Fish River' in the Franklin expedition note found during M'Clintock's expedition (adapted from Beattie and Amy 1990, 78).*

picture puzzle, each expedition added a new piece of geographical information that built on the discoveries of predecessors. The cumulative effect of all of this information provided a vague and still incomplete picture on the geography of the Arctic. It turned out that the Arctic Ocean was filled with many islands, and that the maze of water passages separating these islands produced not a single Northwest passage, but a myriad of possible routes. By 1839 explorers had nearly completed the charting of one passage. Explored and plotted routes from the east and from the west nearly connected along the west coast of King William Island, located in the south-central Arctic (Ross 1835;

[54]

Simpson 1843). Only a 120 km gap in the island's coastline remained to be explored. The east and west routes could be transformed into a single, continuous, unbroken route that would define the first North-west Passage. A final expedition was planned which would eventually clarify this nagging detail of geography.

In May of 1845, John Franklin and his crews departed down the River Thames aboard the royal navy ships *Erebus* and *Terror* on an expedition intent on completing the Northwest Passage (Cyriax 1939; Beattie and Geiger 1993). Supplied for three years, his expedition was considered the best equipped and manned ever sent out by the British in exploration. They never returned. The last Europeans to see them were whalers who, in July, encountered the two ships in Baffin Bay, heading west-ward towards Lancaster Sound, the accepted eastern entrance to the Passage.

It took fourteen years for the world to know what happened to Franklin and his men. In those intervening years until 1859, more than twenty land-based and ship-based expeditions were dispatched from England, first in the role of rescuers, and finally as searchers for the dead.

During these searches, signs of Franklin and his men were found on three islands in the central and southern regions of the Arctic and on part of the mainland of North America (see Fig. 1). At one of these sites, on Beechey Island, the graves of three sailors from the expedition, dating to early 1846, were found. On another, King William Island, the skeletons of a number of sailors were witnessed by searchers as re-presentative of the final disintegration of Franklin's expedition.

Arguably, the most significant event during this intensive search period was the 1859 discovery made by Leopold M'Clintock's expedi-tion of a note left by Franklin's men in a metal cannister placed in a stone marker on the north-west coast of King William Island (M'Clintock 1908). Though probably a survey note originally left at the site on or about the 28th of May, 1847, it also contains marginal notes dated April 25, 1848. These, in part, read as follows (M'Clintock 1908):

> April 25th, 1848 – HM's Ships Terror and Erebus were deserted on 22nd April, 5 leagues N.N.W. of this, having been beset since 12th September 1846. The Officers and crews, consisting of 105 souls, under the command of Captain F. R. M. Crozier, landed here in Lat. 69° 37′ 42″ N, long. 98° 41′ W. Sir John Franklin died on 11th June 1847; and the total loss by deaths in the Ex-pedition has been to this date 9 officers and 15 men. James Fitz-james, Captain HMS *Erebus*. F. R. M. Crozier, Captain and Senior Officer.
>
> . . . and start on tomorrow, 26th, for Back's Fish River.

[55]

On 22 April 1848, the 105 surviving officers and crews of the expedition deserted their two ice-bound ships between 20 and 40 km NNW of where the note was found in 1859. As they progressed along the frozen King William Island coastline, they dragged (in harness) heavily laden life-boats mounted on sledges constructed for this purpose. The physical demands of this project, combined with rapidly deteriorating health and approaching starvation, were insurmountable. Men died along every extent of their route to a place on the adjacent mainland later named Starvation Cove (see Stackpole 1965; Gilder 1881). This appears to be the furthest known point reached by the expedition in their attempt to gain the Back River.

Along this route the expedition connected the two geographical locations achieved by earlier expeditions, thereby completing a North-west Passage. Unfortunately, all expedition members perished, the last survivors likely succumbing during the summer months of 1848. In success, they faced the ultimate failure. Completing the passage, none survived to tell of the victory.

Why?

This question has inspired – and even obsessed – a multitude of explorers, historians, adventurers, and scientists. As part of this legion of Franklin searchers, my project set goals to find and examine the physical remains of Franklin's men in an attempt to use forensic anthropological methods to help explain the disaster. Historically, searchers had keyed on the search for written records (log books, letters, etc.) that could illuminate the events of the expedition. Sailors' remains were encountered and documented their location, but beyond the expected emotional response to these discoveries, the bones were not viewed as a source of significant information. My colleagues and I were to focus on the relocation and recovery of these previously mapped remains and were hopeful of adding new discoveries of skeletal remains through intensive archaeological survey (Beattie 1983).

THE PROJECT

The results of our four field seasons searching for, and recovering, human remains from the third Franklin expedition have been extensively covered elsewhere (Notman and Beattie 1995; Beattie 1993; Beattie and Geiger 1993; Kowal et al. 1991; Kowal et al. 1990; Beattie and Amy 1990; Kowal et al. 1989; Kowalewska-Grochowska et al. 1988; Amy et al. 1986; Beattie 1985; Beattie 1983; Beattie and Savelle 1983). The following is an overview of this research.

During summer surveys of King William Island conducted in 1981 and 1982, the surface-scattered and highly fragmented skeletal remains of a minimum of seven, and a maximum of 15, crew members from the Franklin expedition were found and collected. Later laboratory analysis of these remains failed to provide any positive identifications. Signs of scurvy were observed, and cut marks indicative of cannibalism were found on the femur of one individual. Chemical analysis of the bones (using atomic emission spectrometry) demonstrated elevated levels of the toxic metal lead in amounts suggesting that lead intoxication likely occurred among some or all of these individuals. Relating to the goals of the project – identifying factors from the human remains that could clarify the reasons for the disaster – the discovery that lead was present in the bodies of the sailors provided the basis for formulating an hypothesis that the deleterious physiological and neurological effects of lead played a role in the Franklin expedition disaster. As the bone lead could not tell us the period of exposure for the sailors (weeks, months, years?), and the knowledge of the period of exposure was critical in supporting or rejecting the hypothesis that exposures occurred during the expedition, plans were set in place to investigate the bodies of the first three men to have died on the expedition, and whose bodies were known to be buried in permafrost at Beechey Island. There, the collection and analysis of soft tissues (with lead turnover rates well within the time limits of the expedition) would verify whether or not the men were exposed to lead on the expedition.

During the summers of 1984 and 1986, the bodies of Petty Officer John Torrington (H.M.S. *Terror*, died 1 January 1846, age 20 years – Fig. 2), able bodied seaman John Hartnell (H.M.S. *Erebus*, died 4 January 1846, age 25 years – Fig. 3), and Royal Marine Private William Braine (H.M.S. *Erebus*, died 3 April 1846, age 33 years – not illustrated) were exhumed and full autopsies conducted on their preserved remains. After autopsy (and full x-ray for Hartnell and Braine), the bodies were reburied and the graves reconstructed back to their pre-excavation appearance.

Though we understood that the permafrost conditions would help preserve the soft tissues, we were amazed at the excellent condition of the bodies, particularly that of John Torrington. Freezing by itself will not guarantee preservation for extended periods of time. The tissues become desiccated, and eventually they fully mummify. Such was not the case with the three sailors. In their coffins, they were each encased in solid ice. During the short summer of 1846, when the snow melted on Beechey Island, the melt-water trickled down into the graves, seeped into the coffins, and froze, encapsulating the bodies in a cocoon of ice. This process created an optimal preservation environment for the bodies as well as the clothing and other textiles buried on and with the men. During the exhumation, the ice surrounding the bodies was melted

[57]

Figure 2. The frozen body of John Torrington after ice surrounding his body had been removed.

with running water. Once exposed, the still frozen bodies were moved temporarily to an autopsy tent set up adjacent to each grave. The bodies remained frozen during the x-ray procedure, and most parts of the

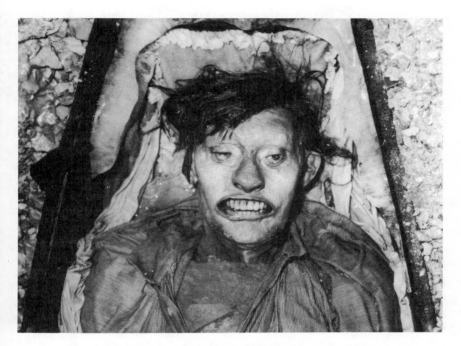

Figure 3. Close-up of John Hartnell after removal of his cap.

bodies were still frozen during the autopsies. Samples collected at autopsy were kept frozen and transported to labs at the University of Alberta for later analysis. All parts of the excavation, exhumation, autopsy, and reconstruction phases of the project were extensively photo-documented.

Among other medical and forensic findings (such as pulmonary tuberculosis, Pott's disease, pneumonia, localised joint trauma, periapical abscessing and caries formation, the identification of viable gut bacteria, and post-mortem skin lesions made by rats), analysis of soft and hard tissues from these sailors revealed highly elevated lead levels, including levels in John Torrington that can be interpreted as life-threatening. Stable lead isotope analysis of the lead in the sailors identified that the likely source for the toxic metal was the solder used in the tinned food supplied in great quantity to the expedition. This mass spectrometry analysis indicated that the lead in the sailors bodies and the lead in the food tin solder were from the same geological source, strongly supporting the interpretation that Franklin's tinned foods, and perhaps all tins made since 1811 and up to the end of the century, posed a significant health risk to consumers. A recent challenge to these objective discoveries suggests that there is no evidence that the lead was from the tins, and that, not knowing the 'average' levels of lead for people back in England, we also cannot conclude that lead poisoning was a factor on the Franklin expedition (Farrer 1993). This is a curious comment, implying that levels in England may have been equally as high as those encountered in the Franklin expedition sailors. If true, one wonders what effect this must have had on English society, for the levels found in the sailors would likely have caused profound physical and neurological pathology – even death – for most English people. Actually, our research has indirectly demonstrated that the sailors likely had not received significant lead exposures prior to the expedition (see Notman and Beattie 1995; Kowal et al. 1991).

That tinned foods were a real health risk in the nineteenth century is supported through documentation in the contemporary medical literature (Beattie 1993; Wightwick 1888; Magruder 1883; Anonymous 1883). Some of the problems of the developing technology related to highly variable quality control due to the tins being made by hand. More importantly, the standard procedure was to solder the tin seams on the inside surfaces of the containers, where the food would be packed and cooked, and ultimately sealed, while in direct contact with the solder. We suggest that the food was contaminated by the lead in the solder and was then consumed by the sailors. At the turn of the century, advances in tin food technology meant tins no longer required soldering on the insides. Today, in North America, the linking of soldered food tins with food contamination is well established, and soldered tins are now a rarity, having been supplanted by forged tin bodies and wire welding techniques (Foulke 1993; US Department of Health and Social Services 1988).

Discussion

The purpose of this paper is not to review and discuss the significance of the medical findings relating to the autopsies of the Franklin expedition sailors buried at Beechey Island, or of the bones from King William Island. What is of interest here is the public reaction to the photographs of the sailors' preserved bodies, particularly a photograph of John Torrington (Fig. 2) that was released by the Public Affairs Office of the University of Alberta in September of 1984, along with a preliminary description of our research findings. The worldwide public reaction to this photograph was – to put it bluntly – staggering. The photograph has stimulated more than a simple interest in the Franklin expedition. The story of this expedition, totally unknown to most, or but a fuzzy recollection in English-speaking countries, was a universal, cross-cultural classic of an heroic endeavour encountering catastrophic defeat. It was irresistible. The ambassador of this expedition was a young sailor, long since dead, but whose body looked not much different to us today than it did to his friends and shipmates who buried him in 1846. His partly opened eyes gave him the appearance of just waking from a long sleep, and his parted lips the impression that he was to tell his story of life and death on the expedition. It was as if the 138 intervening years had disappeared, and the mystery and anonymity of the disaster were to come to an end.

In addition to the general public, playwrights, poets, and artists in various media were influenced by this photograph and the Franklin story. Obviously, the photographic images provided a focusing effect – an anchor – to people struggling to relive the Franklin quest, and all of the human experiences involved in the generation of the myth. Had the remains of John Torrington been represented only by his skeleton, it is doubtful there could have been the same response. It was his preserved body that created the link between us in the present and the sailor from the past.

Of all of the depictions of the disaster completed by artists, the one that I find most stirring is the Washington, D.C. based artist Judy Jashinsky's oil-on-linen triptych entitled 'Sleeping Beauty – John Torrington' (Fig. 4). Its gentle serenity is particularly poignant and reflective. In 1994 Canadian artist Vincent Sheridan exhibited etchings and a 3–D construct of John Torrington in Vancouver, British Columbia. Sculptures of the frozen sailors have recently been displayed in a gallery in Edmonton, Alberta. The Royal London Wax Museum in Victoria, British Columbia, has a theme gallery entitled 'Frozen In Time', highlighting the third Franklin expedition, including wax figures of Sir John Franklin and John Torrington in his 'ice-shrouded grave'.

Canadian artist Robert Tombs has used photography as a vehicle in his 'History of Photography' series, where he asks viewers of his work to re-evaluate what we are actually seeing in an historical photograph. In the early 1990s, a number of Ontario galleries exhibited his 18–photograph series, which included the 1985 image 'Portrait of the Artist as John Torrington'.

A number of theatrical pieces have been written and performed based on the images of the frozen sailors and their role in the Franklin tragedy, the most recent (summer, 1995) being that of the Punchbag Theatre in Galway, Ireland. Edmonton, Alberta's Theatre of the New Heart recently (1993) presented a theatre piece entitled 'then AGLOOKA was the ESHEMUTA', inspired both by the Franklin expedition story and by the photograph of John Torrington. Certainly the earliest dramatic treatment of the disaster – and obviously not influenced by John Torrington's photograph – is the play in three acts 'The Frozen Deep', penned

[61]

Figure 4. 'Sleeping Beauty – John Torrington'. Oil on linen, 72" by 84". 1986, Judy Jashinsky. The painting was destroyed in a studio fire (used with permission of the artist).

by Charles Dickens' contemporary Wilkie Collins (1966). Dickens' influence on the play is seen in the play's prologue, written, and sometimes spoken at performance, by Dickens himself.

Poets and novelists have completed, or are working on pieces inspired by the Franklin expedition. Recent reflections on the disaster have come from German author Sten Nadolny ('The Discovery of Slowness' 1987), and Canadian authors Mordecai Richler ('Solomon Gursky Was Here' 1990) and Margaret Atwood ('The Age of Lead' 1991).

Popular music has also been influenced by the images and the story. For example, singer-songwriter James Taylor's 1991 album 'New Moon Shine' has a track entitled 'The Frozen Man'. In their song 'Stranger in a Strange Land', from the 1986 album 'Somewhere in Time', heavy metal band Iron Maiden tell of a young man on a failed quest, who perishes trapped in a land of ice and snow (Smith 1986):

> One-hundred years have gone and men again they come that way,
> To find the answer to the mystery,
> They found his body lying where it fell on that day,
> Preserved in time for all to see. . . .

Another form of popular cultural expression, the comic book, also dealt with the Franklin expedition and the 'frozen man' in the super hero series Alpha Flight (1986). Not surprisingly, the theme of the frozen sailor also turned up on entertainment television (as well as being extensively covered by news television), including jokes and a skit on Johnny Carson's 'Tonight Show' on a US network.

Two American tabloid newspapers have used photographs of John Torrington on their front pages, one blaring the headlines: 'Man buried in ice in 1845 brought back to life! . . . Hush-hush new drug revives corpse, Doctors say' (*Weekly World News*, 3 March 1992, p. 1). As comical as this last observation may seem, there was considerable interest in our research from companies involved in cryonic suspension of human bodies with the intent of future revival. One French journalist from Paris Match asked if we felt we should have left the bodies alone, considering that some time in the future it may have been possible to revive them. My only comment to these ideas is that, in all three of these sailors, the cellular destruction of two rather critical organs, the brain and pancreas, was complete due to autolysis (the process of the body's own enzymes breaking down cellular structures after death). The possibility of future revival seems very remote.

The power and influence of the photographic image is well demonstrated by these disparate interpretations and uses of the images of the frozen sailors. Though truly dead and gone, the sailors have been forcibly reborn to satisfy various artistic pursuits exploring the complexity of the human condition, and for simple entertainment.

The overwhelming effect that these photographs have had on shaping public opinion about the history of nineteenth-century British exploration has not been well received by a few historians, nor has the hypothesis that lead (especially from tinned foods) played a role in the Franklin expedition disaster (Farrer 1993; Trafton 1989; also see Churchyard's vitriolic and accusatory 1992 booklet 'Arctic Critiques'). The collection of physical evidence from the scenes of the Franklin disaster, the application of new and powerful analytical methods to this evidence, the presenting of the objective data in peer-reviewed scientific journals and professional conferences, and the testing of the interpretations developed by historians from their analysis of archival materials and documents (representing subjective personal accounts and interpretations of the researchers), have been seen by most as a proper, constructive, and complementary process. This is how research and science works. For some, I can only interpret that the new information must pose a threat to a sentiment that 'great men must die of great causes', and that to show otherwise is an unforgivable defamation of the character of each hero (Beattie and Geiger 1993).

[63]

Concluding Comments

The one lesson that must be learned from the Franklin disaster is that new technology invariably brings new challenges and risks that are social, psychological, and physical in nature. The most potent and revolutionary forms of new technology are applied – almost by defini- tion – in exploration. What nation or agency would sanction a danger- ous voyage of discovery knowing that their explorers were not equipped and armed with the best technology that was available? Also by definition, exploration pits human vulnerability against unknown challenges and unpredictable future events. Technology is the protector. When the technology fails, the results can be devastating.

The recent loss of the space shuttle *Challenger* provides an important model that can be successfully applied to the Franklin expedition mass disaster. The psychological trauma that was experienced in the United States with the deaths of seven astronaut-explorers, and even world wide, was extensive. The immediacy, intimacy, and brutality of the disaster as it played out live on television was not conducive to the making of heroes in the traditional sense. Seeing the replays of the breakup over and over again reinforced in the public's minds the fact that the astronauts were victims. The idealised quest was preempted by the stark reality of the accident. People were powerless not to visualise the bodies of the astronauts as part of the trailing cloud of liquid hydro- gen and oxygen vapour and debris of the disintegrating spacecraft. They were forced to contrast that horrific imagined vision with the smiling faces of the astronauts seen on television earlier in the day as they boarded *Challenger*. President Reagan's address to the nation later that same day focused on the memory of the astronauts as they appeared before the flight. Even the quickly convened Presidential Commission (Rogers Commission 1986) on the disaster lacked any significant coverage of the bodies of the astronauts, with the exception of the testimony of a FBI special agent (Larabee 1994, paragraph 9):

> we do have human hair, Negro hair, Oriental hair, and hair from two different brown-haired Caucasians....The hair came from face seals, fragments of helmets, and helmet liners, and headrests.

This cold, impersonal, and sanitised description formed a barrier between the comfortable picture of the living astronauts and any thoughts of what the catastrophic forces induced by such an accident can do to the human body. But the accident had been too public. It was also apparent that the command module was not destroyed during the break-up, but continued hurtling in an arc, with some or all of the astronauts still alive, finally hitting the ocean at a speed of nearly 260 km/hr after a fall of 20,000 metres (Armentrout 1993). How could we not place ourselves in that cabin and play out the last moments of those seven lives?

In her discussion of the *Challenger* disaster, Larabee (1994) asserts that in complex closed environments, catastrophe is inescapable. The victims of the catastrophe do not have a means of self-rescue. The Franklin expedition was such a closed system. The two ships were microcosms of the society they had left behind, '...little worlds unto themselves with the full apparatus of Victorian British ideology, culture, and a considerable degree of self-sufficient comfort (or so they thought)' (Grace 1995, 149). Such a system is inherently unstable, with many interdependent components. The failure of a single, seemingly insignificant component can induce a catastrophe whose outcome is both unpredictable and unpreventable (Larabee 1994). Unlike the televised *Challenger* launch, though, it would take many years to piece together the ultimate fate of the Franklin expedition. There were no eye witnesses; the sailors deaths were mysterious and incomprehensible to those back in England. Heroes were born out of the romantic adventure.

With *Challenger*, the investigation of the disaster fell into a number of concurrent phases, including: recovery and analysis of the hardware; recovery, identification, and medical analysis of the bodies of the astronauts; a recreation of events as the disaster unfolded; and a formal inquiry into the causes of the disaster (Rogers Commission 1986). Failure of the O-ring seal in the right solid rocket booster was eventually isolated as the factor leading to the breakup of *Challenger*. This final determination and ultimate acceptance of the causes of the disaster did not emanate from the testimony and records of the management teams or the agencies and companies responsible for the spacecraft, its hardware, and its systems. The subjectivity and complexity of these sources were incapable of focusing on the root causes. Objective evidence came with the eloquent and simple experiment conducted by physicist and Rogers Commission member Richard Feynman on some 'physical evidence' from the shuttle. He showed that, by immersing O-ring material in ice-water (the temperature on the morning of the launch), the flexibility and resilience of the material disappeared, creating a state that produced the 'blow-by' that resulted in the failure of the right solid rocket booster.

The final *Challenger* mission is an example of the risks of exploration, where new – as well as established – technologies and management styles are pushed to their limits. Forensic science was integrally involved in the investigation of the accident. So, too, with the Franklin expedition. Our research into this earlier disaster has documented some of the circumstances surrounding the deaths of approximately a dozen sailors and was accomplished through the recovery and analysis of items from the expedition and the examination of the skeletal remains and preserved bodies of these sailors. We were also able to isolate a major health problem (lead exposure and poisoning) that we suggest originated from a new technology exploited by the expedition: tinned foods.

However, in investigating their deaths, we did more than provide simple scientific fact relating to their last days of life. By providing faces to the heroes, we regressed; we stepped backwards across the line that had separated myth from reality. The comforting and moving story of the eternal quest becomes the cold and chiseled edge of true and personal human suffering. We now know too much about these people to ascribe to them attributes that make them bigger than life. John Torrington was 162.5 cm tall, he was thin and frail, his health was severely affected by working with coal dust and pipe smoking, and he died an unpleasant death at 20 years of age from poisoning, a kind of death we can document and describe in meticulous detail from modern medical cases. Some people are not happy that we did this. Truth can sometimes threaten heroes. Yet, most see all this from a different perspective. By making the heroes real, we can associate with them on a personal level and relive their true experiences on the expedition, and John Torrington becomes a different kind of hero so much more like ourselves.

ACKNOWLEDGMENTS

I would like to thank the following agencies for supporting the research reported in this paper: the Social Sciences and Humanities Research Council of Canada, the University of Alberta, the Polar Continental Shelf Project, and the Boreal Institute for Northern Studies. Thanks also to Lynda Beattie, Dean Bamber, Pamela Mayne-Correia, and Sabine Stratton for comments on the manuscript.

NOTE

1. *Toronto Globe*, 11 October, 1859.

REFERENCES

Alpha Flight. 1986. *Death/Birth* 1 (37, August).
Amy, R., R. Bahatnagar, E. Damkjar, and O. B. Beattie 1986. The last Franklin expedition: report of a postmortem examination of a crew member. *Canadian Medical Association Journal* 135, 115–117.

Anonymous. 1883. Dangers of canned food. *Medical News* xliii, 270.

Armentrout, T. 1993. Reconstructive analysis of the space shuttle *Challenger*. In *Proceedings of the International Symposium on the Forensic Aspects of Mass Disasters and Crime Scene Reconstruction*, 93–96. Federal Bureau of Investigation, Department of Justice, United States Government Printing Office, Washington, D.C.

Atwood, M. 1991. The Age of Lead. In *Wilderness Tips*, 157–175. McClelland and Stewart, Toronto.

Beattie, O. B. 1983. A report on newly discovered human remains from the last Sir John Franklin expedition. *The Muskox* 33, 68–77.

Beattie, O. B. 1985. Elevated bone lead levels in a crewman from the last Arctic Expedition of Sir John Franklin. In P. Sutherland (ed.), *The Franklin Era in Canadian Arctic History: 1845–1859* 141–148. National Museum of Man (Mercury Series Archaeological Survey of Canada 131), Ottawa.

Beattie, O. B. 1993. Applying forensic anthropology to historical problems. In *Proceedings of the International Symposium on the Forensic Aspects of Mass Disasters and Crime Scene Reconstruction*, 79–92. Federal Bureau of Investigation, Department of Justice, United States Government Printing Office, Washington, D.C.

Beattie, O. B. and R. Amy 1990. A report on present investigations into the loss of the third Franklin expedition (1845–1848), emphasizing the 1984 research on Beechey Island. *Inter-Nord* 19, 77–85.

Beattie, O. B. and J. G. Geiger 1993. *Frozen in Time: the Fate of the Franklin Expedition*. Bloomsbury, London.

Beattie, O. B. and J. M. Savelle 1983. Discovery of human remains from Sir John Franklin's last expedition. *Historical Archaeology* 17, 100–105.

Churchyard, C. 1992. *Arctic Critiques*. Devil's Thumb Press.

Collins, W. 1966. *The Frozen Deep*. Edited by R. L. Brannon. Cornell University Press, Ithaca, N.Y. Note: an edition of the script for the 1857 production of the play, edited and produced by Charles Dickens, pp. 95–160.

Cyriax, R. J. 1939. *Sir John Franklin's Last Arctic Expedition*. Methuen, London.

Farrer, K. T. H. 1993. Lead and the last Franklin expedition. *Journal of Archaeological Science* 20, 399–409.

Foulke, J. E. 1993. Lead threat lessens, but mugs pose problem. *FDA Consumer* 8.

Gilder, W. H. 1881. *Schwatka's Search*. Scribner's Sons, New York.

Grace, S. E. 1995. 'Franklin Lives': Atwood's Northern Ghosts. In L. M. York (ed.), *Various Atwoods: Essays on the Later Poems, Short Fiction, and Novels*, 146–166. House of Anansi Press, Concord, Ontario.

Kottmann, B. [bkottman@erinet.com] 1995. President Reagan's Speech on the *Challenger* Disaster. [http://www.erinet.com/bkottman/speeches/Challenger.html].

Kowal, W., O. B. Beattie, H. Baadsgaard, and P. Krahn 1990. Did solder kill Franklin's men? *Nature* 343, 319–320.

Kowal, W., O. B. Beattie, H. Baadsgaard, and P. Krahn 1991. Source identification of lead found in tissues of sailors from the Franklin arctic expedition of 1845. *Journal of Archaeological Science* 19, 193–203.

Kowal, W., P. Krahn, and O. B. Beattie 1989. Lead levels in human tissues from the Franklin Forensic Project. *International Journal of Analytical Chemistry* 35, 119–126.

Kowalewska-Grochowska, K., R. Amy, B. Lui, R. McWhirter, and H. Merrill 1988. Isolation and sensitivities of century-old bacteria from the Franklin expedition. Poster presented at the Interscience Conference of Antimicrobial Agents and Chemotherapy, Los Angeles, California, 24 October.

Larabee, A. 1994. Remembering the Shuttle, forgetting the loom: interpreting the *Challenger* disaster. *Postmodern Culture* 4(3). [http://jefferson.village.virginia.edu/issue.594/larabee.594.html]

Magruder, W. E. 1883. Lead-poisoning from canned food. *Medical News* 43, 261–263.

M'Clintock, F. L. 1908. *The Voyage of the 'Fox' in Arctic Seas.* John Murray, London.

Nadolny, S. 1987. *The Discovery of Slowness.* Viking, New York.

Neatby, L. H. 1958. *In Quest of the Northwest Passage.* Longmans, Green and Company, Toronto.

Neatby, L. H. 1970. *Search for Franklin.* Hurtig, Edmonton.

Notman, D. and O. B. Beattie 1995. The palaeoimaging and forensic anthropology of frozen sailors from the Franklin arctic expedition mass disaster (1845–1848): a detailed presentation of two radiological surveys. In K. Spindler (ed.), *Der Mann im Eis,* vol. 3. Springer-Verlag, Vienna.

Rogers Commission. 1986. *Report to the President.* U.S. Presidential Commission on the Space Shuttle *Challenger* Accident. Washington, D.C.

Richler, M. 1990. *Solomon Gursky Was Here.* Penguin Books, Markham, Ontario.

Ross, John. 1835. *Narrative of a Second Voyage in Search of a Northwest Passage, and of a Residence in the Arctic Regions During the Years 1829, 1830, 1831, 1832, 1833.* A. W. Webster, London.

Simpson, T. 1843. *Narrative of the Discoveries on the North Coast of America: Effected by the Officers of the Hudson's Bay Company during the Years 1836–39.* Richard Bentley, London.

Smith, A. 1986. *Stranger in a Strange Land.* Zomba Music Publishers, London.

Stackpole, E. A. (ed.) 1965. *The Long Arctic Search: The Narrative of Lieutenant Frederick Schwatka, U.S.A., 1878–1880.* Marine Historical Association, Mystic.

Trafton, S. J. 1989. Did lead poisoning contribute to the deaths of Franklin expedition members? *Information North* 15, 1–4.

U.S. Department of Health and Social Services. 1988. *The Nature and Extent of Lead Poisoning in Children in the United States: A Report to Congress.* Public Health Service, Georgia.

Wightwick, F. 1888. Canned vegetables and lead poisoning. *Lancet* 2, 1121.

6

The landscape context of the Iron-Age square-barrow burials, East Yorkshire

Bill Bevan

What I like about Clive
Is that he is no longer alive.
There is a great deal to be said
For being dead.

– Edmund Clerihew Bentley
(*Biography for Beginners*, '*Clive of India*')

The *application of social theory* and contextualism to the archaeology of death has led to a number of interpretations and reinterpretations of mortuary sites. Of particular relevance to this paper, however, are two areas of research which have *rarely* been addressed by these studies; Iron-Age society and the spatial arrangement of burials in the landscape.

While the more 'processual' approaches in archaeology have promoted landscape studies of Neolithic and Bronze-Age tombs, most contextual studies have focused on the internal structures of the tombs and the deposition of both corpse(s) and grave goods within them (Fleming 1973; Renfrew 1975; Shanks and Tilley 1982; Richards 1988; Thomas 1988; Barrett 1990). The nature, distribution, and interrelationship of activities in the landscape is of vital importance in understanding the past. Topographical features such as valleys, hills, bogs, waterways, woodlands, and grasslands have their own cultural meanings articulated through the social practices of the people who live at a certain place at a certain time (Jackson and Hudman 1990; Bender 1993). In combination with economic, environmental, and climatic factors, these cultural meanings influence how activities within the landscape are structured. The landscape created by these activities is then internalised by societies in their own ways and used in the construction of social perceptions, myths, and attitudes (Cosgrove 1989; Moreland 1992). Relationships between burials, topographical features, and human-made sites, such as settlements and boundaries, can therefore be used to identify and interpret attitudes to death and social structures lying behind the funerary sites (Sharples 1985; Hodder 1991; J. Chapman 1991; Parker-Pearson 1993).

With the exception of Parker-Pearson's (1993) study of the Iron Age in Denmark, much of the archaeological research which views funerary rites and remains as active in the social relations of the living has been on Neolithic and Bronze-Age material. Indeed, the theoretical approach that material culture is active in constructing social relationships has, until recently, largely passed the Iron Age by, producing an interpretative dichotomy between the study of earlier and later prehistory. Society in the Iron Age is still too often assumed to be uniformly 'Celtic' and, interpreted in relation to modern Western concepts, as familiar or similar to our own (Hill 1989). This depiction does little except impose our image of current Western society back onto the Iron Age (for an example see Cunliffe 1991).

Here I will attempt to apply the type of contextual approach employed successfully on Neolithic and Bronze-Age funerary data to the Iron-Age La Tène square-barrow cemeteries in East Yorkshire. These cemeteries are ideal as an object of study. They form one of the largest single group of prehistoric burials in Britain, and the data is extensively recorded and easily accessible (Lang 1986). The Iron Age of East Yorkshire has long been studied by antiquarians and archaeologists, beginning with Stillingfleet, Greenwell, and Mortimer, who opened 'British' barrows and excavated linear earthworks in the nineteenth century, and continuing recently with large-scale excavations of square-barrow cemeteries, field-walking programmes, and plotting of crop-marks (Stillingflett 1846; Greenwell 1865; Mortimer 1905; Sheppard 1939; Stead 1961; 1965; 1975; 1976; 1979; 1991; Ramm 1973; 1974; 1978; Brewster 1980; Dent 1982; 1983; 1984; 1985; Turnbull 1983). These projects have produced records of a large number of Iron-Age square-barrow burial sites.

The data used for this study was provided by the Sites and Monuments Records (SMRs) of Humberside and North Yorkshire County Councils, and the Royal Commission on Historic Monuments (England) (RCHM(E)). There is also a wealth of information available from numerous surveys and excavations, the most useful being the modern, open-area, excavations at Garton Slack, Wetwang Slack, Rudston/Burton Fleming, Bell Slack, Garton Station, and Kirkburn (Brewster 1980; Dent

1982; 1984; Stead 1991).

Much of the archaeological work on square-barrow burials has either been site specific or has mapped cemetery locations. This has been extremely productive in identifying the distribution of square barrows, similarities and variations in the style of funerary monument, the nature of the burial rite within the grave, and the dates for the rite's use. While the topographical and archaeological relationships of some sites have been noted, this has not been approached systematically, but instead has been undertaken as secondary to the discussion of the inhumation rite and barrow morphology (Dent 1982; 1984; Stead 1991; Whimster 1981). The aim of this study is to investigate the square-barrow burials in the context of a landscape of topographical and archaeological relationships beyond the cemeteries. The relationships are interpreted from a predominantly landscape archaeology approach, incorporating excavated and artefactual evidence where available. The internal organisation of cemeteries is also investigated in an attempt to identify whether burials are aligned with natural or archaeological features.

Only those cemeteries consisting of ten or more barrows were used for this study, comprising over half of the known square barrows. Ten barrows is compatible with previous work on the material, making access to, and comparisons with, other information easier because the English Heritage Monument Protection Plan Monument Class Description and the Sites and Monuments Records of Humberside and North Yorkshire County Councils use this figure as a minimum to define square-barrow cemeteries. Groups of spatially adjacent barrows are required to identify confidently relationships between the burials and other archaeological features on aerial photographs and excavation plans. The positive identification of a relationship requires the recognition of the deliberate respect or alignment of the cemetery with the other feature. Without evidence for this alignment, barrows may well have been coincidentally placed near a feature or it may even be later. Cemeteries also become *locales*, specific locations used over a long period for a particular type of use (Bradley 1987). While a single burial could be a 'one off' use of that location for funerary rites or an accident of archaeological survival, the burial of a number of people at one place over a period of time creates a time-depth of use and significance for the community whose dead are buried there.

THE LAY OF THE LAND: GEOGRAPHIC LOCATION

East Yorkshire is a geographically distinct area situated on the northeast coast of England north of the Humber estuary (Fig. 1). It is bordered on the north by the escarpment of the Tabular hills and to the

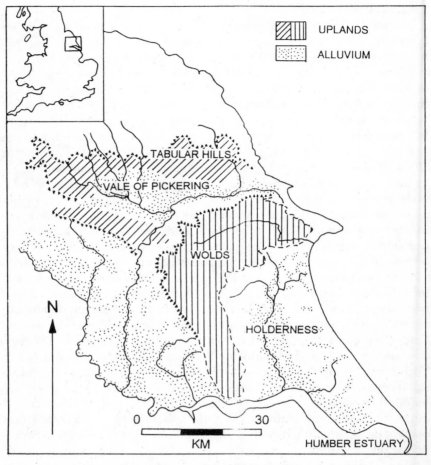

Figure 1. East Yorkshire, location and topography.

west by the rivers Ouse and Derwent. Dominating the region is the crescent-shaped chalk outcrop of the Yorkshire Wolds rising to approximately 160 metres above Ordnance datum.

The wolds are dissected by numerous winding, steep-sided, narrow, dry valleys known as slacks (Foster and Milton 1967). The slacks appear to have been formed by glacial and sub-glacial meltwater action (Foster 1987). Water is usually absent from the surfaces of these valleys and instead follows the lines of the slacks along underground fissures. Except for the Gypsey Race in the Great Wold valley, water only runs along the valley surfaces intermittently (Lewin 1969; Foster and Milton 1976). Known regionally as gypseys (pronounced with a hard g as in 'goat'), these streams are rare today and generally only appear after periods of heavy rainfall. As the wolds become gradually gentler to the south and east, the valleys become wider and shallower until they reach the lower, flatter, ground of the Holderness plain. In the area where the chalk outcrop meets the lowlands, the subterranean streams appear above ground as springs. To the north and west, the wolds drop sharply to the Vales of York and Pickering. Much of the lowlands are drained wetlands, largely comprising glacially deposited clays, silts, sands, and gravels.

THE BODY POLITIC: THE SQUARE-BARROW FUNERAL RITE

Square-barrow burials date from between the mid-fifth and first centuries BC, and form the largest group of Iron-Age inhumations known in Britain (Stead 1991). The majority of those not excavated in the nineteenth century have since been ploughed level and can be identified as crop marks. They are distributed across the region but are concentrated on the lower dip-slope of the southern and eastern wolds (Fig. 2). Relatively few sites have been found on the lowlands, though this may be due to the lowland boulder clay's low susceptibility to aerial photography. Where barrows are identifiable on the lowlands they tend to occur where the underlying chalk becomes the ground level geology through the clay.

The distinctive burial comprises a low square barrow covering an earth-cut grave enclosed within a square plan ditch (Fig. 3). Dimensions of the ditches vary from 3 to 15 metres across. Barrow heights can be estimated from standing sites which survive to between only 8 and 75 centimetres high (Stead 1975). Erosion of the barrows shows that they would have originally been somewhat higher.

Most graves contain a single articulated inhumation, generally lying contracted on one side and orientated north to south (Fig. 3). Males and females appear in similar ratios, but there are only a small number of infant burials and these usually occupy the barrow ditches (Whimster 1981; Dent 1984; Stead. S 1991). Grave goods are common though not universally provided. Of recently excavated burials, approximately 36% included grave goods (Dent 1984; Stead 1991). Most common are La Tène style brooches, pots, and sheep and pig bones. Less customary are finds of glass beads, bracelets, rings, swords, and tools. The square-barrow burials are probably most famous for the well-publicised finds of a small number of vehicles described as chariots or carts (Dent 1985; Stead 1991). However, these vehicle burials only comprise a tiny fraction of the graves excavated and should be thought of as special burials. Other unusual burials include a group of male corpses which

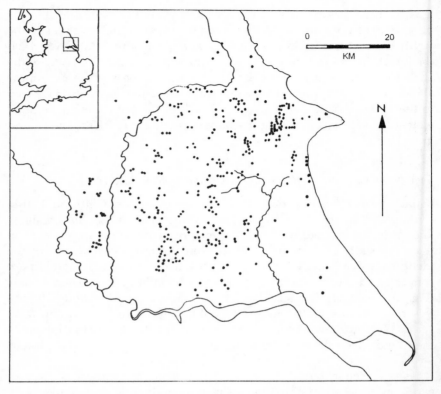

Figure 2. Distribution of square-barrow burials in East Yorkshire.

have had spears thrust into and around them after burial, and a small group of females who died while pregnant or during child-birth and were buried with the foetus or child in place (Stead 1991). A unique find at Garton Slack comprised a male and female double inhumation with a feotus within the pelvis of the female and a wooden stake thrust between the two bodies to which the corpses wrists appear to have been attached (Brewster 1980).

Over half of the square barrows are grouped into cemeteries, some comprising hundreds of graves. At some of the cemeteries, such as at Nunburnholme, the burials are widely dispersed with no evidence of internal organisation (Fig. 4). At others, such as Foxholes and Carnaby, the graves are closer together and arranged into highly structured rows (Fig. 4).

Such groupings of dead people are surely not simply random but represent part of the socially held attitude to the treatment of the community's individuals after death (Bevan, forthcoming). Making

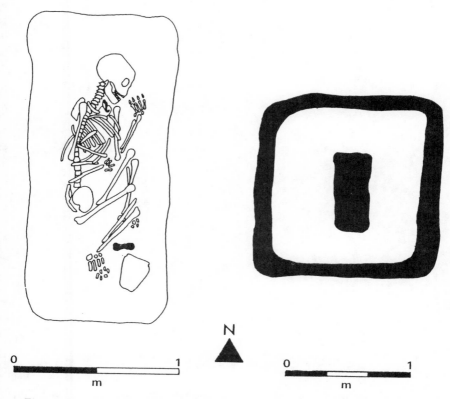

N

0 _____ 1
m

0 _____ 1
m

Figure 3. A typical square barrow in East Yorkshire: whole barrow in plan (right) and inhumation with grave goods (left).

visible a group's ancestors, in this case by creating a mound above the grave, gives physical expression to the dead in the affairs of the living (Parker-Pearson 1982). The deliberate grouping together of these ancestors into discrete locations may be seen as strengthening this expression by forming a wider arena for social discourse (Chapman 1991). The square-barrow cemeteries emphasised common identity and cohesion by symbolising a social ideal of shared descent within a community. This may have formed an idealised kin group, whether or not there was a reality of strong genetic relations. It also established a communal link with a geographic location, so producing as a culturally held concept that a claim to land or resources was ancestrally held (Bloch 1971; Bradley 1984). Because these barrows marked the locations of separate graves, they also symbolised the perceived importance of the individual. This suggests a symbolised balance or conflict between the group and the individual, both of which may be perceived as socially important.

Figure 4. Typical square-barrow cemeteries in East Yorkshire (clockwise from top left): Foxholes, Carnaby, and Nunburnholme (after RCHM(E)).

This ancestral representation of the duality between the individual and the community attempts to reaffirm inter-personal relationships and diminish individuality by incorporation into a society with a set of social rules and norms (Bloch 1971; Giddens 1984). Individual freedom of action is diminished by the benefits of group membership.

[76]

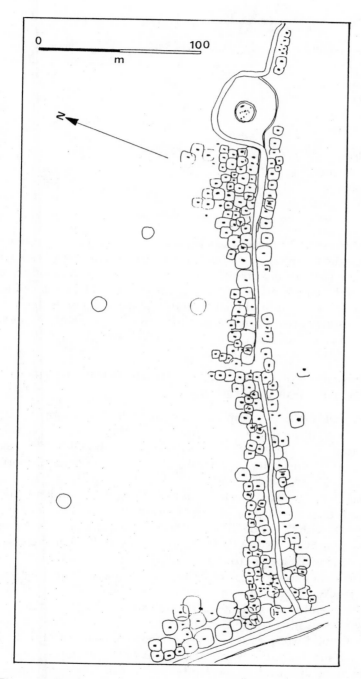

Figure 5. Wetwang Slack square-barrow cemetery (after Dent 1982).

Table 1. *Topographical distribution of La Tène cemeteries in East Yorkshire.*

Topography	number of cemeteries	percentage
Lowland		
plain	14	22.2%
hillside	2	3.2%
hilltop	0	0%
Upland		
valley bottom	22	34.9%
valley side	15	23.8%
watershed	10	15.9%

The difference between dispersed and closely packed cemeteries appears to be a chronological one. This is seen at Wetwang Slack where the more systematically arranged smaller barrows are generally later in date than the larger, more dispersed, barrows (Fig. 5). Evidence for this comes from stratigraphical relationships and dates of grave goods (Dent 1984). This may strengthen the signification of the community at some expense to that of the individual (Bevan, forthcoming).

DEATH IN THE COUNTRYSIDE: THE LANDSCAPE SETTING OF THE SQUARE-BARROW CEMETERIES

Topographical analysis. It can be seen in table 1 that square-barrow cemeteries occur in all but one of the topographical zones which can be identified in East Yorkshire. The results not only show that the majority of sites are found on the wold uplands with a significant minority of sites identified in the lowlands, but that there are preferential topographical zones for the placement of cemeteries. In the uplands there is a strong preference for placing cemeteries in valleys rather than on the watersheds, with 78.7% of all uplands cemeteries located either in valley bottoms or on valley sides (table 2). In the lowlands cemeteries lie predominantly on the lower ground, avoiding the uncommon hills.

This tendency towards lower ground is in contrast to the distribution of Bronze-Age round barrows, which are generally located on the watersheds and tops of slopes. Although the Bronze-Age data has not been systematically studied to allow direct comparisons, and more potential round barrow sites in the lowlands are being identified as ring ditch crop marks, it does seem that a shift in the attitudes towards the placement of the dead in the landscape occurred between these two phases of barrow burial.

Table 2. Topographical distribution of La Tène cemeteries on the Yorkshire Wolds only.

Topography	number of cemeteries	percentage
valley bottom	22	46.8%
valley side	15	31.9%
watershed	10	21.3%

Table 3. Relationship of East Yorkshire La Tène cemeteries to trackways and boundaries.

Relationship to boundary	number of cemeteries	percentage
adjacent to a boundary	17	27%
adjacent to an enclosure	2	3%
adjacent to a trackway	17	27%
at a trackway terminal	2	3%
linear feature of unknown function	6	10%
no observed relationship to a boundary	19	30%

Visibility of the square barrows is reduced by their location within valleys and on lower ground. The small size of the square barrows also reduces their prominence over long distances. Their visibility would have been heightened on the wolds if the chalk-white mound was left or kept exposed after the burial ceremony. To what extent they stood out or blended into the surrounding landscape would have depended on whether they were deliberately returfed, allowed to naturally grass over, or maintained as bared chalk after construction. This visibility relates to how obvious the cemeteries would have been to people over a long distance, but much of the interaction probably occurred at relatively close proximity, as the analysis of the surrounding human-built landscape will show below.

Association with better agricultural soils may have been a reason for the preferential placing of barrows in valleys. All of the wolds are well below the altitude of agricultural marginality reconstructed for the Iron Age (Higham 1987). While there are much deeper soils within the steeper valleys of the central wolds, the valleys along the dip-slope are too shallow for significantly better agricultural soils to be produced lower down slope. Crop marks of field-systems do not concentrate in the valleys but can be found equally on higher ground. It therefore appears that the valleys of the wolds did not have a significantly greater agricultural potential than the hilltops in the Iron Age.

Water is not as notable a feature of today's East Yorkshire landscape as it would have been in the past. In the wolds only the Gypsey Race runs above ground for most of the year. Gypsies used to be more common before the water-table was lowered by industrial and residential water use in Hull from the nineteenth century onwards (Foster, Parry, and Chiltern 1976). The gypseys regularly followed a cyclical pattern, drying out over the summer as the relatively drier weather lowered the water-table and reappearing as fast flowing streams during the wetter winter. Eighteenth-century travellers' accounts refer to the regular appearances after heavy rainfall of the swift-flowing gypseys, surging down the dry valleys as if from nowhere (Woodward 1985). Even in living memory the gypseys were more of a feature of the wolds landscape than they are today (Chris Fenton-Thomas pers. comm.). The main source of groundwater is infiltrating rainfall (Foster, Pary, and Chilton 1976). The level of rainfall was, therefore, the biggest single influence on the absence, presence or permanence of the gypsey streams before the nineteenth century. During the Iron Age, it appears that the climate of East Yorkshire was similar to that of the twentieth century (Higham 1987). It would therefore seem that the intermittent nature of the gypseys would have been a feature during the Iron Age. In the lowlands many of the watercourses are drainage ditches except for the larger rivers. To identify any funerary relationship with water, the hydrology of the Iron-Age landscape has first to be reconstructed.

In the valleys of the wolds the projected most likely course for a stream was taken to be the centre of each valley. This is the lowest part of a valley, and approximately overlies the fissure carrying water underground along the line of the valley. In a number of valleys, sink holes caused by these fissures can be seen into which water flows, collects, and percolates underground during heavy rainstorms. One such sink hole is overlain by a Bronze-Age earthwork and others were identified during excavations of square barrows and the related settlement in Garton Slack (Brewster 1980), showing that they existed in the Iron Age and are not just a modern phenomenon. In the lowlands natural streams have to be recognised from the numerous drainage ditches. Only streams plotted on the earliest available maps, dating from the eighteenth century, or which appear to be natural by their irregular nature and respect shown by later field boundaries have been used. In addition hollows and lower-lying areas which have been heavily drained have also been included as once being natural marshes or meres.

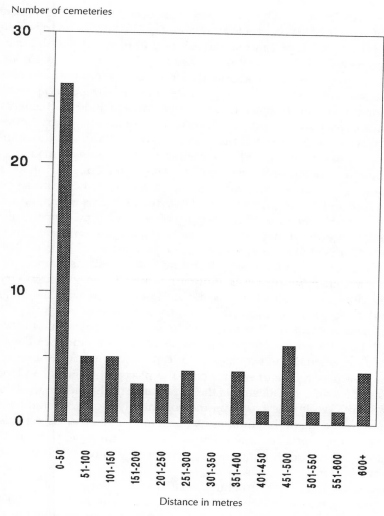

Figure 6. Distance of La Tène cemeteries in East Yorkshire from water.

The results of this analysis show that there was a strong preference for burying the dead of Iron-Age East Yorkshire near to water (Fig. 6). Nearly half of all cemeteries are situated within 50 metres of an actual or potential watercourse. The nearest body of water to three-quarters of all the cemeteries are watercourses, rather than ponds or springs. Of these, 60% are aligned with or orientated in the same direction as the watercourse. Even when at a greater distance from water, almost all of the cemeteries have some line-of-sight relationship with water.

Archaeological analysis. The cemeteries' associations with the non-funerary aspects of the archaeological landscape laid down on top of the topographical landscape can not only be used to interpret possible relationships between life and death, but they can also be used to see if any of these features explain the seemingly strong correspondence between barrows and waterways. The range of features in the landscape pre-dating or contemporary with the square barrows includes settlements, boundaries, enclosures, marked trackways, cursuses, henges, other funerary sites, and cup-and-ring-marked stones. Most of these are visible today as crop marks, while some survive as standing remains.

The relative spatial organisation of funerary and domestic space is important in understanding attitudes to death and the relationship between life and death in any society. Unfortunately, this is unrealisable for East Yorkshire because of the paucity of settlement evidence, which contrasts to the rich funerary data. The only contemporary settlement yet identified is at Wetwang/Garton Slack (Brewster 1980; Dent 1984). The site consists of approximately 80 round houses with associated pits, enclosures, four-post structures, and earthworks. Over 450 burials are situated close to this settlement. Some are interspersed with the buildings but most lie alongside a surrounding bank-and-ditch earthwork, which forms one side of a trackway. There is a close proximity of funerary and domestic space along one of the settlement's boundaries but we do not know whether this arrangement is typical for East Yorkshire.

The construction of barrows to mark the places of the dead in Iron-Age East Yorkshire demonstrates the importance of the past in the Iron-Age present. While this past was the community's own, brought into existence by the life of the community itself, more distant pasts may also have been appropriated and constructed. This may be seen in the archaeological record through the association of features with those of a much earlier date.

There is no observable structured spatial association with any of the earlier settlement sites, cursuses, henges, or cup-and-ring-marked stones (Bevan 1993). While the clearly defined eastern edge of the cemetery at Makeshift is nearly oriented in the same direction as the north-south cursus to the east, the cemetery is actually aligned on the Gypsey Race which used to run between the two but has now been diverted over the cursus (Fig. 7). Boundaries associated with the cemetery cut the cursus showing that it had either been flattened or had become an insignificant site by the Iron Age. A square-barrow cemetery is near to only one of the very small number of henges in the region. This henge lies to the north of Makeshift and can be seen as a clearly defined crop mark (Fig. 7). Adjacent to this is a cemetery but its closeness is likely to be coincidental because no alignment can be seen with the henge, nor

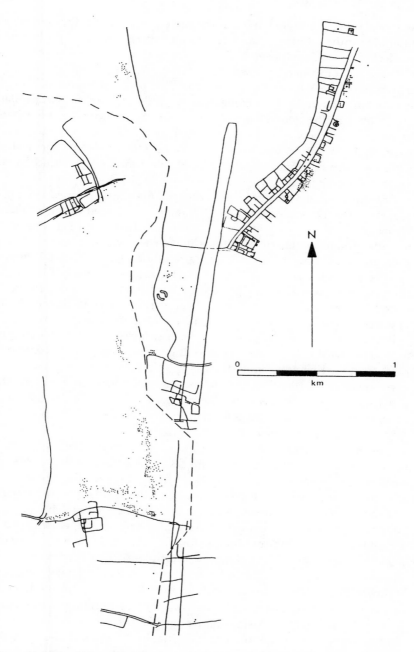

Figure 7. Makeshift and other cemeteries (shown stippled) in the Great Wold valley near Rudston, showing their relationships with the Gypsey Race (shown as a dashed line), boundaries, and trackways (after RCHM(E)).

with the other possible henges in the region. If anything the cemetery is oriented with a linear crop-mark to the west which is probably an earlier course of the Gypsey Race.

There are only minimal associations with earlier funerary sites. The majority of the square-barrow cemeteries have no relationship with earlier barrows at all. Five cemeteries, including those at Garton Slack, are located in the general areas of Bronze-Age barrows without being grouped or aligned with them. However, neither have any of the round barrows been cut by any of the Iron-Age burials except for a single instance of an inhumation being placed in a Bronze-Age round barrow and a square ditch cut around it (Humberside SMR).

Only two square-barrow cemeteries are definitely aligned on earlier barrows. The linear cemetery at Rillington is oriented along a ditched enclosure, part of which at least is later than the burials because one of its outer ditches cuts some of the square barrows, and uses a Bronze-Age group of round barrows as its southern terminal. At Wetwang Slack some of the Iron-Age burials cluster around an early Bronze-Age round barrow which forms the eastern focal point for the cemetery. The round barrow was even respected by an earthwork built during the use of the cemetery which cuts some of the Iron-Age burials (Fig. 5).

While it seems that the presence of earlier barrows was not an important factor in the landscape positioning of square-barrow cemeteries, they were deliberately not disturbed when they were present. The avoidance of earlier burials by square barrows located in their proximity shows the awareness and desire not to disturb the earlier funeral sites but otherwise they had only a limited effect on the Iron-Age mortuary landscape of East Yorkshire.

Boundaries existing in the Iron Age can be identified as standing ditch-and-bank earthworks or as marks created in growing crops. The earliest recognisable boundaries date from the Bronze Age, when a system of dykes was built across much of the wolds, the Tabular hills and parts of the lowlands (Manby 1980; Chris Fenton-Thomas pers. comm.). The dykes represent large-scale land management and its acceptance by the communities using the area covered by the boundaries (Fleming 1988). Most comprise multiple-ditched earthworks, some of which are a number of miles in length and form major landscape features. They were utilised, recut, and elaborated during the Iron Age and were also used as a basic framework for later infilling with less substantial boundaries to form smaller enclosures which were probably field systems. Trackways are also identifiable throughout East Yorkshire when bounded by ditched earthworks. They form an integral part of the enclosed landscape, becoming boundaries in their own right as well as facilitating communication. Some can be interpreted as wide through-routes running along valleys while others are shorter, settlement routes which join different enclosures together. The Iron-Age landscape contemporary with the square-barrow burials was a highly spatially organised one (Bevan 1997) and square-barrow burials have a strong relationship with this enclosed landscape. Approximately 70% of the cemeteries are located next to boundaries or enclosures (table 3). The cemeteries were positioned near either boundaries or tracks in approximately equal numbers. Major boundary dykes and their later subdivisions were both equally chosen as the location for cemeteries.

Neither the relationship between square-barrow cemeteries and boundaries or trackways can be used to explain a coincidental association with water. While some of the trackways follow valleys, there are boundaries and tracks with cemeteries placed next to them across the region in a whole range of topographical settings. Thus, the square-barrow cemeteries of East Yorkshire have highly structured landscape settings, preferentially located within valleys or lower ground and associated with water, boundaries, and trackways.

Interpretation. Elsewhere in Britain there is a late Bronze-Age increase in the deposition of objects in watery places which may be linked to funerary practices (Bradley 1990). This association cannot be identified in East Yorkshire due to the small number of Bronze-Age artefacts discovered in non-funerary contexts (Bevan 1993). But later, the funerary rites in East Yorkshire do occur within the wider context of the deposition of objects and human remains in watery places in Britain throughout the Iron Age. These depositions are predominantly found in the marshes and rivers of eastern England where the range of objects became more general and less related to contemporary grave goods than in the late Bronze Age. During the late Iron Age there was an increase in the deposition of objects in watery places which is contemporary with an increase in burials accompanied by grave goods. The waterways used for these depositions generally formed the boundaries of major territorial areas as identified by coin distributions (ibid.).

A concept which may link the association of death with water, boundaries, and trackways in East Yorkshire is that of liminality. A corpse was conceived as being between the two worlds during this liminal phase of the life-to-death transition. This phase was entered on the physical death of the person for both that person and for the mourners. This phase ended when the corpse reached the world of the dead, while the living were reincorporated into the world of the living. The rate of this process of transition varies in different societies and may be accompanied by distinct ceremonies at each stage. It may take place in specially sanctioned locations, somehow marked off from the world

[85]

of the living, and may be conceived as a physical journey or spiritual transformation (Huntington and Metcalf 1979). The separation and marking off of the world of the dead from the world of the living can be seen in Iron-Age East Yorkshire in the contrast between the burial monuments and contemporary houses – the built structures most associated with death and with life. All of the houses yet discovered from this period (from Wetwang and Garton Slack) are round and have entrances facing east. Round houses have been found elsewhere in the region dating from both earlier and later dates, suggesting that this was the common house form throughout the Iron Age. In opposition to this, the ditches and barrows surrounding and covering the burials are nearly all square and in the very small number of cases where there are deliberate breaks in the ditches these face west.

Water, boundaries, and trackways can all be described as holding liminal locations in the socially constructed landscape. The deposition of objects and human remains in watery places, especially those located on the borders of territories, elsewhere in Britain during the Iron Age implies the liminal position of water at this time. Such a concept could be powerfully developed in the wolds by the intermittent nature of the gypseys. By being above ground for part of the year and underground the rest, gypseys do not hold a permanent place in this world but may be conceived as being between two worlds. Boundaries hold peripheral positions by defining the edges of activity, whether agricultural or territorial. Trackways delineated by earthworks share the peripheral positions of boundaries but may also hold a more liminal social position through their use by people who would, perhaps, be forbidden access to other parts of the landscape. While certain parts of the landscape may be tied to the use of one community, trackways (or at least through-routes) would have been used by different communities and possibly belonged to none. Cemetery association with water, boundaries, and trackways may therefore be related to a desire to place the dead in liminal areas of the landscape where the rite of passage from living to dead could occur. It is also worth noting that many societies perceive death as being a journey across a landscape, whether real or imaginary (Huntington and Metcalf 1979). This journey of the dead could be facilitated by placing them next to trackways.

The late Iron-Age deposition of objects in rivers forming political boundaries has been interpreted as combining ritual and political activities to legitimise social dominance and group identity (Bradley 1990). The visible marking of the dead in the square-barrow cemeteries stressed community identity, linked that community with a geographic location, and could have made a connection with resources believed to be important to the reproduction of the group. In a·sense, the placing of cemeteries next to water, boundaries, and trackways promoted the community's existing use of a resource as an idealised unchallengeable right based on the proclamation of the use of that resource by the community's ancestors. At some locations this association was further strengthened by the deliberate alignment of square barrows in rows parallel or perpendicular to the adjacent feature.

In the wolds, the intermittent nature of the gypseys would have meant that naturally occurring water was a limited resource, access to which may have required strong legitimisation. There is little evidence for artificial water storage in the region during the Iron Age. No wells or cisterns have been discovered from that date, though there is a well approximately 30 metres deep at Garton Slack during the Roman occupation and a number of ponds distributed across the chalk associated with Mesolithic flints (Pat Wagner pers. comm.). Without local water storage, long journeys to the springs situated along the edge of the wolds and the Gypsey Race would have been essential during the dry periods of the gypsey's cycle. The carriage of water and driving of livestock between settlements and springs would have been a regular, probably daily routine.

In the lowlands water may have been perceived differently, but no less socially important, because it dominated the landscape and provided a habitat for much of the food available. Without drainage, arable farming would have been limited to the small areas of higher, drier, ground. Livestock, hunted wild animals and fish, and gathered plants would have been important resources. The linking of burials to the wetter places in the lowlands may have been an attempt to legitimise access to the social resources water supported rather than the water itself.

The placing of burials on boundaries marking limits of land availability and use reinforces symbolism inherent in the boundaries themselves by situating it in ancestral time (Bevan 1997). Earthworks have functional uses, perhaps as stock-proof boundaries or demarcators of different areas of land use. However, they also have a broader significance to the communities who build, maintain and add to them. They can symbolise community identity, status, and rights of access to land. They can also act as boundaries of social exclusion by dividing one group from another, and inclusion by placing a limit around a group of people conceived of as forming one community (Hingley 1987).

The social construction of the boundaries can be identified by the provision of dykes with several ditches, unnecessary if the earthworks were only being used functionally. This implies an important level of symbolism, as well as functionality, within the boundaries, which would contribute to the creation of social relations. These dykes also had a long antiquity by the time of the inception of the square-barrow burial rite.

Through their antiquity the legitimacy of the borders they delineate would have been strengthened, whether agricultural, social, or political. Even a simple single earthwork field boundary has symbolic worth in the social landscape.

When cemeteries are associated with trackways another social dimension is added to the burials in allowing the display of the dead to travellers along those routes. Trackways allow access to the resources utilised by the community within its land, such as fields, woodland, and water. Stock can be moved along bounded tracks without trespassing on neighbouring fields. Tracks also provide the means for inter-communal contact by facilitating the movement of people along mediated and prescribed routes through the landscape. Such contact is necessary in the negotiation of economic and social relations. Inter-personal communication, whether or nor accompanied by some form of exchange or ceremony, is essential to the creation and maintenance of relationships within a region. It allows access to resources not directly controlled within the group and exchange of materials not immediately available. Messages of group identity and legitimate access to land made along trackways are broadcast to a wider audience than would be accessible via boundaries or within settlements.

Who was the recipient of these messages depended upon the type of trackway against which the dead were placed. Routes connecting a settlement with its fields and used primarily by group members directed messages more internally, while through-routes transmitted the symbolism of the burial grounds to other groups (Andrew Fleming pers. comm.). In the small number of cases where the nature of a trackway can be recognised, four times as many cemeteries are adjacent to through-routes as settlement routes. This implies that the symbolism of many of the cemeteries was aimed at a wider audience than just the local settlement group itself.

Also suggested by the association with water is the connection of death with concepts of regeneration and fertility. Idealising fertility is a common theme which can be interpreted in much of the structured deposition in Iron-Age Europe and the funerary rites of many non-Western societies today (Whimster 1981; Bloch and Parry 1982; Bradley 1990). In Iron-Age central southern Britain there is the burial of corpses and querns in the bottom of corn storage pits and of single bones in areas of four-post granaries in settlements (Bradley 1990; Cunliffe 1991). Elsewhere in Britain and Europe there is the placing of corpses, agricultural equipment, animal bones, and pottery food containers in bogs and rivers (Bradley 1990). In East Yorkshire, animal bones and storage or cooking jars are some of the most common grave goods. In some cases animal bones are actually placed within the jars. Agricultural tools are also deposited with some burials. Again this concept may be strengthened in the wolds by the strikingly intermittent nature of the gypseys. Linking death to a cycle which regularly renews itself after a period of dormancy can promote the concept of the community re-generating itself after the loss of an individual. Such a concept is import-ant to communities for which the death of a person is a time of un-certainty and transformation as existing social relations are restructured. It is possible to follow this death/fertility association further in the wolds because of the convergence of the annual gypsey cycle with the agricultural cycle. The coming and going of water in fast-flowing gypseys and sink holes is an extraordinary occurrence, providing a dramatic gateway to another or under world. The flowing of the streams and greater contact with the otherworld of the dead occurs during winter, which is the slack time of the year for agricultural pro-duction. This contact continues until spring when the gypseys begin to dry up again and agricultural fertility is renewed. Simultaneously, water is a source of life, necessary for the survival of people, livestock, and crops. It is essential to fertility and therefore the regeneration of society. Associating burials with water can therefore link concepts of life and death in the form of life from death.

CONCLUSION: THE RETURN OF THE LIVING DEAD

It is through the interrelationship between ideologies and the cultural perception of the landscape that the cemeteries' locations were struc-tured. A fundamental aspect of the rite was the visible marking of the individual grave by a small square barrow. The marking of burials with a small 'monument', and placing them in low visibility areas, meant that the observation of the graves could only have occurred at close proxim-ity. Close association with trackways and in fields where people were working allowed this to happen during everyday activities, in addition to or without the need for special cemetery 'visits'. The intimate level of interaction with the cemeteries was perhaps governed by the enclosed nature of the wolds.

Bringing together individually marked burials into cemeteries sug-gests that both the importance of the individual and that of the com-munity were being signified simultaneously. The importance of the in-dividual was linked to incorporation into a group while the importance of the group was associated with the individuals which form it. The marking of burials placed the symbolised right to existence and occupa-tion of a geographical locality in the past. The dead were turned into the ancestors of the group, who then had an active role in the world and actions of the living. The relationship between individual and group appears to have changed over time. Cemeteries became closer packed with smaller barrows and arranged more formally, placing a greater emphasis on the community's identity over that of the individual. This development was contemporary with increased enclosure of the region (Dent 1982; Bevan 1997).

Cemeteries were near to and oriented along watercourses, marshes, and meres. There is also evidence for relationships with boundaries and tracks. This may be interpreted as related to ideas of liminality and a legitimisation of access to resources. The connection with water may go further. Concepts of fertility and regeneration can be seen in the association between the dead, the seasonally intermittent gypseys, and the agricultural cycle. The latter two are related through the convergence of their annual cycles at spring and autumn. It may be that the placing of the dead adjacent to water linked the three together to ritually encourage the fertility of the arable produce and the regeneration of the community itself from the cyclically returning watercourses.

It is hard to say whether any of the features associated with the cemeteries and the socially constructed concepts they symbolised have primacy over the others. Stressing prime ideological movers too much masks the complexity of human society and action. An individual's conceptualisation of the world may be consciously thought through or subconsciously held, and certain elements may become more important at different times. The liminality of the square-barrow cemeteries have been most relevant during the funerary ceremony of an individual, declining after the person was believed to have reached the world of the dead. Fertility of crops may have been more immediate at sowing time or leading up to harvesting. Some engagement with the cemeteries may have been structured into special ceremonies which formalised the living's relationship with the dead. Most of the time the burials would have been present in the world as people went about their everyday activities. This is to say, the range of placement choices available to the mourners for cemeteries were both socially and historically constrained and enabled.

ACKNOWLEDGEMENTS

This paper is based on an MA dissertation submitted to the Department of Archaeology and Prehistory, University of Sheffield in 1993. I would like especially to thank Mike Parker-Pearson, who prompted me to look at the square-barrow burials in East Yorkshire and gave invaluable guidance along the way. John Collis, Andrew Fairbairn, Andrew Fleming, and Pat Wagner provided useful advice. Some of the ideas in the paper were born out of fruitful discussions with Ross Dean and Chris Fenton-Thomas. Both also took time to visit East Yorkshire with me so that we could observe topographical settings of many of the cemeteries in the field. Much of the primary information used was kindly provided by: the Air Photograph Recording Department, Royal Commission for Historic Monuments (England), especially Cathy Stoertz, who supplied advice on use of the data; Linda Smith of the Sites and Monuments Record, County Planning Department, North Yorkshire County Council; and Gail Falkingham and staff of the Sites and Monuments Record, Archaeology Unit, Estates and Property Management Department, Humberside County Council. Last but not least I thank those poor souls who were asked to read through drafts of the paper: John Barnatt, Chris Cumberpatch, Karen Meadows, and Angela Piccini.

BIBLIOGRAPHY

Barrett, J. 1990. The monumentality of death. *World Archaeology* 22, 96–103.

Bender, B. 1993. Introduction: landscape – meaning and action. In B. Bender (ed.), *Landscape: Politics and Perspectives*, 1–17. Berg, Oxford.

Bevan, B. 1997. Bounded across the landscape: place and identity during the Yorkshire Wolds Iron Age. In C. Haselgrove and A. Gwilt (eds), *Reconstructing Iron Age Societies*, 181–191. Oxbow, Oxford.

Bevan, B. forthcoming. Death becomes them: landscape, square barrow cemeteries and the East Yorkshire Iron Age. In B. Bevan (ed.), *Northern Exposure: Interpretative Devolution and the Iron Age in Britain*.

Bevan, W. 1993. Death, Landscape and Society: the Landscape Context of the East Yorkshire Iron Age Square Barrow Cemeteries. MA dissertation, Department of Archaeology and Prehistory, University of Sheffield. (Unpublished).

Bloch, M. 1971. *Placing the Dead*. Seminar Press, London.

Bloch, M. and J. Parry 1982. Death and the regeneration of life. In M. Bloch and J. Parry (eds), *Death and the Regeneration of Life*, 1–44. Cambridge University Press, Cambridge.

Bradley, R. 1984. *Social Foundations of Prehistoric Britain*. Longman, London.

Bradley, R. 1987. Time regained: the creation of continuity. *Journal of the British Archaeological Association* 140, 1–17.

Bradley, R. 1990. *The Passage of Arms*. Cambridge University Press, Cambridge.

Brewster, T. C. M. 1980. *The Excavations at Garton Slack*. East Riding Archaeological Research Committee, Malton, Yorkshire (microfiche).

Chapman, J. 1991. The creation of social arenas in the Neolithic and Copper Age of S.E. Europe: the case of Varna. In P. Garwood et al. (eds), *Sacred and Profane: Proceedings of a Conference on Archaeology, Ritual and Religion*, 152–171. Oxbow Books, Oxford.

Cosgrove, D. 1989. Geography is everywhere: culture and symbolism in human landscape. In D. Gregory and R. Walford (eds), *Horizons in Human Geography*. MacMillan, London.

Cunliffe, B. 1991. *Iron Age Communities in Britain* (third edition). Routledge, London.

Dent, J. S. 1982. Cemeteries and settlement patterns of the Iron Age on the Yorkshire Wolds. *Proceedings of the Prehistoric Society*, 48, 437–457.

Dent, J. S. 1983. A summary of the excavations carried out in Garton and Wetwang Slack, 1964–1980. *East Riding Archaeologist* 7, 1–14.

Dent, J. S. 1984. Wetwang Slack, an Iron Age cemetery on the Yorkshire Wolds. Thesis (M. Phil.). University of Sheffield: Department of Archaeology and Prehistory.

Dent, J. S. 1985. Three vehicle burials from Wetwang, Yorkshire. *Antiquity* 59, 85–92.

Ellis, S. and D. R. Crowther 1990. *Humber Perspectives: a Region through the Ages*. Hull University Press, Hull.

Fleming, A. 1973. Tombs for the living. *Man* 8, 177–193.

Fleming, A. 1988 *The Dartmoor Reaves*. Batsford, London.

Foster, W. 1987. The dry drainage system on the northern Yorkshire Wolds. In S. Ellis (ed.), *East Yorkshire: Field Guide*, 36–38. Quaternary Research Association, Cambridge.

Foster, S. S. D. and V. A. Milton 1976. Hydrological basis for large-scale development of groundwater storage capacity in the East Yorkshire chalk. *Institute of Geological Sciences Report* 76 (3).

Foster, S. S. D., E. L. Parry, and R. J. Chilton 1976. Groundwater resource development and saline water intrusion in the chalk aquifer of North Humberside. *Institute of Geological Sciences Report* 76 (4).

Giddens, A. 1984. *The Constitution of Society: Outline of the Theory of Structuration*. Polity Press, Cambridge.

Greenwell, W. 1865. Notices of the examination of ancient grave-hills in the North Riding of Yorkshire. *Archaeological Journal* 22, 97–117.

Higham, N. 1987. Landscape and land use in northern England: a survey of agricultural potential c. 500 B.C. – A.D. 1000. *Landscape History* 9, 35–44.

Hill, J. D. 1989. Re-thinking the Iron Age. *Scottish Archaeological Review* 9, 16–24.

Hingley, R. 1987. Boundaries surrounding Iron Age and Romano-British settlements. *Scottish Archaeological Review* 7, 96–103.

Hodder, I. 1991. *Reading the Past* (second edition). Cambridge University Press, Cambridge.

Huntington, R. and Metcalf, P. 1979. *Celebrations of Death: the Anthropology of Mortuary Ritual*. Cambridge University Press, Cambridge.

Jackson, R.. and Hudman, L. 1990. *Cultural Geography, People, Places and Environment*. West, St Paul.

Lang, N. 1986. Crisis and Corporate Expression: an Examination of Iron Age Burial Practices. [typescript].

Lewin, J. 1969. *The Yorkshire Wolds: A Study in Geomorphology*. University of Hull (Occasional Papers in Geography 11), Hull.

Manby, T. G. 1980. Bronze Age settlement in Eastern Yorkshire. In J. Barrett and R. Bradley, *Settlement and Society in the British Later Bronze Age*, 307–370. British Archaeological Reports (Brit. Ser. 83 (ii)), Oxford.

Moreland, J. F. 1992. Restoring the dialectic: settlement patterns and documents in medieval central Italy. In A. B. Knapp (ed.), *Archaeology, Annales and Ethnohistory*, 112–129. Cambridge University Press, Cambridge.

Mortimer, J. R. 1905. *Forty Years' Researches in British and Saxon Burial Mounds of East Yorkshire*. Brown, London.

Parker-Pearson, M. 1982. Mortuary practices, society and ideology: an ethnoarchaeological study. In I. Hodder (ed.), *Symbolic and Structural Archaeology*, 99–113. Cambridge University Press, Cambridge.

Parker-Pearson, M. 1993. The powerful dead: archaeological relationships between the living and the dead. *Cambridge Archaeological Journal* 3 (2), 203–229.

Ramm, H. G. 1973. Aerial reconnaissance and interpretation. *Yorkshire Archaeological Journal* 45, 208–209.

Ramm, H. G. 1974. Aerial reconnaissance and interpretation. *Yorkshire Archaeological Journal* 46, 151–152.

Ramm, H. G. 1978. *The Parisi*. Duckworth, London.

Renfrew, C. 1975. Megaliths, territories and populations. In S. J. De Laet (ed.), *Acculturation and Continuity in Atlantic Europe*, 198–220. International Union of Prehistoric and Protohistoric Sciences, Brugge.

Richards, C. C. 1988. Altered images: a re-examination of Neolithic mortuary practices in Orkney. In R. Hodges and K. Smith (eds), *The Archaeology of Context in the Neolithic and Bronze Age: Recent Trends*, 42–56. J. R. Collis. Sheffield.

Shanks, M. and C. Tilley 1982. Ideology, symbolic power and social organisation in Neolithic Wessex: a reinterpretation of Neolithic mortuary practices. In I. Hodder (ed.), *Symbolic and Structural Archaeology*, 129–154. Cambridge University Press, Cambridge.

Sharples, N. 1985. Individual and community: the changing role of megaliths in the Orcadian Neolithic. *Proceedings of the Prehistoric Society* 5, 59–74.

Sheppard, T. 1939. Excavations at Eastburn, Scorborough. *Yorkshire Archaeological Journal* 39, 35–47.

Stead, I. M. 1961. A distinctive form of La Tène barrow in eastern Yorkshire and on the continent. *Antiquaries Journal* 41, 44–62.

Stead, I. M. 1965. *The La Tène Cultures of Eastern Yorkshire*. York.

Stead, I. M. 1975. The La Tène cemetery at Scorborough, East Riding. *East Riding Archaeologist* 11, 1–11.

Stead, I. M. 1976. La Tène burials between Burton Fleming and Rudston, North Humberside. *Antiquaries Journal* 66, 217–226.

Stead, I. M. 1979. *The Arras Culture*. Yorkshire Philosophical Society, York.

Stead, I. M. 1991. *Iron Age Cemeteries in East Yorkshire*. English Heritage, London.

Stead, S. 1991. The human bones. In I. M. Stead, *Iron Age Cemeteries in East Yorkshire*, 126–139. English Heritage, London.

Stillingfleet, E. W. 1846. Account of the opening of some barrows on the wolds of Yorkshire. *Proceedings of the Archaeological Institute, York*, 26–32.

Thomas, J. 1988. The social significance of Cotswold-Severn burial practices. *Man* 23, 540–559.

Turnbull, P. 1983. Excavations at Rillington, 1980. *Yorkshire Archaeological Journal* 55, 1–10.

Whimster, R. 1981. *Burial Practices in Iron Age Britain*. British Archaeological Reports (British Series, 90 (i)), Oxford .

Woodward, D. (ed.) 1985. *Desciptions of East Yorkshire: Leland to Defoe*. East Yorkshire Local History Society, Beverley.

7

The articulation of disarticulation: preliminary thoughts on the Brochtorff Circle at Xaghra (Gozo)

Simon Stoddart, M. Wysocki, and G. Burgess

with supporting contributions from G. Barber, C. Duhig, C. Malone, and G. Mann

Many mortuary rituals contain several stages (Van Gennep 1909; Huntington and Metcalf 1979). Corpses are frequently given a primary interment and then their constituent parts are reworked and repackaged in subsequent rituals. This type of practice can even be part of Christian ritual (Danforth 1982). One consequence of the practice is disarticulation of the physical (and symbolic) identity of the individual and the re-assembly of body parts in distinctive, often corporate, arrangements.

The general mechanisms of these practices can be readily disentangled in anthropological case studies, indeed some are part of classic social anthropology (Bloch 1971). Time depth is often lacking, but it is possible to proceed rapidly to thick description and alternative interpretations. The mechanisms are still readily accessible in cases of direct historical continuity. The Feast of the Dead of the Huron – comprising primary burial and seasonal mortuary aggregation – was observed in the seventeenth century by Jesuit priests (Trigger 1969; 1978). Very similar practices of mortuary enclosures and ossuary packages have been recovered archaeologically in the Michigan region of the modern United States (Greenman 1967) and can be interpreted in the light of ethno-historic observation.

The dissection of the mechanisms of disarticulation becomes much more complicated in the rituals that are typical of the Neolithic societies

Figure 1. Plan of the Brochtorff Circle (left-hand circle) by Jean Houel (1785).

of Europe. Some scholars, dealing with relatively small samples (41 minimum number of individuals), have worked painstakingly to reconstruct patterns by refitting the most probable combinations of body parts from their final resting places (Saville 1990). Others have moved rapidly towards sophisticated interpretation, without perhaps sufficient consideration of the potential taphonomic contribution to any distribution of body parts (Shanks and Tilley 1982). Still others have been highly successful in unravelling the complex deposition of human and animal bones, vegetal food remains, and material culture and in providing convincing anthropological interpretation (Hedges 1984). Comparable analyses of the significance of disarticulated skeletal material have been undertaken on samples from the Orkney islands (Hedges 1984), Wessex (Thomas and Whittle 1986), and Ireland (Cooney 1992). We will return briefly to compare the Neolithic mortuary practices of the extreme northern and southern limits of Europe in our closing remarks.

The aim of this paper is to make some preliminary observations on the taphonomy, deliberate cultural action, and potential for cultural anthropological interpretation at one site in the southern central Medi-

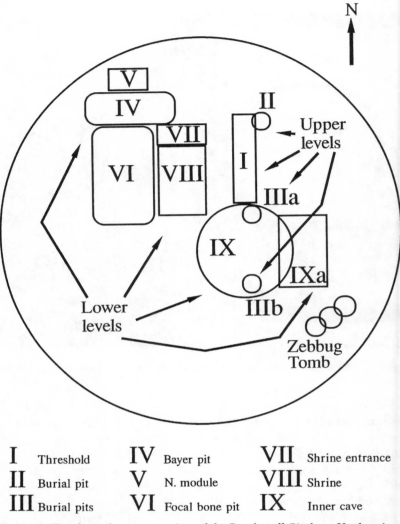

Figure 2. Topological representation of the Brochtorff Circle at Xaghra (not to scale). The large circle represents the line of encircling megaliths.

terranean, where the scale of the bodily remains dwarfs most examples that we are accustomed to in northern Europe. The Brochtorff Circle at Xaghra (Gozo, Malta) (Fig. 1) is a fresh example of the complex deposition of human remains in association with animal remains and intricate (including figurative) material culture in relatively elaborate architectural space. The skeletal parts of more individuals have been recovered from this site than from the whole Irish Neolithic (Cooney 1992, 129).

THE SUBJECT MATTER

The prehistoric mortuary complex at the Brochtorff Circle (Xaghra) on the island of Gozo (Malta) comprises the largest, relatively intact, funerary temple hypogeum discovered and analysed under modern conditions in the central Mediterranean. This site was employed for burial between c. 4000 and 2500 BC and it is on the later Tarxien period phases (c. 3000–2500 BC) that this article will focus. The Maltese islands are well known for the contemporary site of Hal Saflieni, but this was unfortunately unsystematically cleared of its contents at the turn the present century. The Brochtorff Circle, as well as standing in its own right, provides a means of informing on the empty shell of the Hal Saflieni hypogeum. An estimated 250,000 identifiable human bones have been recovered and recorded from distinctively packaged and compartmentalised modules in an artificially modified, *architecturalised*, coralline limestone cave system (Stoddart et al. 1993; Duhig 1994). The earlier material from a self-contained Zebbug period rock-cut tomb within the site (Fig. 2) has been analysed separately (Malone et al. 1995a) and will not be discussed here. Similarly the setting of the site within the Maltese prehistoric sequence and the contextual study of Maltese prehistoric art have been analysed elsewhere (Bonanno et al. 1990; Malone et al. 1995b). The aim here is to place the human bones of the Tarxien phase in focus.

Post-excavation analysis and reconstruction of the excavated data, physical anthropology, pathology, and mortuary ritual of the Tarxien temple hypogeum are currently under way and will be a lengthy and painstaking process. The opportunity is taken here to present a preliminary account of the burial deposits. What follows must be considered anecdotal rather than definitive. It provides an outline of initial impressions and a basis for discussion.

THE DIVERSITY

In the light of our present knowledge of the site the following cultural activities and other site formation processes have provisionally been identified:

Primary interment. 1. The primary mortuary rite and interment of individuals: this appears to have been constrained by permutations of age, sex, location within cave, discrete space within location and architecture. 2. Is a temporal variation of 1.

Cultural secondary processes. 1. Activity is related to the later stages of the multi-stage burial programme, including ritual display. 2. Tomb management aimed to create space or to gain access. 3. Disturbance was a consequence of later primary interments.

4. Accidental processes consisted of knocking and trampling.
5. Damage was done by nineteenth-century excavators.

Natural processes. 1. Processes caused by biological agents: micro-organisms, insects, root, and animal activity. 2. Processes caused by geomorpological processes: flooding, rock falls, chemical activity.

The pattern of bone deposition is highly variable, but nevertheless structured. Cremation is one of the few practices that is missing, although this appears in the subsequent Tarxien Cemetery phase at the site of Tarxien when the Brochtorff Circle was not employed for burial. Human bone appears in almost every archaeological context, but patterned differentiation surfaces from this background noise.

THE SITE

The Brochtorff Circle (Fig. 1) is located at a highpoint of the Xaghra plateau on the island of Gozo, not far from the cluster of monuments which form the Ggantija complex. It is a megalithic circle surrounding a series of interconnected caverns in the coralline limestone, which were enhanced by megalithic architectural devices. The natural compartments in the bedrock have been turned into a series of well-defined modular compartments which are represented diagrammatically in Figure 2. It is on the interplay between these modular compartments and the mortuary remains within them that we will focus.

Threshold flanked by burial pits (Fig. 2, I). The site was most probably entered between two upright monoliths (Fig. 1) which faced towards the Ggantija monumental complex (approximately east). Approaching from the east, one reaches a monumental threshold of coralline slabs with adjacent earthen floors which was flanked by two burial pits, with a third further to the south. The first southerly example contained three stacked supine male (?) inhumations and sheep/goat feasting deposits above the rubble collapse (including a giant stone sphere) from a probable shrine at a higher level. The most southerly example contained a range of skeletons of different age and sex. The pit to the north of the threshold was also adjacent to a number of broken, squared, and worked globigerina limestone (hence imported) blocks which also appear to be the remains a second shrine. This had the remains of a minimum number of 42, predominantly male, disarticulated adults and a minimum number of 25 domestic animals, capped by carefully arranged skulls, above a crouched male skeleton. The excess of skulls and proximal femora shows the deliberate selection of ancestors placed above what appears to be significant male individual at the entrance to the site.

Bayer pit (Fig. 2, IV). A series of rock-cut steps on the ground surface appears to have led down into the caves from the threshold and has provisionally been identified as the entrance to the lower levels of the site. This gives access to a deep depression, fringed with megaliths to the north and west. This area comprised interleaved levels of articulated skeletons, pits filled with human and animal bone and ossuary spreads of human skeletal material. This sequence was capped by a further spread of jumbled human remains which appears to have been a secondary dump or clearance deposit from other parts of the mortuary complex. Firstly, small fragments of distinctive pottery from the inner-most part of the cave system conjoined with large fragments of a distinctive decorated vessel dumped in this area. Secondly, one skull preserved in its interior the white, calcareous sediments typical of many primary burial areas, although recovered from an ochre stained context. Skulls and selected body parts (e.g. mandibles) were stacked against the surrounding megaliths and in rocky niches at a higher level. Bone beads and pottery accompanied these remains.

Northern module (Fig. 2, V). A small modular compartment lay to the north of the central depression. This area was defined by a massive megalithic kerbstone to the south and by several courses of crude dry-stone walling to the east. There was little articulation in this zone with an apparent tendency towards the deposition of juveniles. By contrast, one juvenile corpse had been laid on its back in a shallow scoop, apparently dug only to bury the main trunk area.

The focal bone pit (Fig. 2, VII). Directly to the south of the central depression, a natural plateau contained the large focal bone pit. This module has been almost completely excavated and provides a major contrast in terms of deposition and post-depositional activity. It illustrates the complexity of the mortuary practice and will be described in some detail.

There are indications of periodic flooding or waterlogging, probably seasonal or cyclical, though the possibility of deliberate human agency should not be overlooked. The extensive deposits of human bone and artefacts (to a depth of c. 80 cm) lie in essentially undifferentiated soft pale tufaceous sediments – a homogeneous mixture of alluvial material, calcareous precipitates derived from the limestone bedrock, and frequent fragments of stalactite. A micro-stratigraphy has been noted with small, light skeletal elements – phalanges, carpal bones, vertebrae etc. – frequently overlying deposits of heavier limb bones and crania. It is likely that these have floated off during flood episodes and settled in subsequent silts and precipitates. In some areas these light bones have gathered in small swirls or eddies.

The upper levels of this module contained a distinctive array of disposable portable art (Malone et al. 1995b). These took the form of corpulent, mainly seated clay figurines. Animal phalanges were also carved into minute human heads. The same levels also contained the re-joinable fragments from a larger sculptured stone figure. Relatively few animal remains were recovered; the most prominent were two bovine scapulae, most probably employed in the shaping of the natural depression.

The activity in this module appears to fall into three phases. In the first phase, a natural bowl-shaped depression, originally a cave pool or pond, was reshaped to form an eastern ledge. Crouched/flexed fully articulated skeletons were placed in shallow pits or graves cut into the floor. A small megalithic altar-like (?) structure (later collapsed) was erected north of centre on the eastern ledge. The structure was the focus of activities involving the use of red ochre. Considerable quantities were observed behind and around the fallen stones, on the bedrock. Articulated crouched adult corpses were also placed along the eastern ledge and while originally fleshed were disturbed by later activity.

In the second phase, a further level of articulated individuals were placed over the pit, overlying the primary deposits. The overall impression is of bodies dumped into the bone pit without any formal cutting of pits/graves, and then subject to disturbance. At this level these individuals (typically comprising articulated skull, vertebrae, pelvis, and an odd arm or leg) are intermingled with single or partially articulated limb bones and disassociated skulls and mandibles. The slewed positions, random distribution, and random nature of the disarticulation suggests disturbance by natural processes rather than by deliberate, purposeful, human activity of clearing and pushing away. Some deposits at this level were accompanied by funerary offering bowls which have also been displaced, forming bizarre juxtapositions of material. For example, we have a skull apparently rolling against and into a bowl and smashing in the process. The bowl directly overlays a solitary articulated hand.

The third phase consists primarily of articulated torsos, typically represented only by spinal column, rib-cage, and pelvis. The vertebral columns were extended linearly, not curved, suggesting that these individuals were laid on their backs or in slightly flexed positions, certainly not in the tightly contracted postures of earlier deposits. Reflecting the burials near the outside threshold, two supine torsos, one male, one female, were stacked on top of each other. There is also evidence for a bone collecting and dumping episode focused on the central area of the bone pit. A central mass of disarticulated human bone occupies an area in the middle and spreading towards the north. This consists predominantly of adult limb bones, femora, tibiae, humeri etc. in two to three layers of interlaced bones. This is most likely to have been formed by sweeping or shoving loose limb bones, skulls, and other skeletal fragments together, followed by the collection of loose bundles of long bones which have been dumped on top. A number of skeletal parts within this dump appear to have been crushed or splintered in-situ and were overlain by completely intact specimens suggesting some trampling underfoot during the dumping and collecting episode. At least one skull was brought in from elsewhere since it contained a coarse, dark brown endocranial fill quite foreign to the local matrix. The north-east corner of the bone pit seems to have been given over to deposits of children and infants. Clear concentrations of partly articulated and disarticulated children's remains were recovered. It appears that previous deposits of adult material had been shoved towards the north edge of pit to accommodate these child deposits. The sediments overlying these complex deposits contained less dense inclusions of random disarticulated small bones, vertebrae, bones of hands foot, phalanges, ribs etc.

Northern entrance to the shrine (Fig. 2, VII). To the north-east of the focal bone pit, a narrow corridor or passage marks the probable northern entrance to a demarcated shrine. This area contained a skull cache. The skulls were stacked in a formation similar to drystone walling. The lowest course was well preserved, the skulls carefully laid in a linear arrangement, with a second course of skulls placed on top of these. The structure had tumbled and collapsed.

The shrine (Fig. 2, VIII). The shrine area was dominated by two striking architectural devices and the broken up remains of a third: a megalithic stone bowl (large enough to contain a squatting adult comfortably), placed adjacent to the west wall, a cove-like setting of upright megaliths with lintel, and the broken up remains of a stone trough, with a rope-hole attachment. The latter was associated with a number of sheep/goat horn cores in its final location and it is tempting to think that animals were held in this compartment before employment in mortuary ritual. The upper levels of the shrine contained the collapse of a number of monumental stone blocks and the remains of ritual paraphernalia: the representation in stone of a seated pair of corpulent figures on a wicker bed, a set of schematic stone figures, a ceramic strainer, a small vessel for ochre pigment, small jade pendants, and, from just inside the adjoining inner cave, a shell scoop.

Below this shrine activity, in contrast to other modules, the area contained predominantly undisturbed or partly disturbed individual interments, either in pits, or, at lower levels, possibly laid on an inhumation floor. At the lowest level a pair of black-stained, very friable adult skeletons were recovered from the solid cave floor. Slightly above these, further crouched individuals were recovered, more or less complete and fully articulated. The matrix between these interments was generally sterile, except for residual material. The general impression here is of discrete inhumations arranged around the stone bowl, and in front of the megalithic cove. It is possible that some inhumations have disturbed earlier deposits but effort seems to have been made to maintain the integrity of individual deposits. Among the second 'phase' of inhumations the most notable was a red ochre stained individual buried with a magnificent cowrie-shell head-dress.

At a slightly higher level a fully articulated skeleton squeezed into a small pit marks a change in the mode of interment. The skeleton was accompanied by a Tarxien funerary bowl and, it appears, an infant. The whole appearance of the skeleton suggests that it was thrust into the available space: spine slightly displaced, sacrum twisted and innominates dislocated. This treatment recurs in the area between the shrine and the inner cave.

The upper levels of the shrine area contained only a few discrete child and infant interments, two of which have been partly disturbed in antiquity.

Southern modules. Modules to the south-east of the site were only superficially explored in the sampling design. These explorations revealed multiple entrances to niches containing discrete packages of human and animal bone in the upper levels. The intervening areas contained white sediment with relatively low levels of residual disarticulated material.

Inner cave (Fig. 2, IX). This area was evidently sealed off from the rest of the system at some stage by a rock fall, displacing a globigerina block which had been ineffectively placed to support the roof. Original access to the cave was through a collapsed natural arch. Stone-cobbled flooring led into the deeper inner cave, whose inner section was demarcated by drystone walls and a prominent tapering stone. The roof of this same cave was penetrated by the burial pits to the south of the entrance threshold, adding a three-dimensional complexity to the site.

The upper levels of the cave floor were almost sterile, with only a few scattered disarticulated fragments. Some skulls were stacked against the walls and disarticulated material was placed in a southern niche. A northern niche contained human and pig crania. The sampling strategy restricted excavation at a lower level to the end niche and some burial pits in the floor. Many deposits still remain to be excavated even in these areas.

On the basis of this limited sample, the cave appears to have been sharply divided into an eastern and western section. The demarcated eastern niche, bounded by a drystone wall, contained articulated individuals as well as bone dumps. Two articulated individuals were placed almost in an embrace and associated with Tarxien offering bowls. The western half of the cave contained two pits filled with disarticulated remains in an otherwise relatively level surface. Two curious female torso pendants were also recovered.

DISCUSSION

The broad outlines above give a sense of the complexity of the mortuary deposition, structured by primary and secondary cultural activity and natural processes. Many of these details will have to be verified in detailed statistical and spatial analysis, but from this preliminary analysis, a broad pattern of formal discrete inhumations in individual graves, of the first phase, contrast with the mass of disarticulated and repackaged remains typical of the later phases. Is this a pattern typical of a developing cemetery or a product of changing mortuary practices? The formalisation of the shrine area and the closure deposits of figurines suggests the latter. What begins as a repository for the dead is transformed by tomb architecture into an arena for ritual practices. The changing architecture of the temples above ground in the same period suggests opportunities for misappropriation by sectors of the elite (Bonanno et al. 1990). Special ritual access and rights of mediation between the living and the dead are powerful prerogatives. The pattern of mortuary disposal below ground suggests the merging of the individual within the corporate. The strength of the Maltese evidence is that social interpretation can increasingly be perceived through three dimensions: temple, burial, and settlement. The availability of these three dimensions may allow the detection of contradictions between mortuary evidence and other components of social practice with a facility that is rarely available in Neolithic societies.

The challenge currently met by the post-excavation analysis is to gain a greater understanding of the primary deposition and post-depositional processes outlined above, and the interaction between the two. Hypotheses suggested in this paper for changing mortuary practices will then be accepted, modified, or rejected. When these data are added to the palaeo-demographic information and final stratigraphic analysis, a greater understanding of the ritual and social structure of prehistoric Malta will have been achieved.

CONCLUSION

Two archipelagos at the limits of Europe, Malta and the Orkneys, have provided fascinating evidence of complex deposition of disarticulated human remains broadly within the same third millennium BC. In both cases, meticulous excavation has recovered structured patterns of human and animal bone and material culture within the constraints of architecturally determined modules. At Isbister, excarnation took place outside the burial chambers. At Brochtorff Circle, there appears to be evidence of the principal stages of the doubtless even more elaborate ritual from within the burial complex. At Isbister, the symbolisation of the social components appears to have been done principally through wild animals. At Brochtorff Circle, the symbolisation of the social components appears to have been done through domesticated animals and corpulent images of the human form. These two island contexts at the extreme limits of Europe reveal the diverse strategies of mortuary practice enabled by disarticulation and the possibilities of anthropological interpretation once rearticulation takes place. These were patterns of Neolithic activity not limited to small islands (Thomas and Whittle 1986; Cooney 1992). As Cooney (1992, 140) concludes, sites were made special and sacred by defining architectural space, followed by use of that space for deposition and processing of human remains. Within that framework there were varied strategies; the Maltese example adds to this diversity.

ACKNOWLEDGEMENTS

We are indebted to our co-directors (Prof. A. Bonanno, Mr Anthony Pace, Dr Tancred Gouder, and Dr David Trump) for their assistance, to Mr Simon Mason for his careful overall supervision of the site, and to the principal funding bodies (British Academy, British School at Rome, the McDonald Institute of Cambridge, the Maltese Government and the Society of Antiquaries of London) for making the research possible. We are grateful to G. Barber, C. Duhig, C., C. Malone, and G. Mann for contributing data for this preliminary statement about the mortuary patterns at the Brochtorff Circle. The interpretations, however, remain the opinion of the three main authors and will probably prove wrong when spatial and statistical analysis is completed.

BIBLIOGRAPHY

Bonanno, A., T. Gouder, C. Malone, and S. Stoddart 1990. Monuments in an island society: the Maltese context. *World Archaeology* 22 (2), 190–205.
Bloch, M. 1971. *Placing the Dead. Tombs, Ancestral Villages and Kinship Organisation in Madagascar*. Seminar Press, London.

Cooney, G. 1992. Body politics and grave messages: Irish Neolithic mortuary practices. In N. Sharples and A. Sheridan (eds), *Vessels for the Ancestors: essays on the Neolithic of Britain and Ireland in honour of Audrey Henshall*, 128–142. Edinburgh University Press, Edinburgh.

Danforth, L. M. 1982. *The Death Rituals of Rural Greece*. Princeton University Press, Princeton, New Jersey.

Duhig, C. 1994. Burial practices in a Neolithic Maltese hypogeum – the human remains from the Brochtorff Circle, Gozo. In S. Anderson (ed.), *Ritual Treatment of Human and Animal Remains*. Osteoarchaeological research group, New Buckenham (Norfolk).

Greenman, E. F. 1967. *The Younge Site. An archaeological record from Michigan*. (Occasional contributions from the Museum of Anthropology of the University of Michigan 6), Ann Arbor, Michigan.

Hedges, J. W. 1984. *Tomb of the Eagles. A window on Stone Age tribal Britain*. John Murray, London.

Huntington, R. and P. Metcalf 1979. *Celebrations of Death: the Anthropology of Mortuary Ritual*. Cambridge, Cambridge University Press.

Malone, C., S. Stoddart, A. Bonanno, T. Gouder, and D. Trump 1995a. Mortuary ritual of fourth millennium BC Malta: the Zebbug tomb from the Brochtorff Circle (Gozo). *Proceedings of the Prehistoric Society* 61, 303–345.

Malone, C., S. Stoddart, and A. Townsend 1995b. The landscape of the island goddess? A Maltese perspective of the central Mediterranean. *Caeculus*, 1–15. (Papers on Mediterranean Archaeology, Archaeological Institute, Grüningen University 2), Grüningen.

Saville, A. 1990. *Hazleton North, Gloucestershire, 1979–82. The Excavation of a Neolithic Long Cairn of the Cotswold-Severn Group*. English Heritage, London.

Shanks, M. and Tilley, C. 1982. Ideology, symbolic power and ritual communication: a re-interpretation of Neolithic mortuary practices. In I. Hodder (ed.), *Symbolic and Structural Archaeology*, 129–154. Cambridge University Press, Cambridge.

Stoddart, S., A. Bonanno, T. Gouder, C. Malone, and D. Trump 1993. Cult in an island society: prehistoric Malta in the Tarxien period. *Cambridge Archaeological Journal* 3 (1), 3–19.

Thomas, J. and A. Whittle 1986. Anatomy of a tomb – West Kennet revisited. *Oxford Journal of Archaeology* 5 (2), 129–156.

Trigger, B. G. 1969. *The Huron. Farmers of the North*. Holt, Rinehart and Winston, New York.

Trigger, B. G. 1978. *Handbook of North American Indians*, vol. 15, *Northeast*. Smithsonian Institution, Washington, D.C.

Van Gennep, A. L. 1909. *Les rites de passage*. E. Nourry, Paris.

8

Infanticide in late-Iron-Age Scandinavia

Nancy L. Wicker

The world of the Vikings has often been considered a world of powerful men. Even the word 'Viking' apparently refers specifically to seafaring men, those who pillaged and settled throughout much of Europe and beyond from around AD 800 to 1150 (Jesch 1991, 1). We know much less about women of this Viking period, partly because women seem to be underrepresented in the extant grave material of the Viking period in some areas of Scandinavia. Does this shortage of women appear because they received a burial rite that was different and less ostentatious than that accorded to men? Is it possible that our methods have been biased toward locating male remains? Or were there really fewer women than men?

Old Norse literary and historical material during and shortly after the Viking period shows that there were not as many girls and women as should occur according to natural sex ratios and also indicates that exposure of female infants was practised (Clover 1988). However, these sources have not been correlated with archaeological evidence of the scarcity of women (for instance Solberg 1985, 643) and finds of scattered infant bones, which perhaps indicate exposure of infants. Although archaeological clues that can be marshalled to demonstrate the existence of infanticide are almost all indirect, the dearth of women in graves is so pervasive that it cannot be ignored. We may be witnessing the results of preferential female infanticide compounded by the relative invisibility of low status female graves. Here I investigate whether the archaeological record of the dearth of adult female burials may support the testimony of the written sources indicating exposure of infants.

THE DEARTH OF FEMALE MORTUARY REMAINS

A relative shortage of adult female mortuary remains compared to the expected sex ratio of nearly 1:1 has been noted in many regions of Scandinavia for the Viking period. Norway's Iron-Age population seems to diverge most markedly from average sex ratios. Liv Helga Dommasnes (1979; 1982; 1991) found a much smaller representation of women in studies of Iron-Age burials in four regions of the country. The women's share of graves identifiable by gender in the four areas of Sogn, Gloppen, Nordland, and Upper Telemark varied from only 6% to 32%. Dommasnes (1979, 99–100) found ratios of eight males to one female in Sogn in the seventh century and six to one in the eighth century. The ratios are typical of graves throughout most of Norway in that period. For instance, Ellen Høigård Hofseth (1988, fig. 11) found that women represented only from 8% to 18% of the late-Iron-Age graves in Hordaland. In another study, Trond Løken (1987) found three times as many male as female graves in Iron-Age material from Østfold and Vestfold in Norway.

In Denmark also, sex ratios from cemetery analysis are skewed toward males. A study of all unburnt Danish Iron-Age skeletal remains found during the past century and a half identified 311 Viking-Age individuals (Sellevold et al. 1984). Sex could not be determined for 153 of them, but of the remaining 158, 85 were found to be males and 73 females by skeletal analysis. The numbers represented are small and reflect quite a sampling problem in Denmark where preservation is poor, but fewer women than men were identified and the sex imbalance is even more pronounced in earlier Iron-Age material. In addition, just across the Danish-German border at Viking Hedeby, 62% of adult dead (47 individuals) that could be skeletally sexed were men and only 38% women (29 individuals) (Schaefer 1963).

For Sweden there has been no country-wide re-evaluation of skeletal material as completed for Denmark and in progress for Norway. The situation appears to be quite different with a marked qualitative rather than quantitative difference between the sexes. Studies of Swedish material have concentrated on extraordinary sites such as boat graves at Valsgärde, as well as the large number of burials at Viking-Age Birka. At Valsgärde, men were inhumed in chamber graves and boat graves, but women were cremated (Arwidsson 1942; 1954). At Birka where more than 2,000 grave mounds are visible, sex has been determined for only 415 burials. Anne-Sofie Gräslund (1980) reports that women's graves actually outnumber men's, with women representing 58% of the inhumations (308 burials) and 61% of the cremations (107 burials). However, women were buried in the generally richer chamber graves there less frequently (44%) than men (56%), so there was at least a

[107]

qualitative differentiation between women's and men's graves. Women were more often interred without coffins than men (68% of coffinless graves belonged to women and 32% to men). Rather than indicating a preponderance of women at Birka, Gräslund has suggested that the greater number of women's graves there may merely indicate that their graves are easier to identify because of their contents, especially jewellery. However, Birka is an anomaly – the trading community there should not be considered representative for the Viking period as a whole because of its unusual wealth and early missionary activity.

IDENTIFICATION OF SEX OR GENDER IN GRAVES

A discussion of sex ratios from archaeological remains presupposes that the sex or gender of a buried person can indeed be ascertained. There are two main ways to determine this: by analysis of the human remains or by investigation of grave goods. For Viking finds, both means are used because the preservation of human remains is often not satisfactory enough to allow designations on the basis of osteological analysis alone. Archaeologists are fortunate that many Scandinavians of the Viking period buried their dead with grave goods. Vikings practised both inhumation and cremation, but even cremation graves with only fragments of burnt bone may contain grave goods that possibly may allow gender identification. However, there are many problems associated with the sexing of graves, especially those that have been assigned gender according to objects found in the graves.

The gender of the dead is often ascertained by grave goods when skeletal remains are inadequate. Lewis Binford (1971, 22) proposed that the most important way of displaying gender to the so-called 'invisible society' of burial was by the objects in the grave: clothes, jewellery, other personal equipment, and characteristic tools. However, it is debatable exactly which grave goods can be used reliably as indicators of gender and, indeed, the whole basis for our assumptions of the gender specificity of artefact correlates needs to be re-examined (Brush 1988; Gilchrist 1991, 498).

In Scandinavia, weapons and certain tools buried with skeletons normally indicate males, and jewellery and domestic implements signify females, but it is difficult to make these assignments with certainty. The usual practice has been to assume that a grave is male if, for instance, as few as one weapon was found, or female if five or more beads were found (Solberg 1985, 63). The numbers of objects decided upon may be arbitrary, but no matter what number is chosen as diagnostic, the artefacts used for gender determination normally are jewellery and weapons (Henderson 1989).

[108]

Often there is substantial agreement between results from sexing graves by grave goods and by analysis of skeletal material, but there is not complete accord. Sellevold's study of all unburnt Danish Iron-Age burials (Sellevold et al. 1984) compared results arrived at by skeletal analysis to results indicated from grave goods. For the Viking period there was a strong correlation between the sex of the deceased and the artefacts buried with them. The objects that could be used to distinguish men's graves were: 1) weapons such as swords and spears; 2) axes; 3) riding equipment including stirrups, bits, and spurs; 4) blacksmith's tools such as shears, hammers, tongs, and files; and 5) penannular brooches. Women's graves can be distinguished by the inclusion of: 1) jewellery, including paired oval brooches, trefoil buckles, disc brooches, arm rings, and necklaces, 2) jewel boxes or caskets, and 3) spindle whorls. Objects common to both sexes included buckles, combs, clay pots, wooden vessels, knives, whetstones, coins, and beads.

However, others have shown that results from sexing graves according to grave goods and by analysis of skeletal material do not consistently agree (Henderson 1989; Pader 1981). Berit Sellevold (1985, 67) has demonstrated that only weapons and riding equipment in men's graves and spindle whorls in women's are indicative of gender and that, contrary to common assumptions, beads, sewing needles, and various jewellery types are found in burials of both sexes. Even the common assumption that weapons necessarily indicate males needs to be reassessed in light of a few problematic graves such as at Gerdrup in Denmark (Hemmendorff 1985) and Aurland in Norway (Dommasnes 1982, 77) in which women, as determined by skeletal analysis, have been found with a sword and arrowheads, respectively. Ultimately, however, sexing graves by either method – grave goods or skeletal analysis – indicates that women were scarce.

REASONS FOR A DEARTH OF WOMEN'S GRAVES

Let us now examine possible reasons for the apparent dearth of women's graves. In her analyses of Norwegian material, Dommasnes (1982, 73) assumed that there was a 1:1 ratio of men to women, but perhaps that was not so. The sex ratio from cemetery analysis could be skewed if a portion of the population died elsewhere, away from home (Ehrenberg 1989, 127). One might expect that many men of Viking period Scandinavia died in foreign lands (Gräslund 1989, 236–237), and at least some such deaths are memorialised on runestones which commemorate men and where they travelled and whom they fought. Warfare and migration could have taken such a toll on men that their remains would be scarce in cemeteries at home (as at Birka perhaps). However, in many Scandinavian regions, men are not lacking – women are. William T. Divale and Marvin Harris (1970; 1976) have hypothesised that preferential female infanticide compensates for the loss of adult males due to extra deaths in warfare. Heavy male emigration also would lead to an over-abundance of women without the levelling effect of female infanticide at home.

Some scholars have attempted to discount the dearth of women's remains in Scandinavia by explaining that women only seem to be lacking because they were not memorialised as often with large grave mounds or visible stone settings, so their graves go unnoticed. Dommasnes (1982), for instance, assumes she has not dealt with a representative sample of the Iron-Age population. Women may have been given a different, less ostentatious, burial rite, as at Birka where fewer women than men were interred in coffins and chamber graves. At Valsgärde women were cremated but men were inhumed in chamber graves and boat graves. But perhaps men actually outnumbered women due to selective female infanticide or other factors. The practice of infanticide is difficult to trace in the archaeological record; most of the evidence is only indirect, so first let us consider other testimony that may indicate this practice.

WRITTEN SOURCES RELATING TO INFANTICIDE

Though it may be repugnant to us, infanticide was widespread throughout history and prehistory (Langer 1974; Ehrenberg 1989). Infanticide has had a powerful effect as a conscious or unconscious mechanism of population control and the maintenance of social power. It does not take the form of the cold-blooded murder of babies, occurring instead as the intentional abandonment or 'exposure' of undesired children or as the uncalculated preferential treatment of the favoured sex and neglect of the other sex, both in prehistory and in contemporary societies, such as has been documented in India (George et al. 1992; Krishnaswamy 1984; Miller 1981) and China (Bose 1984; Mirsky 1983; Johansson and Nygren 1991).

The topic of female infanticide in Scandinavia during and shortly after the period of conversion to Christianity, around AD 1000, has been discussed recently by Carol Clover (1988) and Juha Pentikäinen (1990). Clover calls attention to infanticide in eleven Old Norse sources, including references to laws and customs as well as narratives describing specific incidents. The most straightforward Scandinavian accounts of infanticide, usually in the form of exposure, occur in Icelandic sagas. Though written well within the Christian period, such sagas are believed to preserve some material harking back to the Viking period of the late ninth through to the early eleventh centuries. In *Gunnlaugs saga* (chapter 3), Þorsteinn says to his wife Jófriðr: 'It appears . . . that you are with child. If the baby is a girl, it is to be exposed, but reared if it is a boy.' *Hervarar saga* (chapter 3) relates that: 'Now it will be told that Earl Bjartmarr's daughter bore a baby girl, and it seemed advisable to most that it be exposed' (Clover 1988, 157–158).

We have assumed that exposure is a method of infanticide, thus resulting in death for the exposed new-borns. John Boswell (1984; 1988) maintains that exposure in the sagas does not amount to infanticide and that exposed infants were meant to be found. Parents who exposed their offspring may have hoped for a propitious outcome for them. However, one must keep in mind that exposure in the cold harsh climate of the north could be deadly to a new-born much sooner than in southern Christianised Europe where the climate is kinder and the Church's attitude was more pervasive.

Since each of the children intended to be exposed in the sagas was either prevented from being exposed, or discovered and saved before being harmed, Clover (1988, 150–158) contends that these saga examples of exposure were exceptional and that the discovery and adoption of foundling infants in Scandinavia must not have been common. In four instances, boys were put out to die but were discovered; these exposures clearly were considered unusual even within the saga context explicitly because the children were healthy males. Such stories may have been influenced by hero legends or the international Oedipus folklore motif (Pentikäinen 1968, 69–73; Aarne-Thompson 1964, no. 931). These incidents probably were included only because the outcome of exposure was extraordinary and the child would be crucial to the story.

Clover (1988, 151) counters Boswell's thesis by pointing out that law codes such as *Gutalagen* included prohibitions against infanticide. The practice of exposure was apparently common enough that laws against it became necessary in the Christian period. Pentikäinen sees the criminalisation of the exposure of infants as an indication of growing Christianisation. The Swedish *Gutalagen* (chapter 2) states: 'Every child born in our country shall be raised and not gotten rid of' (Thomson 1960, 6). The Icelandic governing body, or *thing*, specifically allowed the heathen practice of the exposure of children during the conversion period (Hovstad 1956, 348). Its tacit acceptance underscores its existence. According to Icelandic sagas, a child could be abandoned until a name-giving rite was carried out, although after this ceremony exposure was considered murder even in the pre-Christian period (Pentikäinen 1990, 79). With Christianisation, all instances of exposure, even before a child was named, were criminalised.

Besides indirect infanticide by abandonment, other methods are attested to in the literature. An Arab traveller, Al Tartushi reported that infanticide was performed at Danish Hedeby, where unwanted infants were thrown into the sea to save the costs of bringing them up (Birke-land 1954, 104). A Christian apologist in *Reykdœla saga* (chapter 7) indirectly substantiates the occurrence of sacrificial infanticide by his report of the assembly's decision not to resort to offering infants and elderly persons to propitiate the weather (Clover 1988, 152).

Old Norse literary sources also mention fewer females than should occur according to natural sex ratios. A suspicious preponderance of male children and a lack of female children, perhaps indirectly reflecting selective female infanticide, are revealed in lists of household membership in the medieval Icelandic *Landnámabók*, concerning the tenth-century settlement of Iceland (Clover 1988, 167–168). The lists of household membership show that there were not as many girls and women as would be expected. Clover estimates that sons usually outnumber daughters at a ratio of four or five to one, occasionally even nine to one. This may indirectly reflect the culling effects of female infanticide. Swedish Upplandic runestones, as counted by Gräslund (1989, 233–40), display similar ratios of sons to daughters. She suggests that female infanticide may account for this scarcity of daughters, though admitting that some might have been left out of inscriptions after marriage into another family.[1]

Some scholars have attempted to discount evidence of infanticide by explaining that women and girls only seem to be lacking because they were not important enough to be mentioned as often. However, even slaves were enumerated in *Landnámabók* (Karras 1988, 80), presumably because of their economic significance. Therefore it would seem logical to assume that each girl should also be noted due to the future negative impact of her dowry, the woman's inheritance which was handed over by her father at marriage (Frank 1973, 475–76). While the scarcity of women and girls in written sources is not conclusive proof of infanticide, it may be seen in conjunction with the explicit saga references to exposure.

ARCHAEOLOGICAL REMAINS OF INFANTS AND CHILDREN

Archaeological evidence that might demonstrate the existence of infanticide is almost all indirect – the most pervasive testimony is still the dearth of women's remains. The frustrations in locating adult female graves wane compared to the difficulties of tracing children and infants in the archaeological record. Interest in the study of women grows, but there has been little research focused on children in prehistory. There is now a growing archaeological literature on children in Scandinavia (Lillehammer 1982; 1986; 1989; 1990), but much of it has been published in regional and university department journals with limited distribution outside Scandinavia (e.g., see Fredriksen 1979; Knutsson 1983; Lindquist 1981; 1989; Rolfsen 1978; Schulze 1978; and Vinsrygg 1979). These references are important as supporting evidence in an investigation of how infanticide may be traced in the archaeological record.

A few very wealthy children's graves are known, as at Luistari in Finland (Lehtosalo-Hilander 1982, 44–46), Birka in Lake Mälaren in Sweden (Gräslund 1973; 1980), and Store Ihre on Gotland, where a young boy was buried with an adult-sized long sword and a horse (Stenberger 1961). A new-born cremated at Mulde in Fröjel parish on Gotland was buried in adult fashion but accompanied by jewellery sized to fit an infant (Lindquist 1989).

Gender- and age-specific grave goods are often all that remain since children's and specifically infants' bones may disintegrate easily depending upon soil conditions. The unossified, cartilaginous skeletal material of infants may be totally destroyed during cremation; all that remains may be the unerupted tooth crowns and the densest temporal area of the skull (Henderson 1989; McKinley 1989, 242). During earlier excavations such scanty remains may often have been missed altogether or discarded as apparent animal bones. Even when bones are preserved, they are fragmentary and have not developed the characteristic sexual dimorphism of adult specimens, so they can rarely be sexed osteologically (Lillehammer 1986, 12; Welinder 1989, 59). The only remaining method for assigning gender to them is according to grave goods, with all the attendant problems of this approach for adult graves.

Even though infant mortality was high in prehistory and the Middle Ages, perhaps as high as 50% for Scandinavia (Welinder 1979, 83), Iron-Age children's graves are rare in Scandinavia. In contrast to the very rich burials mentioned above, many children, particularly those under a certain age, were not given an adult-type burial. In the prehistoric period, infants often were not buried with adults, as for example in a third-century AD cemetery at Udby on Sjælland in Denmark, where no children under five were discovered (Ethelberg 1989, 7). Infants' bodies may often have been deposited without any grave ritual or grave goods (Lillehammer 1986, 13).

Of course, infant bones do not necessarily indicate infanticide as the cause of death, but we can get an idea how infants' remains were treated from the find contexts. Direct evidence of infanticide is particularly difficult to trace in the archaeological record, but a few examples are recognised from diverse settings. Phoenician Carthage, well-known from biblical and other references, is one of the most notable instances where extensive infanticide is attested by archaeological as well as literary evidence (Brown 1986; Stager and Wolff 1984). Other examples of possible infanticide are based only on archaeological remains. A recent article purports to identify the practice of infanticide for the late Roman-early Byzantine periods in Israel where skeletal remains of numerous new-borns were found in a sewer (Smith and Kahila 1992). Louise Robbins (1977) has suggested that sacrificial infanticide occurred at the Incinerator site of the Fort Ancient culture in North America, where some foetal and infant bones were found in burials isolated from cemeteries, unlike those infants buried in household cemeteries with other age groups. According to Robbins, these individuals exhibit cranial depression fractures consistent with being dropped or thrown into pits as sacrifices. Simon Mays (1993) deduces the practice of infanticide for the Romano-British period in England by demonstrating that the age at death of new-born infant remains is not consistent with the distribution of modern stillbirths and natural deaths.

Direct archaeological evidence of infanticide in the Scandinavian region is limited. Malin Lindquist (1981) has proposed that infant bones in stone packing of cairns may be remains of infanticide victims. Inger Saelebakke (1986, 24) suggests that apparently haphazard bone scatters in middens may be interpreted as remains of exposed infants, though she cites no specific instances. At a Norse site at Buckquoy, Orkney, infant bones dispersed through the middens may testify to infanticide (Ritchie 1977, 188 and 220–221). The scattered remains were initially mistaken for animal bones upon discovery; only during osteological analysis were they identified as human. Other examples from such contexts include five infant skeletons strewn through a rubbish pit excavated at Sörby Skola, Gärdslösa, Sweden (Sjöberg and Marnung 1976). Such finds, while scattered and not well known, may exist throughout the Viking world. Many middens from earlier excavations were not investigated as thoroughly as these examples, and one wonders how many infant bones thus have not been discovered. Archaeologists should carefully investigate bone scatters, particularly from middens, to search for infant remains. Old finds need to be re-investigated if the materials have not been discarded.

Infant bones have also been found in wells and bogs, such as at Röekillorna, Skåne, where the skull of a small child was found in a well (Stjernquist 1987) and Bø in Hå kommune, Rogaland, where four new-born skeletons were found in a bog (Haavaldsen 1989). Discoveries of bones in these watery contexts have often been interpreted as evidence of sacrificial infanticide, but are also in accord with Al Tartushi's description of infanticide by drowning at Hedeby (Birkeland 1954).

CONCLUSION

These scattered archaeological sources are direct traces of infants who were not buried with an adult-type burial rite. Admittedly, these sources are problematic, and we must be very careful in deducing the existence of infanticide from them. They serve merely as supporting evidence in an investigation of how infanticide may be traced in the archaeological record, yet we should not underestimate their worth in detecting this practice. Carol Clover has called archaeological evidence one of the 'lesser forms of evidence' (1988, 165), and John Boswell has called the analysis of sex ratios from cemetery remains 'a particularly treacherous methodology' (1988, 44, note 107). Archaeological data have limitations, but the source materials of historical demography, such as taxation lists, court lists, and ecclesiastical records, have their own weaknesses since they also refer to only a portion of the population (Welinder 1979, 33). Although estimating population from archaeological remains is fraught with difficulties, it should not be overlooked. The testimony of hundreds of graves when seen within the context of the literary and historical evidence is a potent source of information.

Even if we can demonstrate that infanticide was practised, we have only indirect grounds for discussing the existence of preferential female infanticide archaeologically. However, female infanticide could account for the dearth of women in literature and in cemetery remains. Only in conjunction with several kinds of evidence can one suggest female infanticide as a factor behind some of these finds. The problem needs to be considered from an interdisciplinary viewpoint.

Infanticide is so pervasive throughout history that it should not be surprising that it occurred in Scandinavia. Studying this practice in the Iron-Age and medieval period may complement other studies of status and social organisation in these societies. Just as few women achieved high status in the sagas (Jochens 1989), few received an honoured status in death. Rich displays such as accompanied the women buried in the Oseberg ship are the exception rather than the rule (Christensen et al. 1992). It seems that many girls were not allowed to live to become women far less powerful women.

NOTES

* I would like to thank Mankato State University for funding the research on which this paper was based and for making it possible to attend the conference, Death and the Supernatural, at which this paper was presented in 1993. This article represents the contribution as read in 1993 and has not been updated. I have incorporated some of this material into an expanded version in 'Selective female infanticide as partial explanation for the dearth of women in Viking period Scandinavia' in *Violence and Society in Medieval Western Europe: Private, Public and Ritual*, pp. 205–221, edited by Guy Halsall (Boydell and Brewer, Woodbridge, Suffolk, 1998).
1. I would like to thank Anders Andrén for drawing my attention to this source.

BIBLIOGRAPHY

Aarne, A. 1964. *The Types of the Folktale. A Classification and Bibliography*, translated and enlarged by Stith Thompson, second revised edition. Suomalainen Tiedeakatemia (FF Communications, no. 184), Helsinki.

Arwidsson, G. 1942. *Die Gräberfund von Valsgärde*, 1. Almqvist and Wiksell (Valsgärde 6), Uppsala.

Arwidsson, G. 1954. *Die Gräberfund von Valsgärde*, 2. Almqvist and Wiksell (Valsgärde 8), Uppsala.

Benediktsson, J. (ed.). 1968. *Landnámabók.* Íslenzk fornrit 1. Hið Íslenzka fornritafélag, Reykjavik.

Binford, L. R. 1971. Mortuary practices: their study and their potential. In J. A. Brown (ed.), *Approaches to the Social Dimensions of Mortuary Practices*, 6–29. (Memoirs of the Society for American Archaeology 25), Washington, D. C.

Birkeland, H. 1954. *Nordens historie i middelalderen efter arabiske kilder.* Norske Videnskapsakademis Skrifter, Oslo.

Bose, A. 1984. Exploring China's population policy. *China Report* 20, 107–114.

Boswell, J. 1984. *Expositio and oblatio:* the abandonment of children and the ancient and medieval family. *American Historical Review* 89, 10–33.

Boswell, J. 1988. *The Kindness of Strangers: The Abandonment of Children in Western Europe from Late Antiquity to the Renaissance.* Pantheon Books, New York.

Brown, S. S. 1986. Late Carthaginian Child Sacrifice and Sacrificial Monuments in Their Mediterranean Context. Ph.D. Dissertation. Indiana University.

Brush, K. 1988. Gender and mortuary analysis in pagan Anglo-Saxon archaeology. *Archaeological Review from Cambridge* 1, 76–89.

Christensen, A. E., A. S. Ingstad, and B. Myhre 1992. *Oseberg Dronningens Grav: Vår arkeologiske nasjonalskatt i nytt lys.* Schibstad, Oslo.

Clover, C. J. 1988. The politics of scarcity: notes on the sex ratio in early Scandinavia. *Scandinavian Studies* 60 (2), 147–188.

Divale, W. T. 1970. An explanation for primitive warfare: population control and the significance of primitive sex ratios. *The New Scholar* 2, 173–179.

Divale, W. T. and M. Harris 1976. Population, warfare, and the male suprematist complex. *American Anthropologist* 78, 521–538.

Dommasnes, L. H. 1979. Et gravmateriale fra yngre jernalder brukt til å belyse kvinners stilling. *Viking* 1978, 95–114.

Dommasnes, L. H. 1982. Late Iron Age in western Norway. Female roles and ranks as deduced from an analysis of burial customs. *Norwegian Archaeological Review* 15, 70–84.

Dommasnes, L. H. 1991. Women, kinship, and the basis of power in the Norwegian Viking Age. In R. Samson (ed.), *Social Approaches to Viking Studies*, 65–74. Cruithne Press, Glasgow.

Ehrenberg, M. 1989. *Women in Prehistory.* British Museum Publications, London.

Ethelberg, P. 1989. Skrålbanken. *Skalk 1989* (2), 3–9.

Frank, R. 1973. Marriage in twelfth- and thirteenth-century Iceland. *Viator* 4, 473–484.

Fredriksen, G. 1979. Barnegraven fra Leirhol i Valdres. *AmS-småtryck* 5, 20–24.

George, S., A. Rajaratnam, and B. D. Miller 1992. Female infanticide in rural south India. *Economic and Political Weekly* 27 (22), 1153–1156.

Gilchrist, R. 1991. Women's archaeology? Political feminism, gender theory and historical revision. *Antiquity* 65, 495–501.

Gräslund, A.-S. 1973. Barn i Birka. *Tor* 15 (1972–73), 161–179.

Gräslund, A.-S. 1980. *Birka IV. The Burial Customs. A Study of the Graves on Björkö.* Almqvist and Wiksell International (Birka, Untersuchungen und Studien. K. Vitterhets Historie och Antikvitets Akademien), Stockholm.

Gräslund, A.-S. 1989. 'Gud hjälpe nu väl hennes själ': Om runstenskvinnorna, deras roll vid kristnandet och deras plats i familj och samhälle. *Tor* 22 (1988–89), 223–244.

Gunnlaugs saga. 1933. Íslenzk fornrit. Hið Íslenzka fornritafélag, Reykjavik.

Haavaldsen, P. 1989. Pojken må förast ut i kärret . . . . *Frá haug ok heiðni* 12, 174–176.

Hemmendorff, O. 1985. Gravens bipersoner. In *Skalks Gæstebog*, 13–20. Wormianum, Højbjerg.

Henderson, J. 1989. Pagan saxon cemeteries: a study of the problems of sexing by grave goods and bones. In C. A. Roberts, F. Lee, and J. Bintliff (eds), *Burial Archaeology: Current Methods and Developments*, 77–83. British Archaeological Reports (British Series 211), Oxford.

Helgason, J. (ed.) 1924. *Hervarar saga. Heiðreks saga (Hervarar saga ok Heiðreks konungs).* Jørgensen (Samfund til Udgivelse af Gammel Nordisk Litteratur 48), Copenhagen.

Høigård Hofseth, E. 1988. Liten tue velter . . . problemer knyttet til mann- sog kvinnegravenes i fordeling i Nord-Rogaland. In *Artikkel-samling II*, 5–38. Arkeologisk Museum i Stavanger (AmS Skrifter 12), Stavanger.

Hovstad, J. 1956. Barneutbering. In J. Granlund (ed.), *Kulturhistoriskt Lexikon för Nordisk Medeltid från Vikingatid till Reformationstid*, vol. 1 Allhems Förlag, Malmö.

Jesch, J. 1991. *Women in the Viking Age.* Boydell and Brewer, Woodbridge, Suffolk.

Jochens, J. 1989. The medieval icelandic heroine: fact or fiction? In J. Tucker (ed.), *Sagas of the Icelanders: A Book of Essays*, 99–125. Garland Publishing, New York.

Johansson, S. and O. Nygren 1991. The missing girls of China. *Population and Development Review* 17, 35–51.

Karras, R. M. 1988. *Slavery and Society in Medieval Scandinavia.* Yale University Press, New Haven.

Knutsson, K. 1983. Barn, finns dom? *Fjølnir* 2, 8–11.

Krishnaswamy, S. 1984. A note on female infanticide – an anthropological inquiry. *Indian Journal of Social Work* 45, 297–302.

Langer, William L. 1974. Infanticide: a historical survey. *History of Childhood Quarterly* 1, 353–365.

Lehtosalo-Hilander, P.-L. 1982. *Luistari III. A Burial-Ground Reflecting The Finnish Viking Age Society.* (Suomen Muinaismuistoyhdistyksen Aika- kauskirja, Finska Fornminnesföreningens Tidskrift 82 (3)), Helsinki.

Lillehammer, G. 1982. Med barnet på vei inn i forhistorien. In A. Lille- hammer (ed.), *Faggrenser brytes. Artikler tileigna Odmund Møllerup, 7. desember 1982*, 97–102. Arkeologisk museum (AmS-Skrifter), Sta- vanger.

Lillehammer, G. 1986. Barna i Nordens forhistorie. Drøft metodegrunn- laget og kildenes bærekraft. *KAN (Kvinner i Arkeologi i Norge)* 2, 321.

Lillehammer, G. 1989. A child is born: the child's world in an archaeological perspective. *Norwegian Archaeological Review* 22, 89–105.

Lillehammer, Grete. 1990. Barn av sin tid. *Arkeo* 1, 9–12.

Lindquist, M. 1981. Mylingar-offer, utsatta barn eller förhistoriska barnbe-
gravningar? *Gotländskt arkiv* 53, 7–12.

Lindquist, M. 1989. Barngravar vid Mulde i Fröjel sn. *Gotländskt arkiv* 61,
241–242.

Løken, T. 1987. The correlation between the shape of grave monuments
and sex in the Iron Age, based on material from Østfold and Vestfold.
In R. Bertelsen, A. Lillehammer, and J.-R. Næss (eds), *Were They All
Men?: An Examination of Sex Roles in Prehistoric Society*, 53–63. Arkeologisk Museum i Stavanger (Ams Varia 17), Stavanger.

McKinley, J. 1989. Spong Hill, Anglo-Saxon cremation cemetery. In C. A.
Roberts, F. Lee, and J. Bintliff (eds), *Burial Archaeology: Current Methods
and Developments*, 241–248. British Archaeological Reports (British
Series 211), Oxford.

Mays, Simon 1993. Infanticide in Roman Britain. *Antiquity* 67, 883–888.

Miller, B. D. 1981. *The Endangered Sex: Neglect of Female Children in Rural
North India*. Cornell University Press, Ithaca, New York.

Mirsky, J. 1983. One child per family (no girls) – the infanticide tragedy in
China. *The Nation* 137, 12–14.

O'Connor, A. 1991. *Child Murderess and Dead Child Traditions*. Suomalainen Tiedeakatemia (FF Communications 249), Helsinki.

Pader, E.-J. 1982. *Symbolism, Social Relations and the Interpretation of Mortuary Remains*. British Archaeological Reports (International Series 130),
Oxford.

Pentikäinen, J. 1968. *The Nordic Dead-Child Tradition*. Suomalainen Tiedeakatemia (FF Communications 202), Helsinki.

Pentikäinen, J. 1990. Child abandonment as an indicator of Christianiza-
tion in the Nordic countries. In T. Ahlbäck (ed.), *Old Norse and Finnish
Religions and Cultic Place-Names*, 72–91. The Donner Institute for
Research in Religions and Cultural History, Åbo, Finland.

Ritchie, A. 1977. Excavation of Pictish and Viking-age farmsteads at
Buckquoy, Orkney. *Proceedings of the Society of Antiquaries of Scotland*
108 (1976–1977), 174–227.

Robbins, L. M. 1977. The story of life revealed by the dead. In R. L.
Blakely (ed.), *Biocultural Adaptation in Prehistoric America*, 10–25.
University of Georgia Press, Athens, Georgia.

Rolfsen, P. 1978. En barnegrav fra romertid. *Agder historielag årskrift* 56, 56.

Saelebakke, I. 1986. Noen förelöbige inntrykk fra en middelalder-kirke-
gård i Tönsberg. *META* 2–3, 21–25.

Schaefer, U. 1963. *Anthropologische Untersuchung der Skelette von Haithabu*.
K. Wachholz (Die Ausgrabungen in Haithabu 4), Neumünster.

Schulze, H. 1978. Barngravfältet i Bjärby, Kastlösa sn. *Kalmar län* 63, 59–
62.

Sellevold, B. J., U. Lund Hansen, and J. Balslev Jørgensen 1984. *Iron Age
Man in Denmark*. Det Kongelige Nordiske Oldskriftselskab (Nordiske
Fortidsminder 8), Copenhagen.

Sellevold, B. J. 1985. Knokler, Oldsaker og Kvinner. Fysisk antropolgi som
metode til kunnskap om kvinner i middelalderen. In *Kvinnearbeid i
Norden fra vikingtiden til reformasjonen*. (Foredrag fra et nordisk kvinne-
historisk seminar i Bergen 3–7 august 1983, 63–77), Bergen.

Sigfússon B. (ed.) 1940. *Reykdœla saga ok Víga-Skútu*. Hið Íslenzka fornritafélag (Íslenzk fornrit), Reykjavik.

Sjöberg, M. and B. Marnung 1976. *Fornldmning 126. Gravfält, Äldre Järnålder, Sörby Skola, Öster Sörby, Gärdslösa socken, Öland.* Riksantikvarieämbetet (Rapport B44), Stockholm.

Smith, P. and G. Kahila 1992. Identification of infanticide in archaeological sites: a case study from the late Roman-early Byzantine periods at Ashkelon, Israel. *Journal of Archaeological Science* 19, 667–675.

Solberg, B. 1985. Social status in the Merovingian and Viking periods in Norway from archaeological and historical sources. *Norwegian Archaeological Review* 18, 61–76.

Stager, L. E. and S. R. Wolff 1984. Child sacrifice at Carthage: religious rite or population control? *Biblical Archaeology* (Jan.-Feb.), 30–51.

Stenberger, M. 1961. Das Gräberfeld bei Ihre im Kirchspiel Hellvi auf Gotland. Der wikingerzeitliche Abschnitt. *Acta Archaeologica* 32, 1–134.

Stjernquist, B. 1987. Spring-cults in Scandinavian prehistory. In T. Linders and G. Nordquist (eds), *Gifts to the Gods,* 149–157. Uppsala Universitetet (Acta Universitatis Upsaliensis Boreas 15), Uppsala.

Thomson, A. 1960. *Barnkvävningen: En rättshistorisk Studie.* (Skrifter utgivna af Kungliga Humanistiska Vetenskapssamfundet i Lund 58), Lund, Gleerup.

Vinsrygg, S. 1979. Våre 'eldste' barn. *Ottar* 115, 30–34.

Welinder, S. 1979. *Prehistoric Demography.* CWK Gleerup (Acta Archaeologica Lundensia, Series in 8° Minore, 8), Lund and Rudolf Habelt, Bonn.

Welinder, S. 1989. An experiment with the analysis of sex and gender of cremated bones. *Tor* 22 (1988–89), 29–41.

9

The church lends a hand

Ross Samson

It thus appears certain that the deposition, in the German manner, of grave goods destined for service in the hereafter ought to have clashed with the beliefs of Christians. And yet, no conciliar canon was produced against such a custom.

That was Eduard Salin writing in the early 1950s about the Merovingian, i.e. sixth- and seventh-century (the name derives from the royal line of Merovech), burial custom in northern France, Belgium, and along the Rhine into south-western Germany[1] (quoted as preface to Young 1977; all translations of modern texts are my own unless otherwise stated). Across the English Channel we similarly find the great misconception that 'burial with grave goods', as archaeologists insist on calling the practice of burying bodies fully dressed,[2] was pagan and was actively stopped by the church. Meaney and Hawkes (1970, 53) wrote of the Anglo-Saxon practice of burial with grave goods in the so-called Final Phase (roughly late seventh century):

This was one of the old customs which died hard ... it was a custom the Church was at first prepared to wink at. In our late cemeteries offerings of food and drink had become infrequent ... only the fastening and ornaments worn on the garments in which the dead were buried, and indispensable adjuncts of everyday wear such as knives [continued]. ... By the 1st half of the 8th century the custom seems virtually to have been stamped out ... even dress-fasteners were now frowned on ... the archaeological poverty of a cemetery like Winnall II is a demonstration of the Church's success in combating one of the outward shows of heathenism.

The Anglo-Saxons most emphatically were pagan; they had to be converted by Christian missionaries. The *Reihengräber* 'row-graves' of the continent are similarly associated with Germans who entered the Roman empire late: the Franks of northern Gaul, the Alamanni of south-western Germany and northern Switzerland, the Lombards of northern Italy, and the Visigoths of northern Spain. Most of these Germans entered the empire as pagans (although some Goths came as 'bad' Christians, in other words as Arians). The Franks of northern Gaul lived in the least urban part of Gaul, usually considered the earliest and core area of the custom of burying the dead fully clothed in graves laid out in rows, sometimes creating huge cemeteries. Much of the population, therefore, was countryfolk, *pagani*, from which the word pagan is derived, and for good reason. Gregory of Tours (*HF* X §31) gives a potted history of the extension of parish churches through his diocese in the sixth century, and it is clear that the more remote rural areas still lacked theirs. It was probably not until the end of the seventh century or even the eighth century that Gaul was more or less completely furnished with parish churches (Imbart de la Tour 1900). The simple, democratic, freedom-loving, Dark-Age, bellicose, country-dwelling German (of Victorian histories) was pagan. The now entrenched Victorian mythology of the early church sees the Roman church as a late developer in the missionary field, which was supposedly the particular expertise of the Celtic church. Thus it was once easy to accept that not until Columbanus came to Gaul in the early seventh century, followed by further waves of Irish monks, did missionary activity really make headway in northern Gaul. It was there that saints Eligius and Amand were active in the mid-seventh to early eighth century, after which came Willibrord, Boniface, and the Anglo-Saxon missionaries. The disappearance of the *Reihengräber* in northern Gaul – and they were always more common in northern Gaul than in southern Gaul – in the late seventh century was easily seen as the result of this Christian missionary activity (indeed, below we will find Frederick Paxton still attributing the supposedly enormous spirituality of the Gaels to the end of this burial practice).

In truth, many *pagani* (people of the *pagus*, the Roman rural district which often became the medieval parish) in northern Gaul were more country bumpkins than pagans and the documented seventh- and eighth-century missionary activity took place in the far north of *Reihengräber* territory. In other words, few of those buried in their clothes would have been called pagans by, for example, the bishop of Tours. Yet most archaeologists still cling to the myth that the church somehow brought an end to these burial rites because they were not properly 'Christian'. Thus Alain Dierkens (1981, 62) says that

> The slow abandonment of funerary grave goods at the end of the Merovingian period was indisputably the consequence of the growing strength of Christianity just as, from the fourth and fifth centuries, it [the abandonment of grave goods] had been the direct or indirect reflection in Gaul . . . of philosophical and religious ideas that insisted on the immaterial state of the soul. From then, we should recognise that the church, with its spiritualist, metaphysical ideas and with its continual and violent reactions against certain, visibly excessively materialist, aspects of the Gallo-Roman world, influenced the evolution of funerary customs in a decisive way.

Now, all these archaeologists have struggled with the perceived 'slowness' of the church in stopping 'un-Christian' burial practices. The internal intellectual struggle is most clearly seen in Salin when he wrote 'and yet' there was no prohibition by the church. He obviously thought there should have been. The others dissemble: the church was biding its time, it was gathering strength, it was chipping away at 'old habits' with its metaphysics. We will see plenty more of this struggle with the intellectual contradictions created by the explanations offered by archaeologists before the end of this essay.

The mental dilemma is posed by the simple problem that the evidence is overwhelming that in the sixth and seventh centuries good Christians were indeed buried dressed, that clothed inhumation was not even remotely perceived as 'anti-Christian', that perhaps the bulk of the population who came to rest in *Reihengräber* were probably Christians. So strong is the desire by archaeologists to cling to the traditional explanation of the disappearance of grave goods as somehow pagan in spirit that they consistently fail to see the obvious.

THE WELL-DRESSED CHRISTIAN CORPSE

King Childeric, whose famous grave was found in Tournai in 1653, was probably pagan, having died some time around AD 481, long before his famous son, Clovis, was converted to Christianity. Childeric's burial was an archetypal, well-furnished, Dark-Age inhumation, and one that dates to the very start of the period when this burial custom blossomed (a good little introductory guide to these funerary rites and their chronology is Halsall 1995). Later royal burials differed little. Archaeologists have uncovered in St Denis Abbey the tomb of one Arnegunde, archaeologically dated to c. 600. She was immediately identified as

Queen Aregunde (without the first 'n'), who died around 570 (see Halsall 1995, 33–34 for who she might really be). In any case, she was near enough royal to be buried at St Denis. Enough of the fabric of her clothing survived to let us know that she had been buried in a white head cloth, purple dress, white stockings, and a long red coat/cloak. Gregory of Tours, writing his *Histories of the Franks* (as it used to be called, and still is by me) at the end of the sixth century, related descriptions of three royal burials: Chilperic, with his wife and sons, 'dressed Sigibert's corpse and buried it in the villa of Lambres' *(HF IV §51)*; the bishop of Senlis 'washed the body [of King Chilperic] and dressed it in more seemly garments' *(HF VI §46)*; and after being killed in battle, the body of King Theudebert was picked up 'by a certain Aunulf, washed and wrapped in decent vestments', and buried in Angoulême *(HF IV §50)*. These members of the royal family were all decidedly 'Christian', even if murderous Christians. The powerful aristocracy were buried in no different manner. Gregory of Tours described the burial of a female relative of Duke Guntram Boso's wife, who was buried in a church near Metz, with 'much gold and a profusion of jewellery' *(HF VIII §21)*. A young boy, richly equipped in his coffin, has been excavated from under the cathedral at Köln. We must assume that all these powerful people who died in the sixth and seventh century were devout Christians.

The same assumption can presumably be made about the now nameless who have been excavated from Dark-Age churches. Rainer Christlein (1974) considered some fifty such burials from Germany and Switzerland: a remarkably large number given the questionable evidence for the existence of Christianity east of the Rhine before the late eighth century. These people were presumably very powerful, and have been interpreted as nobles who founded the churches (Burnell 1989). Certainly, Christlein showed that they were buried with a great deal of expensive jewellery and weaponry. Only fifteen (30%) fell into the 'poor' category, whereas 'poor' accounted for 97% of burials in the great field cemeteries. In short, those seventh-century Alamanni whom we can most confidently suggest were Christian (church founders) were also the most lavishly dressed in death.

If the laity were not necessarily the best Christians, by Dark-Age standards the best Christians, important churchmen, were buried in the same way in northern Gaul. Gregory of Tours described the burial of three men of the cloth. 'Bishop Felix visited him [St Friard] just as he was dying. . . . The bishop washed his body, dressed it in seemly clothing and buried it' *(HF IV §37)*. Gregory's own father had been cured by Abbot, later Saint, Martius, who died at the age of ninety. 'His body was washed with great honour and dressed in suitable clothes, and buried in the oratory of the monastery' (*Lifes of the Fathers* XIV §4).

> There was a hermit named Marianus . . . The men who came to search for him . . . found him dead, lying beneath an apple tree. Hence it was widely circulated among the people that he had slipped from the tree and exhaled his spirit; but it was not known for certain, because no one had been an eyewitness. The men who had come lifted [his body] and brought it to the village of Evaux. After washing the body and dressing it in worthy garments the people buried it in a church. Each year they celebrated the festival commemorating his death (*Glory of the Confessors* §80).

The manner of the religious person's burial did not differ from that of the lay. At Lindisfarne, archaeology has uncovered the burial of St Cuthbert, who died in AD 687. He had gone to his tomb in his finest suit with a lavish jewel-bedecked pectoral cross.

The two elements of preparation for burial that we find over and over again in sixth- and seventh-century literary sources, washing and dressing a corpse, are alluded to in one of the earliest surviving Christian prayers relating to death. Paxton (1990, 64–65) claims that a Spanish (Visigothic) origin is recognisable in the wording:

> Receive, Lord, the soul of your servant . . . clothe it in heavenly vestments and wash it in the holy font of eternal life.

An unusual description of a burial was that of Gertrude, abbess of Nivelles, a noble woman, daughter of Itta and Pepin of Landen, who instructed her nuns just before she died in 659 (*Life of St Gertrude* §7; Effros 1996, 1 for translation) that[3]

> they should not put woollen or linen clothing upon her in that place of burial, but rather one very paltry veil, which a certain holy pilgrimess had used there many days before in order to cover her head, and a hair shirt placed beneath it, so that she should rest in peace and be covered with no other cloth, excepting these two, that is, in the hair shirt in which she had been dressed, and in an old veil with which the hair shirt was covered.

As Effros stresses, Gertrude's deathbed wish 'reflected her lifelong pursuit of chastity and humility'; it was 'radically ascetic' and arose from 'penitential behaviour'. But her wish bears the inescapable implication of her expectation to be dressed for burial in linen or wollen *clothes*. We must assume, along with Effros, that the dress would have been that of, or appropriate to, a nun. Wool was more humble than linen, but silk and linen would have been more appropriate to a noble lay woman. But regardless of the humility or ostentation, in AD 659 an abbess in northern Gaul might expect to go to the grave in clothes.

What seems even more remarkable is that a late-eighth-century text, the Berlin Sacramentary (Sicard 1978, 108–111), continued to present humble clothes as appropriate for the burial of a nun at a time when the practice of dressing a corpse had probably stopped. [4]

If we find kings and queens and nobles and great churchmen and saints buried clothed, with fine jewellery, weapons, cups, and buckets (to hold alcohol? Woolf and Eldridge 1995) in sixth- and seventh-century Gaul, it seems unreasonable to assume that rustics buried at the same time with a small iron belt buckle and knife and perhaps a string of cheap beads were therefore pagan.

That Christians were buried with worldly possessions in the sixth and seventh century in western Europe is inescapable. And yet Lloyd and Jennifer Laing (1993, 25) tell us that

> archaeological evidence for early Christianity is extremely difficult to date, since Christian burials are *always* devoid of datable goods.

Now, why is it that archaeologists write such nonsense? [5]

LIFE AFTER DEATH

Sonia Hawkes, like most archaeologists of the Anglo-Saxons, is never quite explicit why burial with grave goods or items of dress should be offensive to Christians, or why the church should have to 'wink' at them. Of seventh-century England she (1982, 48) writes:

> We thus have a series of early or proto-Christian cemeteries, often quite short-lived, in which deposition of grave-goods was not yet abandoned and pagan practices still lingered. Indeed, it has been suggested that there is increased evidence of superstitious behaviour in the seventh century, from decapitation or stoning of corpses to simple provision of more pagan amulets, as if people doubted the power of the new religion over potentially unquiet dead who had been denied accustomed pagan rituals.

Well, perhaps we should not rush to use pejorative terms such as superstitious when describing customs and beliefs not in accordance with the early church. Just how rational was the behaviour of the former queen and founder of the great nunnery in Poitiers, Radegund (Fortunatus's *Life of Radegund* § 26)?

One Quadragesima, she devised a still more terrible agony to torture herself in addition to the severe hunger and burning thirst of her fast. She forced her tender limbs, already suppurating and scraped raw by the hard bristles of a hair cloth, to carry a water basin full of burning coals. Then, isolated from the rest, though her limbs were quivering, her soul was steeled for the pain. She drew it to herself, so that she might be a martyr though it was not an age of persecution. To cool her fervent soul, she thought to burn her body. She imposed the glowing brass and her burning limbs hissed. Her skin was consumed and a deep furrow remained where the brand had touched her. Silently, she concealed the holes, but the putrefying blood betrayed the pain that her voice did not reveal.

What Hawkes stopped short of saying was what Salin came right out and said: everyday objects in the graves, to his mind, reflect a common superstitious belief in a *physical* rather than a spiritual life after death. Dierkens (1981, 60) expands:

The reasons for this abandonment have often been sought in the growing influence of Christianity: it was against the concept of an immaterial soul to offer the corpse gifts of food and it was a failure to recognise the essence of the Last Judgement to furnish the deceased with objects of everyday life or those recalling social position.

Dierkens takes these commonly held assumptions to be not entirely false, but flawed for giving Christianity too much credit. He seems to hold that indeed the church should have attacked these rites for being spiritually un-Christian, but did not do so actively. It acted by example and only eventually won the day.

Bailey Young (1977) has tried to resolve Salin's paradox of pagan beliefs in life after death *supposedly* reflected in grave goods and the lack of concern on the part of the church to condemn them. He proposed that *Reihengräber* were not pagan, but that ultimately they were un-Christian. Because they were not pagan they were not condemned outright, but eventually they succumbed to the pressure of the church and disappeared because somehow 'wrong'. Christianisation supposedly proceeded in two phases, the first was a violent assault on the outward material expressions of paganism, including sanctuaries, temples, sacred trees, and idols, while the second phase was a subtle attack on popular superstitions. Young's awkward argument is the result of trying to explain that the disappearance of clothed inhumation really was the result of Christian *belief*, while recognising that Christian contemporaries accepted the practice and never once commented upon its supposed improper spirituality. The argument rests ultimately on the advice Pope Gregory is meant to have given St Augustine on his mission to the Anglo-Saxons to use pagan sites rather than destroy them if it achieved better results. Perhaps I should say that it rests on the historical gloss this advice has received by historians, who have used this almost off-the-cuff remark to represent church policy during conversion. Saints' lives, on the other hand, show an almost unremitting violent onslaught against pagan trees, idols, and assorted paraphernalia. The supposed subversive 'winking' policy of the church is little evidenced from our surviving evidence.

Young's theory also relies on a so-called 'popular religious mentality' which is meant to lie behind these burial practices, and is largely defined by Young as containing the beliefs of 'the survival of the personality' and 'collectivity'. In the former belief, death is not conceived of as being the obliteration of the personality, but rather that something akin to the spirit remains and continues to function within society, often as a malign force. The individual, according to the latter belief, is part of the community or tribe, from which he or she cannot be removed. The community itself forms a *continuum*, which includes deceased members of the community, at the extremity of which stand divinities. Burial of the deceased, clothed and equipped for life, is interpreted by Young (1977, 65, my italics) as revealing a belief in the survival of the personality, from which the church took two centuries to 'convert to its more *rational* conceptions'.

Young's 'popular religious belief' may be criticised for the implications of how such a popular belief and its presumed counterpart an 'unpopular' belief existed. Peter Brown (1981, 13–21) argues that the source of such an idea was David Hume's essay, 'The Natural History of Religion', written in the 1750s. In essence Hume pictured 'the vulgar, that is, indeed, all mankind a few excepted, being ignorant and uninstructed', as incapable of abstract thought. Their fragmented view of the universe resulted in polytheistic ways of thinking. The cultured elite who benefitted from instruction were able to abstract an 'original providence' from the general order of the universe. Brown notes the association of 'popular religion' with 'vulgar' or 'superstition', pejorative terms. Because 'popular belief' is founded on the bedrock of general intellectual stupor, Brown suggests it cannot but be revealed as a 'monotonous continuity'. Indeed, this must be true of Young's 'popular religious mentality' for many of its characteristics are revealed to him in *modern* folkloric studies, which are used to recreate ancient beliefs. The folklore is in most cases drawn from fully orthodox Catholic Christian, if parochial, peasants. Thus the popular religious mentality Young

[127]

details has clearly been very popular indeed, having survived at least one and a half millennia of Christian disapproval!

Archaeology suffers from a widespread, unexamined, and fairly witless idea that pagans and primitives have a physical rather than metaphysical belief in an afterlife and that Christians and moderns have a spiritual rather than corporeal view of existence hereafter. One of the universal laws of archaeology is that all well-'equipped' burials, in all parts of the world, in all periods (indeed, from Neanderthal), are interpreted as the result of a belief in 'life after death'. Surprisingly few have commented, if they have noticed, on how unvaryingly narrow the interpretation is. Archaeologists seem to have no other way of understanding the role of such supposedly 'superstitious' practices. In their interpretations, archaeologists stress the 'everyday', so that hunter-gatherers are made to go to a happy hunting ground and members of a stratified agrarian society go to a pseudo-Valhalla to battle all day and drink all night. Emphasis on the mundane real-life activities in the vision (manufactured by archaeologists, let us not forget) of a life-to-come and the apparent one-track minds of the dead makes the ancients appear to lack sophistication in metaphysical belief. And yet, strangely, although prehistoric after-lives are said to be similar to the former earthly one – hence the 'need' for a variety of everyday items – when the qualities of an after-life are described or postulated by archaeologists they often embody characteristics antithetical to normal life. The constraints of time and space and geometry are frequently suspended for the dead. For instance, the dead can 'use' objects that are broken, worn beyond normal functioning, or are only represented symbolically.[6] It is archaeologists who force the simple, physical, everyday-life-after-death spirituality on almost every past culture, even when it clearly defies the non-physical and unreal symbolism surrounding the corpse or its treatment (pennies placed on eyes or in the mouth are hardly everyday ways of paying a ferry fare, for example).

The single greatest reason for holding our hands up in the air, shaking our heads slowly with a pained expression on our face, and muttering 'fools' at those who interpret objects in the grave as pagan because they are supposedly meant to reflect a superstitious belief in life after death is that Christians believe utterly and *fundamentally* in life after death: the resurrection of Christ is the cornerstone of orthodox belief. In a debate with one of his priests over the reality of resurrection, Bishop Gregory of Tours (*HF* X §13) put forward these thoughts.

> We believe, I answered, that even if a man were reduced to very fine dust and then scattered over the land and sea in the face of a keen wind it would still not be difficult for God to restore that dust to life.

It is clear from this that although a fish may have swallowed part of a body, or a bird torn sections of it away, or a wild animal devoured it, it will still be joined together again and restored by our Lord for the resurrection.

Gregory of Tours reveals less about the reality of resurrection (although that was his intention) than he does an underlying feeling that life in Christ will be *corporeal*. No ethereal spirits for that Gregory.

A superb reason for questioning the materialist, mundane, life-as-usual, corporeal *pagan* version of what follows death offered by many an archaeologist is that pagan peoples in the early Middle Ages (the Anglo-Saxons, the Saxons, and all the Slavic peoples) often cremated their dead. It seems unlikely that this was just a hygenic way of ridding the farm of a smelly body, as the ashes were regularly placed in pots, in some cases highly ornate pots, and buried in 'cemeteries' rather than 'middens' (and Downes reminds us in this volume that cremation is expensive in labour, technoology, and materials). If this suggests anything, it suggests that a *spiritual* rather than physical form of post-humous existence was understood. While the pagan Saxons east of the Rhine cremated their dead, perhaps releasing their inner spirits to the heavens above, Gregory of Tours had to dispel the fears of Christian Franks west of the Rhine that life after death was impossible if their physical bodies were destroyed by fire or nibbled away by fishes. Bonnie Effros (1996) draws attention to the evidence of embalming or efforts to retard decay by Merovingian Christians, partly the result of a link between sanctity and bodily preservation (saints' bodies were regularly discovered 'uncorrupt') and partly 'to diminish fears associated with the decomposition of human corpses prior to the final resurrection.' Indeed, such fears may have contributed to the demise of cremation as a common burial practice in the late Roman empire. Thus, the average Christian may well have had a less spiritual conception of heavenly existence than did their pagan neighbours in the early Middle Ages.

The continuation of the classical funerary tradition of mourners, oftentimes hired wailers, weeping and shrieking publically caused the early church some concern, especially in the eastern Mediterranean. Several early church fathers felt that excessive mourning implied a lack of belief in resurrection, and that one should weep for *one's own* grief, but not for the dead. The home-spun counselling offered was that the dead should be thought of as 'leaving on a journey' (and what better preparation for a journey than warm clothing, stout shoes, and a drink or two?). The 'journey' being exceeding long meant the sadness could be commensurate but not hysterical.

Gregory of Tours, like most early medieval churchmen, stopped short of suggesting what exactly came after the resurrection. In the seventh century two visions of heaven and hell were committed to vellum, that of the Irish saint, Fursey, and that of Barontus, a monk from the diocese of Bourges in Gaul. Demons tormenting the vain, murderers, and adulterers are fine set pieces that have not changed in thirteen hundred years. Bede's (*History* V §12) account of the vision of Drycthelm, who almost saw the pleasures of heaven and horrors of hell (he only got to the mouth of hell and close enough to smell heaven), dwelt mainly on the ghastly torture suffered by the souls that had repented and confessed, and were seemingly being purified, for these unfortunates were actually destined for the kingdom of heaven! The horrors of hell were clear enough, but the pleasures of heaven were far less obvious. Countless thousands of children or throngs of virgins standing in crowds bearing candles do not create, in my mind at least, an image of unimaginable joy for the masses. For Bede's Drycthelm the happy people, in white robes, sat in a sweet-smelling meadow. Heaven offered more scope for active afterliving for the elite. Barontus (§8) recognised some of the other monks of his monastery who had died before him. Some were apparently just sitting about, chewing the fat, at the first gate of paradise. By today's secular standards this was perhaps the most pleasurable vision of heaven produced by a medieval cleric. Another former brother had a house of gold by the second gate (impressive but cold, you might think). While yet another, Betolemus, was at the fourth gate. He was in charge of the lighting of all the churches in the world. He was upset that the candles at Barontus's monastery were not kept lit all through the night. Job-related stress was not avoidable even in paradise.

These visions were but tableaux of heaven. Pope Gregory the Great was one of the few to attempt to describe what *life* after death would be like for a Christian. It is the subject of the fourth of his dialogues, in the aptly named *Dialogues*, from which five major points may be extracted. At death the invisible soul departs for heaven or hell, whichever it is judged (prejudged might be better) to have merited. Prayer by the living is beneficial for the soul of the deceased in arranging a preferential final judgement (Bede believed this too). Although invisible, the individual personality of the soul remains clear to other souls, which can simultaneously view those suffering in hell and rejoicing in heaven. The incorporeal spirit may, however, take on corporeal forms. Finally, when the real Judgement Day arrives, the body, uncorrupted, shall rejoin the soul.

In one anecdote of the *Dialogues* (IV §57) a priest is served faithfully on several occasions by an unknown servant at the baths to whom the priest offers bread in thanks. The stranger, 'a spirit disguised as a man', asks for the priest's prayers instead, as he had been a sinner in life and hoped for the priest's timely intercession with God. Following

THE CHURCH LENDS A HAND

Gregory's frank interpretation of what he held to happen after death, we can assume that this spirit was the soul of a man in hell, suffering great torment. But not as great a torment as would come after the Judgement Day when his uncorrupted body would join in the pain, making it that much worse. No wonder the spirit went in search of some help. Gregory the Great thus believed that souls could linger on this earth, make themselves be seen and felt by the living, could continue to have their personality recognised even though invisible, and ultimately would rejoin their physical body – the very definition of what constitutes a living person: physical body animated by an invisible soul. How does this differ from Young's interpretation of burial of a corpse, clothed as in life, as embodying 'popular religious belief' in the 'survival of personality'? Obviously not by one iota. And what of Dierkens's suggestion that apparel appropriate to social rank in life transgressed the philosophy of resurrected life? The vision of Barontus clearly reveals that those who ranked higher in life were to be found further in heaven (by the fourth gate, for instance) and better accommodated. Mere children and virgins only had roles as extras in the crowd scenes.

If archaeologists (most either devoutly or superficially Christian) have smugly maintained a superior air when interpreting physical, materialist, happy-hunting-ground-inhabiting-lives-after-death beliefs as 'pagan', it has only been possible by the Christian church's almost total silence on the subject, allowing Christian after-life to appear more purely spiritual. 'Christianity left the theme of the restoration of all things in God relatively undeveloped' (Markus 1974, 165). Even today heaven and hell owe far more to popularist images and home-spun philosophies than canonical, theological teaching. Christain thinkers have largely avoided the tricky question of what exactly it means to live eternally in Christ by placing most emphasis on the day of resurrection, Domesday, the Day of Judgement. The fear of one's guilt keeps the day in front of the all-knowing judge foremost in the thoughts of what follows death, not whether there is music, dancing, and drinking thereafter. There is much truth in the popular joking today about heaven being boring, 'a place where nothing ever happens'. Barontus's vision of heaven was a striking one to *see*, but there was little to suggest any particular pleasure awaiting the poor common individual, apart from endless Monty Pythonesque 'rejoicing' in torch-lit processions.

The Anglo-Saxon poem *Seafarer* preached the traditional sermon on how to attain life everlasting.

> A man may bury his brother with dead
> And strew his grave with the golden things
> He would have him take, treasures of all kinds,

> But gold hoarded when he here lived
> Cannot allay the anger of God
> Toward a soul sin-freighted.

Boddington (1991, 177) wrongly claims that this captures 'the senti-ments of a Christian recalling the heathen practice of burial with grave-goods and preaching its futility'. The poet was not intimating that bury-ing the deceased in fine clothes would enrage Jehovah, but certainly that it would not impress Him: it is easier for a camel to pass through the eye of a needle than for a rich man to get through the gates of heaven. Indeed, the poet almost implies that the dead *may* take their gold with them, but that they cannot then buy God's forgiveness with it.

So why did grave goods disappear? Why were the dead no longer buried in their clothes after the Final Period?

CHANGE IN BURIAL RITUAL

From archaeology we can infer that the year AD 700 roughly marked a turning point in the burial customs of Christians in western Europe. A custom that had long been practised in some places was now almost universal: corpses were inhumed in or around churches, following its orientation, or directed east towards the rising reborn sun, and without adornment, although this almost certainly was the result of being buried unclothed, in a shroud or naked, rather than being due to a sense of Christian humility or an avoidance of pagan beliefs in life after death, which of course Christians believed in most fervently. The wealth of data (and objects for museum collections) in the shape of buckles, brooches, knives, and beer mugs dries up for large parts of western Europe (southern and eastern England, northern France, Belgium, Switzerland, south-western Germany, and northern Italy in particular).

In terms of the burial ritual the change was far from dramatic in most places. Even in some areas settled by the Anglo-Saxons, where crema-tion had been common, it had been replaced by the inhumation of dressed bodies before the change I am outlining (Halsall 1995, 13 is one of the few who draws attention to this). Inhumation had been common in the west and north of Britain from the late Roman empire (if not before). Indeed, the fifth century in most of Europe (including almost all of eastern Europe) was truly the Dark Ages in archaeological terms:[7] we have no idea how most corpses were disposed of either because the method of disposal left no archaeological evidence or because the in-humations have been excavated but remain unrecognised and undated because the bodies were buried without imperishable items (usually clothes fasteners or pottery). This practice continued throughout the sixth and seventh centuries in much of southern France, Wales, Spain, and Italy.

While most archaeologists have assumed that the disappearance of objects in graves at the end of the seventh century in the *Reihengräber* was a natural, logical conclusion to the general reduction in the number of objects found in graves throughout the seventh century, this is surely a terrible mistake. The excavation of a skeleton with a meagre mid-seventh-century iron knife and small belt-buckle strikes the archaeologist as markedly different from that of a skeleton with a superabundance of mid-sixth-century artefacts. But that is because archaeologists love 'goodies' – there is something of the Victorian antiquarian in all of us. Perhaps had all the organic material not disappeared, archaeologists would recognise the important similarity: both were buried in their clothes. The excavation of a mid-eighth-century skeleton with no more than a meagre bone or bronze pin might seem to the archaeologist in the field as disappointingly much like the mid-seventh-century burial remains, but the important distinction has been lost with the decayed fabrics. The mid-eighth-century corpse was probably buried wrapped in a shroud, held together by a pin or stitched so no artefact remained to be found by the archaeologist.

That this transition often goes unnoticed is revealed by one French archaeologist's observation of the changing burial rituals: the eighth century saw the abandonment of many rural cemeteries and the only objects found now are '*l'agrafe à double crochet*, which could be used to fasten a simple piece of clothing, almost always found on the chest'. But the 'double-crotchetted hook' on the chest presumably fastened a shroud not a simple chemise.

There are many possible causes for the 'drying up' of grave goods in the course of the seventh century. The one that makes the least sense is the one that is generally held, but rarely stated openly. Presumably if two brooches, a belt buckle, and a string of beads were 'pagan' or 'un-Christian', reducing the ensemble to one brooch and a belt-buckle would somehow be less pagan and more Christian. This is just what Meaney and Hawkes seem to imply when they suppose that at first the church 'winked at' food and drink going into the grave, but later its approval was reduced to the bear necessities of daily wear, and finally it 'stamped out' even the belt straps and pins holding clothes together.

The most obvious possible cause is the one that no one mentions, namely a change in dress fashions. A broad perspective detects a marked difference between the artefacts found in cemeteries of the sixth and the seventh century on the continent, from which it can confidently be inferred that somewhere around AD 600 there was a change in clothing styles. This fashion change is patently obvious to the all-too-few students of early medieval dress. Iron inlaid with silver was all the rage in buckles for men and women in the seventh century, a style which certainly looks impoverished compared to some of the lavish gold and garnets of a hundred years earlier. In comparative terms, the archae-ological residue of seventh-century dress is thinner than the residue of sixth-century costume. But, admittedly, not so poor that it can explain all the 'drying up'. Guy Halsall (1992) suggests a socio-political process by which people had less need to reinforce their political claims through elaborate, conspicuous consumption of wealth. This interpretation of social 'process' is common enough among prehistorians, and appeals to a younger generation of medieval archaeologists. But as an explanation it suffers from two weaknesses. First, was the late fifth century and early sixth so unique? Did the source of wealth, rank, power, and status change that much through the early Middle Ages that the elite of, say, the Meuse valley were 'insecure' about their position in 525, less so in 625, and hardly at all in 725? Second, why should changing political structures impinge on the treatment of a loved one's body?

Whether or not politics or economics or cultural notions had some-thing to do with a decline in the lavishness with which the deceased's body was dressed for burial, the answer can only be found in terms of burial practices. Changing practices, whether or not they derived from a process of social, political, or economic development, might easily result in less emphasis being placed on the corpse itself. It is easy to imagine the actual burial becoming more private, attended by only close family, a modest affair. But that does not mean that the whole business of burial did not become grander. Perhaps ever more numerous participants were involved in events away from the body, at a feast, at a public gathering, at the dispersal of gifts and alms, at the home of the dead. Perhaps the crowds assembled at church.

The assumption that fewer objects in the grave equals less attention to the corpse is not necessarily true. It is quite plausible that the seventh century saw a shift not only in the fashions of clothes worn everyday, but also in the type of dress worn *by the deceased*. Rather than dress the loved one in their everyday best, such as might be worn at a wedding or a meeting of the local court, people may have laid out a dead relative in somber attire suitable to attendance of a church service or festival.

Gregory of Tours's story of 'the broken tomb in the church of St Venerandus' may reveal that dress in death was not always everyday (*GC* §34):

> In this chamber were many tombs sculpted from Parian marble,
> in which some holy men and ascetic women were buried. There
> is therefore no doubt that they were Christians, because the

historical scenes on their tombs are revealed to be about the miracles of the Lord and his apostles. During the time when Georgius, a citizen of Velay, was count at Clermont, a section of the vaulting that was soaked with rain because of long neglect from lack of repair fell on one of the sarcophagi. The lid of the sarcophagus was struck and shattered into pieces. A girl was visible, lying in the sarcophagus; all her limbs were as intact as if she had been recently taken from this world. Her face, her hands, and her remaining limbs were without blemish; her hair was very long; I believe that she had been buried with spices. The robe that covered her lifeless limbs was as white as a lamb and intact, neither mutilated by any decay nor discoloured by any blackness. Why say more? She appeared to be so robust that she was thought to be sleeping rather than dead. Because of the shiny whiteness of her silk robe some of us thought that she had died while wearing the white robes [of baptism]. Some said that rings and gold necklaces were found on her and secretly removed, so that the bishop did not know.

The unknown woman was buried dressed, her jewellery was pilfered. Her silk white clothing immediately reminds me of St Bathilda's gorgeous white silk chemise at the Alfred Bono Museum, Chelles, on which was embroidered a golden cross. These white blouses were perhaps not every-day wear, but especially Christian, worn at mass or death. In short, the difference in the wealth of the dress adorning the noble woman Arnegunde and Balthild in death, separated by some seven or eight decades, was perhaps not the result of Byzantine dress fashion effecting the Merovingian court, as Vierck (1978) suggested, but the result of dressing the dead 'for church' rather than for a secular extravaganza.[8] It seems quite likely that even the most expensive and competitively fine outfit for church attendance in the seventh century, white, silk, and beautifully embroidered, might have left only pitifully poor archaeological residue.

In one last odd twist, Bailey Young (1986) suggests an aristocratic impetus, and subsequent emulation by the lesser folk, for the demise of grave goods. Getrude of Nivelles' ascetic burial (described above) was, according to Young, 'a break with old custom' and provided 'a deliberate Christian example'. Because from a noble family, Getrude was meant to have inspired hair shirts as the lastest in Christian funeral fashions. Young's interpretation has been adopted by Paxton (1990, 63), who explicitly accepts that 'her example was followed', and suggests that the seventh-century 'retreat from ostentatious burial' was the result of 'the penetration of Irish monasticism', which supposedly 'reoriented power

[135]

and spirituality in Gaul.' Somehow I doubt it. Put bluntly, this is to argue that nobles displayed greater humility in the seventh century than in the sixth, which is codswallup. Humility has always been a Christian precept and St Augustine of Hippo had explicitly preached against funeral extravagences two and a half centuries before Getrude died. John Chrysostom (d. 407) in his *Homily on Hebrews* and *Homily on John* suggested which psalms were appropriate to funerals and said that exaggerated funeral pomp should be avoided, including rich grave clothes and sumptuous trappings. According to Chrysostom, a simple shroud for the body and the giving of alms as a memorial were all that was needful (Rowell 1977). The point about Gertrude was her aeseticism. She was barking mad; not really a role model for the rich. And a hairshirt worn in death only made sense in her own self-punishing world because those of her class expected to be well dressed on Judgement Day.

This supposed fashion for humility is simply the last logical scramble to maintain the Christian *spiritual* explanation for the abandonment of the deceased's clothing. Now, instead of the church 'winking' at practices with un-Christian undertones, it is seen, unrealistically, as spawning a new generation that was super-spiritual in its humble rituals.

If there was anything logical about the total disappearance of grave goods in the eighth century after the decrease in the quantity and quality of objects during the seventh, it was *not spiritual*. It seems possible that in the seventh century rather than dress the loved body in its secular finest as was customary in the sixth century, people dressed it in its best church clothes (the corpse was probably taken into the church before burial). Or possibly less emphasis was placed on the body as increasingly important parts of the funeral ceremony occurred away from the grave-side, and presumably in church. The two probably went together. But the difference in the treatment of the corpse between the seventh and eighth century was a fundamental one. Instead of clothed for inhumation, the loved body went to the grave naked in a shroud. One cannot use the metaphor of drying up for the disappearance of 'grave goods', the dead did not get buried in increasingly fewer clothes over a hundred years, becoming ever more risqué, before finally ending naked.

My assumption is that in the sixth and seventh century the dead body was prepared and dressed for burial by the family; in the eighth century it was prepared and wrapped in a shroud by the church.

Evidence for the family burying their dead before the eighth century is varied. The protection of graves afforded by law codes has been interpreted as the protection of kin rights over their 'property' and a continuation of Roman practice. The clustering of graves in *Reihengräber* cemeteries has been plausibly interpreted as 'family plots'. Gregory of Tours related miracles worked at 'the tombs that rose from the ground' (*Glory of the Confessors* §51), during which he especially noted that although the three sarcophagi were buried together, the three were *not* related by blood. The very fact that he mentioned this suggests that the audience would have expected family to be buried together. There are also textual anecdotes of kin burying their dead. I have already mentioned that of King Chilperic burying Sigibert. Gregory of Tours (*GC* §15) related a miracle that occurred when a poor man went looking to 'steal' a sarcophagus lid to be used for the sarcophagus of his dead son. He also told this story (*GC* §102)

> Pelagia was a devout ascetic . . . she called her son and said: 'I ask, my most beloved son, that you not bury me for four days, so that all the servants and maids [i.e. slaves] might come and see my body and so that none of those whom I have most care-fully supported might be excluded from my funeral.' As she said this, she sent forth her spirit. After being washed according to custom she was placed on a bier and brought to the church.

And he told a story (*Glory of the Martyrs* §70) involving his own family:

> Once it happened that the husband of my sister was very ill with a high fever. Already he had lain gasping on his bed for four months. Since his grieving wife could think of nothing else except what was required for his funeral, she wept and in her unhappiness went to the church of the saints [Ferreolus and Ferrucio].

Naturally there was a happy ending. What constituted the 'require-ments of the funeral' we are not told, neither here nor in any hagio-graphic story. We do read of arrangements made by people before their death. St Amand's will reveals an obsession with the danger of his body not being buried in his monastery. Presumably, he already knew that his bones would become relics. Pelagia asked for a four-day extension of her wake so her many dependants could pay their respects. Bishop Reticius's wife said to him on her death bed (*Glory of the Confessors* §78) 'I pray that after my death and after the passage of time you may be placed in the tomb in which I am placed. Then the partnership of a single tomb will hold those whom the love of a single chastity preserved in one marriage bed.' The story naturally ends with Reticius being buried alongside his wife in the same tomb, but only after his instruc-tions are nearly ignored and after the corpse of Reticius announces its happiness at being reunited with his wife. Archaeology has documented

[137]

a great number of 'multiple graves', but their discussion has been dominated by the assumption that this represents an illegitimate reuse of previous graves and sarcophagi, which the church itself legislated against at, for instance, the Council of Mâcon in 585 (see Effros 1997a, 6).

In the case of Bishop Reticius and his wife, family and church were the same thing. But even when the church was involved before the eighth century, there are hints that it did so at the request of the family. Pope Gregory the Great, who did not favour people having their family buried in churches,[9] nevertheless took up the case of a high-ranking woman, Nereida, who complained to him that the bishop of Caralis had charged her a hundred shillings for her daughter's burial in church (Ep. IX §3). The pope was not pleased at the idea of a bishop charging a fee for singing a mass. It is possible that there was no other involvement of the clergy, that the family had more or less organised the interment. The pope's letter also leads me to infer that the fee was not customary, a sign perhaps that ecclesiastical involvement was in its infancy.

While this is fairly circumstantial textual evidence of practices, archaeology reveals an eighth-century abandonment of most rural cemeteries in favour (we often have to assume this) of churchyard burial grounds. Early medieval and prehistoric cemeteries started anew and lapsed all the time, but moments of widespread abandonment or commencement were regularly associated with new rituals. It is next to impossible to prove that one cemetery was abandoned for another, but several southern German sites seem to be good examples of *Reihengräber* rural burial grounds abandoned for a new church cemetery. And by the way, it was only in the Carolingian period (the eighth century, the name derives from the royal line of Charles or Carolus) that the Greek word *coemeterium* made a regular appearance in texts.

Textual evidence similarly suggests an increase in ecclesiastical interest in burial in the eighth century.[10] Bullough documents Carolingian, liturgical texts relating to funerals. In particular there was the handbook of liturgical rituals at Rome, the *Ordines romani*, and sacramentaries. The Gelasian Sacramentary contains a number of *orationes ad defunctum*, including a prayer by Alcuin, and formulae for *missae in cymeteriis*. The commendation of the dying from the Sacramentary of Gellone, written c. 760, contained these lines among others (Hillgarth 1986, 193–4):

> Go forth, O soul, from this world, in the Name of the Father Almighty who created you. . . . Today your servant's place is established in peace and his dwelling in Jerusalem on high. Receive your servant, Lord.
>
> Free, O Lord, the soul of your servant from all the perils of hell and from the snares of sin and from all tribulations. . . .
>
> Receive, O Lord, the soul of your servant, returning to you;

clothe him with a heavenly garment and wash him in the holy spring to eternal life, that he may rejoice among those who rejoice, and be wise with those who are wise. . . .

In the eighth century burial practice also appears in other texts, such as the so-called Penitential of Theodore, which (Bullough 1983, 191):

explicitly follows 'Roman custom': the corpses of monks and clergy are taken into church where they are anointed with chrism and a mass celebrated for them; they are then carried out for burial. There are corresponding provisions for laity, for whom however commemorative masses may be offered on the third or later days, preferably after a period of fasting by the dead man's kindred.

I assume it is no coincidence that the first evidence we have for liturgical collections dealing with burial rites and prayers date to around the eighth century, although for this period the only three certain liturgical elements are the singing of psalms during the funeral procession and burial – Psalm 50 was popular – the recitation of prayers, and the singing of special masses. Variations on the prayer *Suscipe, domine* ('Receive, Lord . . .') make clear reference to the bearing of the body to burial or depositing 'the body from the bier into the grave' (Paxton 1990, 65). Enough literary descriptions exist that we can be certain that the body was usually taken to a church before being borne to the grave.

In the second half of the seventh century, St Amand cut down a man hanged by Count Dotto, took the body back to his cell, and prayed for his soul to be returned to his body. After successfully resurrecting the man, Amand called for water to be brought to his cell. The brothers 'supposed that it was to wash the body before burial' (*Life of St Amand* §14 quoted in Hillgarth 1983, 143–4). Of course we cannot know whether the monks thought it extraordinary that Amand should be preparing the corpse rather than the man's kin (who certainly existed, for the man is returned to them amid much rejoicing). But the anecdote does reveal one of the few elements in the burial ritual that we know the church practised: washing the body. St Papula lived for thirty years in a monastery in the diocese of Tours, disguised as a man. Three days before she died she revealed the secret to the other monks. 'When she died, she was washed by other women and buried' (Gregory of Tours, *Glory of the Confessors* §16). Bishop Reticius's body 'was washed and placed on the funeral bier' (Gregory of Tours, *History of the Confessors* §74); 'his [Charlemagne's] body was washed and prepared for burial in the usual way. It was then borne into the cathedral and interred there' (Einhard, *Life of Charlemagne* §31).

How and why the ritual bathing of the dead body began, I cannot say. Certainly washing was also carried out by the family (several instances were quoted earlier). But even if the church inherited an ancient Jewish or pagan practice, the similarity to baptism could not have been plainer. One version of the Dark-Age burial prayer *Suscipe, domine* could not be clearer: 'Lord, wash the soul of your servant in the holy font of eternal life'. The Greek text of c. 500, *Ecclesiastical Hierarchy*, explicitly drew the parallel of anointing the 'one in sleep' with baptism. A seventh-century Visigothic deathbed penance has the sick person changed into clean clothes after penance 'if death is imminent' in a direct echo of baptism (Paxton 1990, 77). It may well be the closeness of the two that made the council of Auxerre ban the burial of dead *in baptisterio* (Effros 1997a, 15 for reference). Baptism was also a popular ritual. The early medieval church banned people from being baptised more than once. It was a fitting ritual to echo in death: coming into the Christian flock in one, going out of the community of believers in this world in the other.

Although largely silent on the subject, the little precedent that is offered by the bible in matters of how to treat the corpse involved a shroud (wrapped around Lazarus, for instance). The shroud, particularly a *white* shroud, was an echo of the baptismal robes. Baptism may thus hold the key to the disappearance of so-called 'grave goods'; there was no room in this pseudo-baptism for brooch, belt-buckles, and knife.

The same church fathers who worried about wailing at funerals also tried to stamp out the Roman pagan custom of wearing black. White, for rebirth, was considered appropriate. When the monk, Eadmer, had a vision of St Anselm's death, 'the room was filled with a host of people most wonderfully and beautifully arrayed in white apparel'. The church, however, was unable to stop the living from mourning in traditional black (our own sombre mourning dress thus has an unbroken tradition more than two millennia old). Gregory of Tours tells of a religious procession at Saragossa (in Visigothic and hated Arian Spain) in which all the women wore black garments 'so that they might have been burying their dead husbands' (*HF* III §29). If the church had no impact on the mourners' attire, it had more influence over the dead.

At the end of the sixth century, Gregory of Tours expected the dead to go to their grave clothed (and in or by a church), but wrapped in a shroud would not have surprised him. St Cuthbert, if the *Life of St Cuthbert* is to be believed (and it was more or less contemporary), was buried clothed *and* wrapped in a shroud. The white clothing worn by a dead woman reminded Gregory of baptismal robes and some churchmen in the east had long been trying to get participants at funerals to dress in white. At the end of the seventh century, it seems likely that the church had finally concocted a funeral rite drawing on elements of the mass and baptism, with the logical conclusion that the dead should go out of the world as they came in, ashes to ashes, dust to dust, born naked into the world and borne in white into the community of Christ.

I can even suggest what happened to the clothes. One of the most common themes of saintly Merovingian living, especially of women, was the donation of their good clothes as alms to the poor. Perhaps half a dozen such incidents are recorded in the *Life of St Radegund* by Fortunatus alone. While Chrysostom in the eastern Mediterranean had suggested a simple shroud and alms as memorial as more suitable than extravagent funeral pomp, the giving of alms itself developed into an extravagent pompous ceremony. Think of our specially minted Maundy silver coins for the queen to give away to the poor! Emperor Charlemagne did something similar from a special balcony of his palace. It is all too easy to imagine that the unprepossessing burials of the eighth century did not represent 'the Church's success in combating one of the outward shows of heathenism' as Meaney and Hawkes so implausibly hold. Rather they represent the final capitulation of the church to the demands of the people to take final care for the loved body in death, while the outward shows of ostention and bad taste by the rich were directed at the deserving poor.

NOTES

1. Throughout I write effectively about these regions and Anglo-Saxon England. The burial practices of Mediterranean Europe were different. There, the absence of datable objects in graves and sarcophagi make it difficult to discuss sixth- and seventh-century burial. It seems quite likely that the eighth-century burial practices adopted in temperate Christian Europe that I document here had already developed perhaps by the sixth century in Italy and southern France.

2. The limitations of language have an adverse affect on British archaeology in this instance. In French, the word *habillé* is generally used, meaning 'dressed', reinforcing the idea of the body being buried in clothing. The general use of 'grave goods' in British archaeology increases the tendency to see artefacts as objects rather than parts of costume. Moreover, its helps to create an image of the body being *given* objects such as belts or swords, placed around it as the body lay in the ground, rather than being formally *dressed* and taken to the grave.

   This linguistic phenomenon makes it all the more remarkable that Salin, who more often wrote of 'dressed inhumation' than of 'grave goods', should prefer the latter precisely when concerned with how the church might view the ritual.

   I imply no distinction when I write grave goods or clothes, objects or dress in the course of this paper.

3. I must thank Bonnie Effros especially for letting me see the typescript of her articles for the *Revue belge* and *Viator* in early stages, as well as offering me much advice and criticism. I was sadly unable to see her unpublished thesis before writing or revising this paper.

4. Effros footnotes a short article by Roosens (1985) as relevant to the question of Merovingian religious women and men being buried in humble garments rather than a shroud. I was unable to see this when writing.

5. Some who read this in draft insisted that there are archaeologists who recognise that burial of dressed and equipped corpses in the sixth century was acceptable Christian practice. Yet the names put forward, such as Young, are often precisely those of people whom I quote here to demonstrate their reluctance to accept just that. Guy Halsall remains one of the few in print who is explicitly happy to see *Reihengräber* burial practices as fully acceptable to the church. He (1995) makes the important observation that British archaeologists are led astray by the coincidental and vague contemporaneity of the success of missionary activity among the Anglo-Saxons in the century after St Augustine and the changes in burial rites. The result is the widespread (mis)use of the term 'pagan' for cremations and well-equipped inhumations in Britain.

6. I was thinking of 'accidentally' broken or poorly mended objects. Effros drew my attention to 'purposefully' broken objects, and the more complex implication of preventing future use of the object on earth but perhaps allowing continued use elsewhere or in another time. Even this convoluted notion of an afterlife that might be both physical, allowing intercourse with the living, and non-physical is in keeping with Christian beliefs. In the following text Pope Gregory the Great's example is of a soul that *walks, talks, serves,* and *eats* with a priest.

7. Archaeologists do not yet seem to appreciate just how universal is the dearth of recognisable burials from the fifth century across the whole of Europe, from Scotland to Poland, although perhaps less so around the Mediterranean. Heiko Steuer once roughly calculated that perhaps a quarter of a million *Reihengräber* of the fifth, sixth, and seventh century had been excavated in western Europe. Only five per cent came from the fifth century. Throughout the whole of the Slavic areas of Europe fifth-century burials are almost non-existent.

Because the phenomenon has yet to be recognised there are no explanations presently on offer. The tendency is for archaeologists to explain the paucity only in their own locality, and usually by inferring an absence of population.

8. The possibility of a sober, presumably white, church outfit offered here is either pure speculation or I have read contemporary anecdotes suggesting this possibility to me, but now have no conscious recollection of the evidence.

9. Perhaps because burial within a church seems so natural to us today, archaeologists seem oblivious to the fact that churchmen in the early Middle Ages were not keen on this practice. While theologians never even so much as mentioned the burying of the deceased in their clothes, there was plenty of condemnation of the practice of burying the dead in a place of worship. Paxton (1990, 186) notes that at 'Ravenna the founder of the church of Saint Vitale had the bronze doors engraved with an inscription to the effect that only bishops could be buried there. At the Council of Mainz in 813 the decree was repeated that "no dead body was to be buried within a church, except those of bishops and abbots, or worthy priests or faithful laity".'

10. See Bullough 1983, Paxton 1990, and McLaughlin 1994 for the most accessible studies in English.

BIBLIOGRAPHY

Anonymous (c. 679). Vision of Barontus, monk of Longoretus. In *Christianity and Paganism, 350–750. The conversion of western Europe*, 195–204, edited and trans. by J. N. Hillgarth, 1986. University of Pennsylvania Press, Philadelphia.

Anonymous (c. 760). Sacrementary of Gellone. In *Christianity and Paganism, 350–750. The conversion of western Europe*, 193–195, edited and trans. by J. N. Hillgarth, 1986. University of Pennsylvania Press, Philadelphia.

Anonymous (c. 665). Life of St Gertrude. In *Late Meovingian France. History and hagiography 640–720*, 301–326, edited and trans. by Paul Fouracre and Richard A. Gerberding, 1996. Manchester University Press, Manchester.

Bede (c. 731). *A History of the English Church and People*, translated by Leo Sherley-Price, revised 1968. Penguin, Harmondsworth.

Boddington, Andy 1991. Models of burial, settlement and worship: the final phase reviewed. In Edmund Southworth (ed.), *Anglo-Saxon Cemeteries. A reappraisal*, 177–199. Allan Sutton, Stroud, Gloucestershire.

Brown, Peter 1981. *The Cult of the Saints. Its rise and function in Latin Christianity*. University of Chicago Press, Chicago.

Bullough, Donald 1983. Burial, community and belief in the early medieval west. In Patrick Wormald (ed.), *Ideal and Reality in Frankish and Anglo-Saxon Society*, 177–201. Blackwell, Oxford.

Burnell, Simon 1989. Merovingian to Early Carolingian Churches and Their Founder Graves in Southern Germany and Switzerland: the Impact of Christianity upon the Alamans and the Bavarians. Unpublished D.Phil. thesis, Oxford University.

Christlein, Rainer 1974. Merowingerzeitliche Grabfunde unter der Pfarrkirche St. Dionysius zu Dettingen und verwandte Denkmale in Süddeutschland. *Fundberichte aus Baden-Württemberg* 1, 573ff.

Dierkens, Alain 1981. Cimetières mérovingiens et histoire du haut moyen âge. Chronologie – société – religion. In *Histoire et Méthode*, 15–70. (Acta Historica Bruxellensia 4) Brussels: Université de Bruxelles.

Dierkens, Alain 1984. Superstitions, christainisme et paganisme à la fin de l'époque mérovingienne: à propos l'Indiculus superstitionum et paganiarum. In Hervé Hasquin (ed.), *Magie, sorcellerie, parapsychologie*, 9–26. Bruxelles: Éd. de l'Université de Bruxelles.

Effros, Bonnie 1994. From Grave Goods to Christian Epitaphs: Evolution in Burial Tradition and the Expression of Social Status in Merovingian Society. Unpublished Ph.D. dissertation, University of California, Los Angeles.

Effros, Bonnie 1996. Symbolic expressions of sanctity: Gertrude of Nivelles in the context of Merovingian mortuary custom. *Viator* 27, 1–10.

Effros, Bonnie 1997a. Beyond cemetery walls: early medieval funerary topography and Christian salvation. *Early Medieval Europe* 6, 1–23.

Effros, Bonnie 1997b. *De partibus Saxoniae* and the regulation of mortuary custom: a Carolingian campaign of Christianization or the suppression of Saxon identity? *Revue Belge de philologie et d'histoire*.

Einhard (d. 840), Life of Charlemagne. In *Einhard and Notker the Stammerer Two Lives of Charlemagne*, trans. by Lewis Thorpe, 1969. Penguin, Harmondsworth.

Fortunatus c. 590. Life of Radegund. In *Sainted Women of the Dark Ages*, 60–105, trans. by Jo Ann McNamara and John E. Halborg, 1992. Duke University Press, Durham, North Carolina.

Gregory of Tours (d. circa 594), *Glory of the Confessors*, trans. by Raymond Van Dam, 1988. Liverpool University Press, Liverpool. *Glory of the Martyrs*, trans. by Raymond Van Dam, 1988. Liverpool University Press, Liverpool. *History of the Franks*, trans. by Lewis Thorpe, 1974. Penguin, Harmondsworth.

Gregory the Great ca. 593. Book of Dialogues. In *Saint Gregory The Great. Dialogues*, trans. by Odo John Zimmerman, 1959. Fathers of the Church, Inc., New York.

Halsall, Guy 1992. Socal change around A.D. 600: an Austrasian perspective. In Martin O. H. Carver (ed.), *The Age of Sutton Hoo: the Seventh Century in North-Western Europe*, 269–270. Boydell and Brewer, Woodbridge, Suffolk.

Halsall, Guy 1995. *Early Medieval Cemeteries. An introduction to burial archaeology in the post-Roman west.* Cruithne Press, Glasgow.

Imbart de la Tour, Pierre 1900. *Les paroisses rurales du 4e au 11e siècles* (reprinted c. 1979). Picard, Paris.

Laing, Lloyd and Jenny Laing 1993. *The Picts and the Scots.* Alan Sutton Publishing, Stroud, Gloucestershire.

Markus, Robert Austin 1974. *Christianity in the Roman World.* Thames and Hudson, London.

McLaughlin, M. 1994. *Consorting with Saints: Prayer for the Dead in Early Medieval Europe.* Cornell University Press, Ithaca, New York.

Meaney, A. L. and Sonia C. Hawkes 1970. *Two Anglo-Saxon Cemeteries at Winnall, Winchester, Hampshire.* (Society for Medieval Archaeology Monograph Series 4), London.

Paxton, Frederick S. 1990. *Christianizing Death. The creation of a ritual process in early medieval Europe.* Cornell University Press, Ithaca, New York.

Roosens, H. 1985. Reflets de christianisation dans les cimetières mérovingiens. *Les études classiques* 53: 132–134.

Rowell, Geoffrey 1977. *The Liturgy of Christian Burial. An introductory survey of the historical development of Christian burial.* Alcuin Club/ S.P.C.K., London.

Salin, Edouard 1950–59. *La Civilisation Mérovingienne*, 4 vols. Picard, Paris.

Sicard, Damien 1978. *La liturgie de la mort dans l'église latine des origines à la reforme carolingienne.* Aschendorff, Münster.

Venantius Fortunatus (d. 609), *The Life of the Holy Radegund.* In *Sainted Women of the Dark Ages*, trans. by Jo Ann Mcnamara and John E. Halborg, 1992, 70–105. Duke University, Durham, North Carolina.

Vierck, Hayo E. F. 1978. La 'chemise de Sainte-Bathilde' à Chelles et l'influence byzantine sur l'art de cour mérovingien au VIIe siècle. In *Actes du Colloque international d'archéologie: centenaire de l'abbé Cochet*, 521–570. Rouen.

Young, Bailey K. 1977. Paganisme, christianisation et rites funéraires mérovingiens. *Archéologie Médiévale* 2: 7–81.

Young, Bailey K. 1986. Exemple aristocratique et mode funéraire dans la Gaule mérovingienne. *Annales Économies, Sociétés, Civilisations* 41, 379–383.

Woolf, Alex and Roy Eldridge 1994. Sharing a drink with Marcel Mauss: the uses and abuses of alcohol in early medieval Europe. *Journal of European Archaeology* 2.2, 327–340.

10

Archaeologia Victoriana: the archaeology of the Victorian funeral

Melanie Richmond

I am told he makes a very handsome corpse, and becomes his coffin prodigiously.

– Oliver Goldsmith, 'The Good-Natured Man'

The Victorians took death to heart, it was an ever-present condition of life. For a large number of the population, life was (in the words of Thomas Hobbes) 'solitary, poore, nasty, brutish and short', particularly for the underprivileged or vulnerable, e.g. the working classes in industrialised Britain and children (Morley 1971, 7). Industrialisation created a well-to-do middle class which acquired the means and opportunity to display their affluence both in life and death, and affluence was equated with respectability. This credo was not the sole preserve of the middle class, who themselves were emulating those at the top of the class structure, as it percolated to the very body of people who could least afford to invest their funerals with ostentatious display of wealth or social standing. It seems almost perverted to modern sensibilities that financial resources that could have enriched the lives of the lower and middle classes were, on occasion, reserved solely for the funeral and interment costs at the expense of general welfare and education whilst alive.

It is within this social context that we are able to set the Victorian funeral and its attendant material culture. It is this social background which provided a fertile breeding ground for extravagance and sentimentality. By contrast, these same social conditions engendered the formation of burial reform and pressure groups, such as the Ecclesiologists, who produced their own unique material culture and archaeology. Since fashion and custom dictated the demeanour and grandeur of funerals, it is hardly surprising that similar items of conspicuous consumption played a role in the realm of mourning, added to which a panoply of rigid social mores and restrictions governed the social behaviour of those in varying degrees of mourning. Thus, a comprehensive 'language' of actions and objects (from the mourning teapot to the mourning ear-trumpet [Morley 1971, pls 14 and 33]) was constructed around death and reactions to death which can be detected in the archaeology and physical remains of that period. Coffin furniture of the eighteenth and nineteenth centuries also belongs within this framework, and from it we can infer symbolic and social meaning particular to death and mourning.

Social conditions in Victorian Britain

A combination of elements conspired to produce the Victorian funeral. Much was invested in funerals of the early to mid-nineteenth century both in terms of finance and visual display as a continuation of the decorative preferences of the previous century. The industrialisation of urban centres allowed for the mass-production of coffin furniture; the squalid and hazardous living conditions of populations doubled or trebled through influxes from rural communities promoted by clearances and famine in these areas (e.g. from Ireland and the Scottish Highlands to Edinburgh and Glasgow). This in turn encouraged the spread of disease of epidemic proportions (such as cholera and typhus), causing mortality rates to soar in communities whose sanitary conditions could not cope with the teeming masses it had to support. From 1831–32 cholera made its biggest impact in Scotland, causing the deaths of some 10,000 inhabitants of the, by now, densely populated cities, towns, and rural agricultural centres (Devine and Mitchison 1988, 47). Typhus made its impact in Scotland during each of the three major industrial depressions of 1816–18, 1827–28, and 1837–39, so it can be said that population increases coupled with poverty compounded the rise in mortality rates in urban areas (Devine and Mitchison 1988, 49).

A symbiotic relationship had now evolved between industrialised Britain and the elaborate coffin furnishings of the nineteenth century. Industrialisation promoted urban living and concomitant biological hazards which in turn allowed urban mortality rates to rise. Elaborate coffin fitting were only able to be mass produced because large-scale industrialisation had taken place.

[146]

Figure 1. 'Motherless' plaster by George A. Lawson, 1832–1901, Kelvingrove Museum and Art Gallery, Glasgow.

Morality and decency also played their part in the Victorian celebration of death. Social guidelines and morality tales in the form of children's periodicals of the 1820s (Dixon 1989, 141), and monumental art or religious statuary taught the population that death was, for the unblemished soul, something to be looked forward to. Disease, poverty, and starvation would no longer haunt a short and hard life when you eventually went to rest in the arms of Jesus, so the sentimental element, which cannot be separated from Victorian mentality, crept into death and dying (see Fig. 1). The Victorians saw their urban cemeteries as pleasant, instructive, and reflective idylls where the genteel could take their Sunday constitutional down the winding, tree-lined paths and carriage drives. There they could read the epitaphs of the great and the good, they could marvel at the statuary of the monuments, they could (if, like the Glasgow Necropolis, the city of the dead was built into a hill) gaze upon the vista of the industrialised metropolis, and they could enjoy the merits of inventive planting in what was often the nearest accessible 'parkland' (Brooks 1989, 58).

VICTORIAN ATTITUDES TO DEATH

The funeral trade was already well established when the young Victoria came to the throne in 1837. Many stockholders' investments in urban cemeteries were proving financially successful by this time, for example Liverpool and Glasgow Necropolises and Kensal Green Cemetery. The social framework was already in place for the Victorian funeral (Richardson 1989, 107). It is the Victorian era more than any other which is synonymous with elaborate and ostentatious funerals. Clearly, mourning in all its various socially prescriptive forms had never been so 'deep' nor – a favourite Victorian sentiment – respectable. In fact, one ran the risk of morally offensive behaviour and scandal if one inadvertently flouted public decency by, say, mourning for the wrong length of time or with the wrong depth of crepe on one's skirts (Morley 1971, 68). The Victorian imagination was gripped by the horrors of the resurrectionists and the terror of premature burial, which, because precautionary measures were taken, resulted in specific burial practices with distinct and clearly identifiable funerary archaeology. Examples of nineteenth-century fears transmuted into physical realities include graveyard watch-houses, mortsafes, and an ingenious device developed by a Russian count allowing an alarm flag to be raised by the would-be corpse from inside the coffin if buried alive (Wilkins 1990, 51).

The very real fear of becoming an anatomy lesson in front of a roomful of gentlemen scholars after one's death is perhaps more understandable to the modern mind. It is timely to note here that in the crypt of Glasgow Cathedral there was uncovered a cache of disarticulated bone deposited in a small shaft sunk flush against the brickwork of the Victorian heating system installed at the turn of the century, which included a skull that had had its crown surgically removed post mortem

Figure 2. Skull recovered from excavations at Glasgow Cathedral.

(Driscoll 1992). Until 1888 the original site of Glasgow University, which had a long history of teaching anatomy and dissection, was but a short distance away from the cathedral (see Fig. 2). Added to the perceived potential problem of being physically incomplete when the final trump sounded on the day of resurrection, there was a uniquely Victorian worry in terms of respectability and social standing posed by the dirty deeds of body-snatchers. After all, until the passing of the Anatomy Act in 1832, the only legitimate supply for the demand for cadavers were the bodies of those who died at the end of a rope, i.e. convicted criminals (Richardson 1987). The social indignity of suffering the same posthumous fate as those of the largely poor, criminal fraternity was unthinkable to the middle and lower classes alike.

The literary influences of writers such as Edgar Allan Poe, who tapped directly into the dark veins of a generation and played on their widespread morbidity, also shaped the embodiment of the Victorian funeral. Other spectres of specifically British Victoriana such as death and madness brought about by opium addiction, syphilis, or absinthe abuse plagued a society that thrilled to the tales of Varney the Vampire in the 'penny dreadfuls' (Rymer 1991, 145) or the real-life crimes of Burke and Hare. To cap it all, the monarch herself actively participated in and tacitly encouraged widespread adoption of the material culture and emotional culture of death. In effect, after the death of Prince Albert, she never came out of mourning until she herself died.

[149]

THE FUNERAL INDUSTRY

Despite the vast quantities of cash that were spent on funerary expenses, undertakers were generally not, as one might imagine, excessively wealthy as a result. The reasons for this were two-fold. Firstly, the undertaker himself 'sub-contracted' various duties to an assortment of middlemen – the carpenter, plumber, upholsterer, and doctor (Morley 1971, 24) – and therefore the income was split accordingly. Secondly, the trade was over-subscribed as virtually anyone with the inclination to do so could set themselves up in the undertaking business. Thus despite the climbing mortality rate due to the cramped and unsanitary conditions worsened by the industrial revolution there were more establishments to deal with the dead than was necessary. So undertaking was not necessarily a lucrative business despite the large sums of money which, as the documentary evidence bears out, was changing hands (see the appendix).

Funeral expenses included the purchase of a suitable coffin and the choice of materials, upholstery, and exterior decoration was bewildering, from the simple elm case to the triple-shelled lead structure and many permutations in between. Coffin furniture in the form of grips, grip-plates, coffin lace, escutcheons, and depositum plates also formed part of the vigorous array of decorative elements which could be incorporated into the fashionable coffin.

It appears to be the case that, once a style or design became popular, fashions were extremely slow to change; presumably this has its roots in the manufacturing processes as well as questions of taste and fashion. Methods of manufacture dictated the pace of change, but tradition also played a part in the development and diversity of designs available. Power-assisted die-stamping machines were introduced in 1769 (Litten 1991, 106) and the intricate die-stamps used could only be altered or redesigned at some cost of time and money. It was not until the 1950s that moulding and casting replaced stamping in the manufacturing process. This, coupled with the fact that the undertaking business is a relatively traditional industry not given to innovative changes which prefers to follow the 'tried and tested' methods of market forces, may do much to explain the slow pace of change.

THE MATERIAL CULTURE: VICTORIAN FUNERARY PRACTICE

There was by the late 1870s a bewildering array of coffin furniture, coffin types, hearses and shrouds/grave clothes to choose from, and the larger funerary establishments were able to cater for all tastes and ideological requirements. The designs of coffin furniture which are illustrated in the three extant trade catalogues of the eighteenth and

[150]

Symbol	Immortality/mortality	Meaning
winged cherub's head	immortality	winged soul – resurrection
sun's rays	immortality	The Glory of God / The Radiance
angel with crown and trumpet	immortality	Angel of Resurrection
dove with sun's rays	immortality	Holy Spirit in Radiance
winged skull	mortality	*memento mori*
lighted torch	immortality	*flambeau* – eternal life
skull and crossed bones	mortality	*memento mori*
crown	immortality	Crown of Righteousness
Father Time	mortality	*memento mori*
palm fronds	immortality	victory over death
weepers with extinguished torch	mortality	mourning over the end of earthly life

nineteenth centuries can be compared with the analysis of symbolism inherent in the patterns which decorate Scottish gravestones of the same period (Willsher 1990, 25–31). The symbols carry particular meaning and values in the Christian tradition, despite the fact that these designs were criticised by reform groups such as the Ecclesiologists as being too pagan in origin. They can be divided into two types, those that represent immortality (i.e. as part of the Christian belief system) and those that represent mortality. A number of these designs can be found incorporated in the patterns of coffin furniture; the table above details their form and symbolic meaning based on the interpretations given by Willsher (1990).

The English post-Reformation funeral has received due attention from interested academics such as Julian Litten (1991) and John Morley (1971) and high-profile excavations such as those at Christchurch, Spitalfields (Reeve and Adams 1993) and Sevenoaks, Kent (CBA News 1994) have highlighted the archaeology associated with studies of this type of funerary activity. However, the same cannot be said of the Scottish material, which has been little studied. Clearly some differences existed, even within the legislative framework for burial. For example, intramural inhumation was made illegal in London as part of the more general burial reforms of 1852, whereas it was not outlawed in the rest of England and Wales until 1853, Scotland in 1855, and Ireland in 1856 (Brooks 1989, 48). Other acts of parliament which directly affected encoffined burials in Scotland include An Act for Burying in Woollen of 1677, the Act anent for burying in Scotts Linnen of 1686 (Gordon 1984, 29–30), and a Proclamation of Council in 1684 forbidding the use of coffins decorated with metalwork. The latter stated that it would 'prohibit and discharge the makeing use of any coffins covered with silk cloath or fringes; as likewayes all coffins whereon ther is any carveing or mouldering or brasse or irone worke thereupon for ornament more then for necessar use' (*The Acts of Parliament of Scotland*, vol. VIII, 1684. 497).

These laws had direct repercussions for the style and appearance of coffins and consequently for the archaeology itself. It was felt necessary to impose restrictions on the 'exorbitant expences of burialls' (*The Acts of Parliament of Scotland*, vol. VIII, 1684. 476), which continued to escalate, and, some two hundred years later, the location of the interment. Fashionable society now placed such an enormous emphasis on status in funerals that it was becoming more costly than the conditions of living itself. Legislation, however, did not deter those intent on having an elaborate coffin in Scotland, so the mort cloth was developed to provide decoration and still remain within the letter of the law. Few surviving examples exist today but their appearance and cost to hire can be deduced from extant kirk session records of the time, that is, post-1684. The mort cloth was a decorative covering for a plain coffin which was removed before the coffin was lowered into the grave, and re-used, so it does not form part of the material remains from interments. However, its absence highlights the fact that plain coffins were not necessarily chosen because they were popular or fashionable, but because there was little choice for the Scottish parishioner (unless a stiff fine was a legitimate financial consideration and subsumed as a funerary cost).

By 1886, Andrew Edgar (1886, 259), the minister at Mauchline, Ayrshire was able to declare, 'But now that coffins are all covered with cloth, or else made of fancy wood, and are more or less ornamented, mortcloths are no longer required as trappings.' It is to this ornamentation, or coffin furniture, that I now wish to turn. Coffin decoration is the last affirmation of the status of an individual in terms of wealth and social importance within the community. This symbol of status is conferred by the remaining family of the deceased upon the material culture of funerary rites.

THE ARCHAEOLOGY: COFFIN FURNITURE FROM GLASGOW CATHEDRAL

In November 1992 Glasgow University Archaeological Research Division undertook excavations in the choir, crypt, and nave of Glasgow Cathedral (Driscoll 1992), which revealed eight intact coffined inhumations (four from the crypt and four from the nave) and several fragments of unstratified coffin furniture. It is the intention here to use the archaeological evidence from one such intramural inhumation to illustrate just how elaborate and visually impressive a Victorian coffin could be, and to assess how status in life could be transferred to status in death.

The most complete examples come from a coffin in lair 24 in the east end of the crypt (Driscoll 1992), which is unfortunately listed as unsold on the only lair plan so far discovered; consequently the corpse is as yet unnamed. However, from skeletal analysis carried out by Sarah King, we can say that the individual was a mature adult female between 5'2" and 5'5" tall and with arthritis in the joints of her feet and spine. She had been interred in a wooden coffin of the classic flat-lidded shouldered type, which, when new, would have been covered in a piled fabric (probably coloured velvet), traces of which were discovered still adhering to the reverse of the coffin furniture sandwiched between this and the coffin wood. When uncovered the lid was found to have collapsed, but the coffin outline could easily be discerned as could the metal of the coffin furniture. The latter was given basic conservation *in situ* to strengthen the decoration enough for it to be retrieved in almost one piece. This was successfully achieved with the grip-plate from the left-hand side panel nearest the foot and it remains the best-preserved example. There were four pairs of grips and grip-plates on this coffin; one on the head end panel, one on the foot end panel, one each on the left- and right-hand shoulder panels and two each on the left- and right-hand lower panels. Each panel was bordered with coffin lace, and enough was retrieved of this and the grip plates to identify the pattern of both.

The grip plate measures 20 x 14 cm and is formed of an extremely thin metal, which analysis has shown to be a tin pewter (70–80% tin and 20–30% lead). This bears an embossed decoration consisting of a raised oval cartouche (somewhat compressed by the action of the weight and pressure of the soil in which it was buried) surrounded by rococo style design which incorporates a pair of winged cherubs' heads. The surface has been damaged and the embossed pattern is now quite flat. It is difficult to make out the decorative elements, but when viewed from the reverse side it is possible to see the outline of the wings and the faces of a pair of cherubs above the convex oval. It is very similar in design and form to the grip-plates which adorn one of the coffins in the Bell vault at Milton St John, Kent which is reproduced in a photograph by Litten (1991, 115). This coffin houses Eleanor Bell, who died in 1827, and has 'a scarlet velvet upholstered elm case, with its cherub grip-plates, which might have been equally at home in the 1720's' (ibid., 114).

Since its introduction in the seventeenth century, coffin furniture designs were slow to change. Elements of the designs for coffin furniture in Tuesby and Cooper's 1783 catalogue, such as the border of bell or husk flower garlands, the rococo style designs, the oval cartouche,

Figure 3. Plate from eighteenth-century pattern book (reproduced by courtesy of the Victoria and Albert Museum).

and the winged cherub's head (Litten 1992, 106) have many points of similarity with the nineteenth-century grip plate from Glasgow Cathedral. The precise date of interment has not yet been confirmed, and despite intramural burial having been outlawed in Scotland in 1855, burials were still taking place in the crypt of Glasgow Cathedral in 1886 (Glasgow Cathedral Register of Burials Jan. 1873 – May 1942). Firmer identification of this grip-plate, coffin lace and much of the unstratified and complete coffin furniture was made possible by comparison with three extant trade catalogues which are held by the Victoria and Albert Museum, whose kind permission allows reference to be made to them here. One of the catalogues dates to the 1790s, the other to the 1820s, and the third consists of a portfolio of loose prints from a second eighteenth-century pattern book. One of the illustrations displayed in the latter is virtually identical to the grip-plate from Glasgow Cathedral, although it does not show a handle attached to the embossed plate, it may also have been available with grips (see Fig. 3). Much of the coffin furniture shown in the trade catalogues came in different finishes, including white, white and black, gilt lacquered, or black, and although no traces of colour survive on this particular grip-plate, it may be that the passage of time has removed it; certainly traces of colour have been detected on other examples from the cathedral.

Also from this coffin were strips of coffin lace that formed a border around the panels of the coffin sides and may have originally have formed an edging on the circumference of the lid, similar to one which was uncovered during the excavations at Govan Old Parish Church (Cullen and Driscoll 1994, 268). The longest piece of lace which was conserved measures c. 11 cm, and can be identified as matching a design from the 1820s catalogue. The illustrations in the catalogue were drawn at a scale of 1:1, hence a direct comparison can be made. The lace measured 3.2 cm wide and the pattern consisted of a double raised line of rope embossing which bisected the lace lengthways. The pattern of each half is the same and consisted of a line of pyramidal lozenges arranged with their longer axis running horizontally. The background is embossed with fine, closely set horizontal lines. Again, this type of coffin furniture was available in a number of coloured finishes; it was sold by the dozen yards, and was used as an alternative to upholstery nails, which were both decorative and functional, fixing the fabric to the exterior of the coffin.

RECONSTRUCTION OF A VICTORIAN FUNERAL

When new, this coffin would have presented quite a colourful spectacle, covered with the best quality black or scarlet velvet, perhaps with grip-plates finished in gilt lacquer and edged in coffin lace to match; it may also have had a decorative and coloured depositum plate in addition to any number or combination of lid escutcheons. Once installed in the rear of an etched glass-sided hearse, it may also have been covered by a fine quality silk velvet pall with silk 'family ropes' attached to the grips (the hearse itself may have been draped in black velvet). The hearse would then have been drawn along at a stately pace by perhaps four horses plumed with black ostrich feathers, led by two mutes bearing draped staves and escorted by pages and attendants carrying wands and truncheons, all wearing new black silk hatbands (or 'weepers'). Bringing up the rear would have been two mourning coaches with fours, also draped and plumed. This is a picture of a typical early Victorian funeral which could have been seen arriving at the great west doors of Glasgow Cathedral in the mid-nineteenth century (Morley 1971, 113 and pl. 76).

A mid-nineteenth-century middle-class funeral represented the apogee of funeral pomp and display, and, despite the dubious morality or idealism which drove this costly respectability, it has furnished a rich and detailed glimpse into the funerary customs of the relatively recent past. It combined a great many elements into a funeral procession which had its symbolic roots in the heraldic funeral and no doubt would have presented the assembled band of mourners (or more pertinently, their neighbours) with a spectacular and sombre ceremonial crocodile wind-

ing its way from the abode of the deceased to the churchyard or cemetery whence the carnival continued.

CONCLUSION

Despite the obvious folly of generalisation it is hard to imagine a Victorian era *not* entrenched in morbidity given its social circumstances. The
exciting aspect of that which historians of death have documented is
that we can see and study the society behind this flamboyant cultural
response to death through their funerary archaeology. However, the
opportunity for studying any material from a Scottish Victorian funeral
has not often been grasped. Why, given the relatively rare conditions in
which nineteenth-century burials are disinterred, should this be so? It is
my contention that nineteenth-century archaeology is not widely considered to be 'real' archaeology, in effect, it is too modern. Certainly
post-Reformation funerary practices do not receive nearly as much
scholarly attention as their prehistoric counterparts. This paper has tried
to redress this imbalance. Despite having access to historical documentary sources it does not preclude artefactual research of the material
remains as a useful adjunct to a fuller understanding of the Victorian
funeral. I propose that this is a valid area of study, and I take this
opportunity to emphasise the ephemeral nature of the material itself
which imposes some sense of immediacy. After all, the majority of
coffins intended for churchyard or cemetery inhumation were designed
to be broken down in the sod – 'ashes to ashes, dust to dust'.

APPENDIX

Entries taken from old parish records.
Burial Register of High Church (Glasgow Cathedral).
Intramural Inhumations, February 1837 – July 1846.

Margaret McNair / *Died* 14 March 1837 *1 Buried* 20 March 1837 / *Occupation* –
Widow of the late John Black, merchant / *Address* – Bath Street / *Undertaker* – unknown / Buried in the lair of the late John Black / *Location* – in back of Cathedral /
Cause of death – Heart / *Age* – 60 / *Funeral* – hearse, 4 horses, 10 ushers / *Cost* – £
1. 5 sh. 6 d.

Elizabeth Dennistoun / *Died* 29 August 1837 / *Buried* 2 September 1837 / *Occupation* Widow of the late John Ward, merchant / *Address* – Moore Park / *Undertaker* – Wylie and Lochhead / Buried in the lair of James Dennistoun / *Location* – in
back of Cathedral / *Cause of death* – Palsy / *Age* – 50 / *Funeral* – hearse, 4 horses,
4 ushers / *Cost* – £ 1. 15 sh. 6 d.

John McCulloch / *Died* 25 December 1837 / *Buried* 27 December 1837 / *Occupation* Founder / *Address* – Charlotte Street / *Undertaker* – William Gilbert / Buried
in the lair of McCulloch / *Location* – Crypt / *Cause of death* – Typhus fever / *Age* –
17 / *Funeral* – hearse, 4 horses, 8 ushers / *Cost* – £ ?

[156]

George Miller / *Died* 7 December 1838 / *Buried* 10 December 1838 / *Occupation* – Merchant / *Address* – St Vincent Street / *Undertaker* – Wylie and Lochhead / Buried in the lair of Laing Turnbull / *Location* – in back of Cathedral / *Cause of death* – Decline / *Age* – 39 / *Funeral* hearse, 4 horses, 4 ushers / *Cost* – £ 1. 15 sh. 6 d.

Rabina C. Black / *Died* 21 March 1840 / *Buried* 25 March 1840 / *Occupation* – Daughter of John Black, merchant / *Address* – Woodside / *Undertaker* – Donald / Buried in the lair of J. Black / *Location* – within railings, back of Cathedral / *Cause of death* – Hooping cough (sic) / *Age* – 2 years 6 months / *Funeral* – chaise, 2 horses, 4 ushers / *Cost* – £ 1. 7 sh. 6 d.

Robert Haldane / *Died* 12 December 1842 / *Buried* 20 December 1842 / *Occupation* – ? / *Address* – Auchengay, Edinburgh / *Undertaker* – John Boyd / Buried in the lair of Oswald of Scotstoun / *Location* – Nave / *Cause of death* – ? / *Age* – 78 / *Funeral* – hearse, 4 horses, 10 ushers / *Cost* – £ 1. 5 sh. 6 d.

Katherine Haldane / *Died* 14 June 1843 / *Buried* 20 June 1843 / *Occupation* – Widow of the late Robert Haldane / *Address* – Auchengay, Edinburgh / *Undertaker* – John Boyd / Buried in the lair of Oswald of Scotstoun / *Location* – Nave / *Cause of death* – Decline / *Age* – 74 / *Funeral* – hearse, 4 horses, 10 ushers / *Cost* – £ 1. 5 sh. 6 d.

Marion Hamilton / *Died* 31 August 1843 / *Buried* 8 September 1843 / *Occupation* – Daughter of Claude Hamilton, major in Army / *Address* – Portobello / *Undertaker* – McDougal / Buried in the lair of Dreghorn / *Location* – Crypt / *Cause of death* – Bilious fever / *Age* – 56 / *Funeral* hearse, 2 horses / *Cost* – 15. sh. 6d.

Ann Louise Oswald / *Died* ? / *Buried* 2 March 1844 / *Occupation* – Daughter of George Oswald, merchant / *Address* – Newton Place / *Undertaker* – Colquhoun / Buried in the lair of R. A. Oswald / *Location* – Nave / *Cause of death* – Scarlet fever / *Age* – 4 / *Funeral* – chaise and carriages, 2 horses, 2 ushers / *Cost* – 7 sh. 6 d.

Lidia Mary Himan /*Died* 6 March 1844 / *Buried* 9 March 1844 / *Occupation* – Wife of George Oswald, merchant / *Address* – Newton Place / *Undertaker* – Wylie and Lochhead / Buried in the lair R. A. Oswald / *Location* – Nave / *Cause of death* – Peurepal fever / *Age* – 30 / *Funeral* buried in the same coffin as James Oswald, hearse, 3 carriages, 4 horses, 4 ushers / *Cost* – £ 1 .

James Oswald / *Died* 4 March 1844 / *Buried* 9 March 1844 / *Occupation* – Son of George Oswald, merchant / *Address* – Newton Place / *Undertaker* – Wylie and Lochhead / Buried in the lair of R. A. Oswald / *Location* – Nave / *Cause of death* – Fever / *Age* – 7 days / *Funeral* buried in the same coffin as Lidia Mary Himan.

John Ryburn / *Died* 30 November 1844 / *Buried* 5 December 1844 / *Occupation* – Merchant / *Address* – Bath Street / *Undertaker* – White and Son / Buried in the lair of John Ryburn / *Location* – Crypt / *Cause of death* – Water in the chest / *Age* – 79 / *Funeral* – hearse, 12 carriages, 4 horses, 12 ushers / *Cost* – £ 1. 5 sh. 6d.

Kippen (female) / *Died* 27 October 1845 / *Buried* 6 November 1845 / *Occupation* – Relict of James Hill / *Address* – Gartloch, Edinburgh / *Undertaker* – John Boyd / Buried in the lair of James Hill / *Location* – Crypt / *Cause of death* – Decay of nature / *Age* – 76 / *Funeral* – hearse, 8 carriages, 4 horses. 1 *Cost* – 15.sh.

Margaret Laird / *Died* 12 November 1845 / *Buried* 17 November 1845 / *Occupation* Daughter of the late William Laird, merchant / *Address* – Edinburgh / *Undertaker* – Dowel / Buried in the lair of Miss Oswald / *Location* – Nave / *Cause of death* – ? / *Age* – 82 / *Funeral* hearse, 4 carriages, 4 horses, 6 ushers / *Cost* – £1.

[157]

BIBLIOGRAPHY

The Acts of Parliament of Scotland, vol. 8, 1684.

Andrews, W. 1899. *Bygone Church Life in Scotland*. Hull.

Bennet, M. 1992. *Scottish Customs from the Cradle to the Grave*. Polygon, Edinburgh.

Brooks, C. 1989. *Mortal Remains*. Wheaton Publishers, Devon.

Burial Register of the High Church, February 1837 – July 1846. MS. Glasgow Room, Mitchell Library.

Burial Register of the High Church, January 1973 – May 1942. MS. Glasgow Room, Mitchell Library.

CBA 1994. Church reveals secrets of the grave. *Council for British Archaeology News*, 1994 Sept., 1.

Cullen, I. S. and S. T. Driscoll 1994. *Excavations at Govan Old Parish Church*. GUARD, Glasgow.

Devine, T. M. and R. Mitchison (eds) 1988. *People and Society in Scotland*, vol. 1. John Donald, Edinburgh.

Dixon, D. 1989. The two faces of death: children's magazines and their treatment of death in the nineteenth century. In R. Houlbrooke (ed.), *Death, Ritual and Bereavement*, 136–150. Routledge, London.

Driscoll, S. T. 1992. Excavations at Glasgow Cathedral. *Glasgow Archaeological Journal* 17, 63–76.

Edgar, A. 1885. *Old Church Life in Scotland*. Paisley.

Edgar, A. 1886. *Old Church Life in Scotland*, second series. Paisley.

Frayling, C. 1991. *Vampyres*. Faber and Faber, London.

Glasgow Cathedral Register of Burials, January 1873 – May 1942. MS. Glasgow Room, Mitchell Library.

Gordon, A. 1984. *Death Is for the Living*. Paul Harris Publishing, Edinburgh.

Gorer, G. 1965. *Death, Grief and Mourning*. P. Cresset, London.

Hobbes, T. 1986. *Leviathan*. Penguin, Harmondsworth, Middlesex.

Houlbrooke, R. (ed.) 1989. *Death, Ritual, and Bereavement*. Routledge, London.

Litten, J. 1991. *The English Way of Death*. Robert Hale, London.

Love, D. 1989. *Scottish Kirkyards*. Robert Hale, London.

Molleson, T., M. Cox, A. H. Waldron, and D. K. Whittaker 1993. *The Spitalfields Project*, vol. 2, *The middling sort*. Council for British Archaeology, York.

Morley, J. 1971. *Death, Heaven and the Victorians*. University of Pittsburgh Press, Pittsburgh.

Reeve, J. and M. Adams 1993. *The Spitalfields Project*, vol. 1, *The archaeology. Across the Styx*. British Council for Archaeology, York.

Richardson, R. 1987. *Death, Dissection and the Destitute*. Routledge, London.

Richardson, R. 1989. Why was death so big in Victorian Britain? In R. Houlbrooke (ed.), *Death, Ritual and Bereavement*, 105–117. Routledge, London.

Rymer, J. M. 1991. Varney, the Vampyre. In C. Frayling, *Vampyres*, 145–161. Faber and Faber, London.

Wilkins, R. 1990. *The Fireside Book of Death*. Robert Hale, London.

Willsher, B. 1990. *Understanding Scottish Graveyards*. Council for Scottish Archaeology, Edinburgh.

11

Research and our recent ancestors: post-medieval burial grounds

Jez Reeve and Margaret Cox

This *paper sets out* research considerations for application to the partial or complete clearance of post-medieval burial grounds, including crypts (Fig. 1), vaults, graveyards (Fig. 2), and cemeteries. It is intended not to make a case for the full excavation of every post-medieval burial ground but to assist in the selection of suitable candidates for examination (those that can advance knowledge in a number of specific research areas) and suggest appropriate methods for the treatment of sites. The recommendations in this paper are those of two experienced funerary archaeologists who are keen to widen the debate. As would be expected, the contents reflect the authors' wide-ranging experience of such sites.

The belief that archaeological investigation has nothing to add to the historic past has been discounted (e.g. Grauer 1995) and it is generally acknowledged that formal written histories do not record all the activities and processes which represent the pragmatic approach to belief systems and rules and regulations. Nevertheless, there is presently little agreement on how church officials, local planning authorities, professional undertakers, and archaeological curators and contractors should deal with the ever increasing threat to post-medieval funerary contexts. It is these groups as well as the general public who must engage in debate to ensure an outcome that satisfies the majority.

CURRENT STATE OF RESEARCH ON POST-MEDIEVAL BURIAL GROUNDS

While many post-medieval burial grounds have been subject to commercial clearance, on occasion accompanied by a last-minute watching brief (e.g. St Nicholas, Bathampton, Cox and Stock 1995, Fig. 3), there

Figure 1. Excavation of the crypt beneath Christ Church, Spitalfields. The clearance of this crypt was achieved via an appropriate programme of archaeological works. The site has subsequently proved to be one of the most important cemetery excavations in Europe.

appear to have been few which have been cleared with some level of archaeological supervision. Those that have include St Nicholas, Sevenoaks; Islington Green burial ground, London; disused burial ground, Marylebone Road, London; Quaker burial ground, Kingston-upon-Thames; Quaker burial ground, Bathford (Stock 1998). Even fewer have been published (St Augustine the Less, Bristol, interim report, Boore 1985 and 1998; Christ Church, Spitalfields, Reeve and Adams 1993, Molleson and Cox 1993 and Cox 1996a; Kellington, North Yorkshire; St Brides, Farringdon Street, London). With such a limited source of published material and only accidentally retrieved material to complement it, it is considered necessary to recommend an archaeological approach for such sites.

Despite a thorough custom-designed archaeological approach to the clearance of the crypt at Christ Church, Spitalfields, which has advanced our understanding in a large number of areas (particularly demographic aspects of human skeletal material and funerary practice) it is only as a result of post-excavation analyses and subsequent scientific advance that areas for future research have been highlighted. Archaeological investigation of further sites comprising large samples of closely dated in-

Figure 2. The graveyard of St Nicholas' Church, Bathampton. An extension to the east end of the chancel led to the destruction of eighteenth- and nineteenth-century shaft graves (photograph by Margaret Cox).

dividuals, with secure biographical information, are required to pursue some of the methodological, taphonomic, socio-economic, and historical questions the Spitalfields sample raised. The funereal furnishings, which were only lightly treated in the Spitalfields publication (Reeve and Adams 1993), require further analysis in respect of their perceived role in the funeral and the undertaking industry (see Richmond this volume), as well as consideration of their use of symbolism in comparison to contemporary above-ground monuments.

NATURE OF THE THREAT

There are a number of reasons why burial grounds come under threat of disturbance. Sometimes remains are exposed by accident or unexpectedly during the course of redevelopment. Often, in the case of a disused burial ground, the pressure for land development overrides the desire for open space, and the local planning authorities are prepared to grant permission for clearance if undertaken by suitable organisations. In the case of crypt or vault clearance the opposite consideration may be to the fore; clearance is required to reclaim more open space, that beneath the floor of the church, for either ecclesiastic or secular use (e.g. Christ

*Figure 3. The exhumation of a coffin by commercial undertakers at St Nicholas'
Church, Bathampton. This modus operandus took place because the archaeological curators failed to appreciate the archaeological importance of the site in respect of development proposals. A last-minute watching brief was implemented
when the impact of the development was appreciated. Archaeological considerations aside it should be considered if such a method of exhuming human
remains is either appropriate or respectful (photograph by Margaret Cox).*

Church, Spitalfields). Other pressures, such as the need for underpinning (Kellington, North Yorkshire), redundancy of churches and sale of church land for non-ecclesiastic use, or extension to the church by the active church community (as at St Nicholas, Bathampton), all threaten the archaeological remains.

THE QUESTION OF OWNERSHIP AND RESPONSIBILITY

When approached to define the archaeological importance of a particular burial ground the first consideration is to understand the nature of the value attached to the site and its contents by those who are responsible for, or own it. Such ownership can be defined on three levels: legal, spiritual, and intellectual.

The *legal* responsibility for human remains is discussed elsewhere (Garratt-Frost et al. 1992) and the position has not changed substantially since that publication (Garratt-Frost pers. comm.). In England, whether civil or ecclesiastical, the division of responsibility between the archaeologist and the legal owner is not set down explicitly, whereas in Scotland an attempt has been made by Historic Scotland (1996).

The *spiritual* value of a burial ground to contemporary groups of people, which amounts to an expression of ownership, can effect the type of approach taken to wholesale clearance, whether archaeological or commercial, and particularly to the issues of repatriation and reburial (Bray et al. 1994; Bray 1996). Opposing stances are evident within different religious denominations within the UK. These range from the lack of spiritual interest in mortal remains and their place of burial by Quakers (Stock 1998) to total abhorrence of the disturbance of the dead in Judaism (see for example Jewbury, York 1983–84 in Lilley et al. 1994).

The expressed academic research objectives which a particular site can address provide the context for a third type of ownership, *intellectual* ownership. The extent of this ranges from archaeological and historic communities, forensic and medical scientists, and individuals undertaking genealogical research.

There has been and continues to be considerable debate about the appropriateness of defining human remains as an archaeological and intellectual resource (see for example the debate in *British Archaeological News* 1994 Oct. and Nov.; Parker Pearson 1995; Cox 1997). This is an issue that deserves the attention of a wider group and its participation in debate. English examples highlighting the diversity of views are illustrated below.

First, let us consider the judgement of the Arches Court of Canterbury (26 Oct. 1995) on whether the proposed church extension should take place at St Michael and All Angels, Tettenhall Regis. In this case the court agreed with the chancellor, who had ruled against the proposal, which would cause extensive and wholesale disruption to human remains until, at the very least, further efforts were made to trace the relatives of those buried within the last fifty years.

In this case, investigative archaeological trial trenches had been undertaken to inform the decision, following which the excavated human remains were cremated before reburial. Both the chancellor and the court agreed that this action was wrong in consideration of section 3 of the Burial Act of 1853. The decision attempted to clarify the law on the disruption of human remains in consecrated ground (Arches Court 1996):

> The petitioner will not be able to do this [convince the Chancellor] unless they ascertain and bear in mind the views of relatives, even distant relatives, of those whose ancestors have been, or may have been interred in the burial ground and also the views of parishioners who are not necessarily churchgoers.

The second case is that of the Quaker burial ground at 84 London Road, Kingston-upon-Thames. On consultation with the Kingston Friends Trust, their response to the proposed wholesale clearance of the eighteenth-century burial ground was as follows (Kingston Friends Trust, Minute 96.6):

> We have no objection should a full archaeological investigation take place. Neither do we object to the use of any remains as a teaching resource. We would prefer the remains to be cremated and the ashes passes on to us for disposal at a Quaker cemetery, rather than be reinterred in separate containers.

The site was excavated with specific research priorities geared towards enhancing our understanding of Quaker burial practice. The results are in preparation and selected skeletal remains have become part of Bournemouth University's teaching collection while the remainder has been cremated.

RESEARCH CRITERIA

Post-medieval funerary deposits require the same procedures for assessing research potential and value as any other type of archaeology (see *Planning Policy Guidance 16, Archaeology and Planning* 1990 Nov.) and the results of such work must then be assessed against accepted research priorities.

Thorough desk-based assessment is crucial to assessing both the site's history and the availability and quality of relevant historical documentation. Historical sources include parish registers, death certificates, trade directories, vestry minutes, wills and probate records, insurance policies, and bills of mortality. If the indications are that the site has other than low archaeological potential then a programme of site evaluation will be required to establish the nature, condition, and extent of the site/material. Subject to the results of evaluation procedures, either an appropriate programme of low, high, or variable resolution works should take place. It should be remembered that the site's potential, and that of its various component parts, may be of national, regional, or local archaeological importance and, in some cases, a mixture of all three (Reeve 1998).

Research priorities arguably fall into three main subject areas. These include funerary archaeology, osteoarchaeology, and the complex issue of burial environments, preservation, and taphonomy. The examination of human remains from the post-medieval period is essential to complement documentary information about the aetiology of disease, the history of dentistry and medicine, demography, and local history, and genealogical studies. At present only the Christ Church sample is published in depth (Molleson and Cox 1993; Cox 1996a), other groups of individuals such as that from St Barnabas, London remain unpublished. Crypt samples from this period have enormous potential for enhancing biomolecular studies such as DNA analyses, diagenesis, and taphonomy. This coincides with an area of archaeological research which is attracting considerable attention at the moment, that of in-situ preservation and the interaction between the burial environment and buried remains. Where possible, it is desirable to monitor the burial environment in advance of detailed archaeological examination of a site (Cox 1996b). This approach will facilitate correlation of the condition and state of preservation of a wide range of artefacts (both organic and inorganic) and ecofacts with environmental and physical parameters. Such a monitoring programme was in place at St Pancras Church, Euston Road, London from August 1995 until September 1997 (ibid.). Where such schemes are not practical, every effort should be taken to discern information relating to the history of the burial environment via other sources (e.g. remedial works noted in vestry minutes).

In order for skeletal samples to have high research potential it is essential that the size of the group is large and that they have accompanying biographical information. The issue of representativeness is also important (Molleson and Cox 1993; Waldron 1994). The scientific excavation and examination of an entire burial context from a rural area will provide data for a much more representative sample of the population than one from an urban context, which may be numerically larger, but which will almost certainly only be representative of a small sub-set of the living population.

APPROPRIATE METHODOLOGY

Having assessed the site's archaeological potential, completeness, and importance, it will be possible to judge which level of treatment and what sampling strategies are appropriate. The levels of treatment (or resolution) can crudely be expressed on three levels:

Option 1: no site investigation. The material is considered to be of such value to the legal or spiritual owners that it should not be disturbed (in line with the Vermillion Accord 1989) despite development pressures and intellectual and scientific justification. Alternatively, the site is considered to be of such low research potential, due to poor preservation or completeness and/or lack of documentation, that no investigation is justified.

Option 2: minimal recording. Where the potential of the deposits is largely low (poor condition, incompleteness, etc.), there may still be local or other specific research objectives which can be met by summary and tactical observations (watching briefs or an appropriate sampling strategy). Recording can be limited and might take place alongside a non-archaeological clearance operation.

Option 3: structured investigation and analysis. Where the potential of a site is moderate or high, an academically credible and reasoned project design with detailed methodologies is essential, illustrating how the identified research criteria are to be met. It might include detailed on-site recording and sampling or it might take the form of a very focused sampling and collection policy. Alternatively, it might be appropriate to devise a programme of work employing different levels of resolution of recording and recovery in certain areas based upon specific research criteria.

WORKING PRACTICES

Having defined the site's potential, objectives, and level of treatment and having obtained the agreement of the appropriate statutory and non-statutory authorities a risk assessment should be carried out with reference to current statutory and regulatory obligations (see Kneller 1998). The relevance of CDM regulations should be considered.

The discipline standards as set out by the IFA *Code of conduct, Bylaws and Standards* will act as the basis for all archaeological work. Any work associated with disturbing human remains requires the involvement of the local authority Environmental Health Officer acting as agent for the

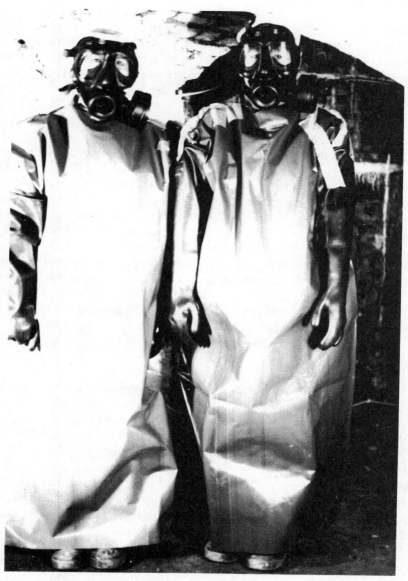

Figure 4. Personal protective equipment at Christ Church, Spitalfields for dealing with 'sealed' lead coffins.

Health and Safety Executive. When disturbing post-medieval funerary deposits, the implications for health and safety are potentially serious. They range from the small but nevertheless significant risks associated with conditions such as smallpox (see Young 1998) and anthrax to the topical issue of post-traumatic-stress disorder (see Thompson 1998). Issues that must be considered range from appropriate use of personal protective equipment (for crypt excavation, level three will be required, see Fig. 4) to the involvement of non-archaeological but nevertheless highly specialised staff for specific tasks such as those that are potentially traumatising.

A further factor to consider is that if the objectives of an excavation include biomolecular research then meticulous measures will have to be taken to avoid the contamination of materials. This extends beyond the obvious level of contamination between archaeologist and human remains, to contamination during post-excavation processes (both assessment and full analyses). Particular care must be taken to prevent cross-contamination between skeletons at all stages of recovery, analysis, and curation. Furthermore, any conservation strategy must consider the likely effects of conservation treatment and storage upon the biomolecular status of material. (The latter issue is one that urgently requires appropriate research particularly as most bone recovered from post-medieval contexts retains a higher than usual level of organic material.) Specific constraints such as those discussed here will effect not only working practice but also budgets and timetables.

POST-EXCAVATION

There are published guidelines on the selection and retention of archaeological material for long-term storage (Museums and Galleries Commission 1992; Society of Museum Archaeologists 1993). Reserving the ethical considerations for wider discussion (Parker Pearson 1995; Cox 1997), if it is decided that material from a funerary context is to be retained, the above guidelines will apply. The only material that should be retained for permanent storage should have informed the eventual analysis, have the potential to address unanswered questions about the site, or have long-term research potential in light of developing scientific methodologies and priorities. Permanent storage should be in an appropriately licensed and respectful environment with adequate environmental controls to ensure the long-term survival of such material.

Publication policies for post-medieval sites should be as for any other archaeological site and should bear in mind that such sites seem to attract very wide public interest and may merit a popular publication (Cox 1996a).

SUMMARY

Post-medieval funerary archaeology is an area of research that can offer enormous scientific and academic potential to a wide range of disciplines. In order to realise that potential it is essential to engage in dialogue with relevant organisations, interest groups, and specialists and define an ethical code and working practices conducive to realising that potential. This should be undertaken with full recognition of the legitimate interest of a wide range of participants. It is outside the scope of this paper to consider the ethical issues implicated in the clearance of burial grounds, what is set out here is a framework within which to approach, and do justice to, a complex and often neglected archaeological resource.

BIBLIOGRAPHY

Arches Court 1996. St Michael and All Angels, Tettenhall Regis.

Boore, E. 1985. Excavations at St. Augustine the Less, Bristol 1983–4. *Bristol and Avon Archaeology* 4, 21–33.

Boore, E. 1998. Burial vaults and doffin furniture in the West Country. In M. Cox (ed.), *Grave Concerns: Death and Burial in Post-Medieval England*, 67–84. Council for British Archaeology, York.

Bray, T. L. 1996. Repatriation, power relations and the politics of the past. *Antiquity* 70, 440–44.

Bray, T. L. and T. W. Killion (eds) 1994. *Reckoning with the Dead: the Larson Bay Repatriation and the Smithsonian Institute*. Smithsonian Institution Press, Washington.

Cox, M. 1994. On excavating the recent dead. *British Archaeological News* 18, 8.

Cox, M. 1996a. *Life and Death in Spitalfields 1700 to 1850*. Council for British Archaeology, York.

Cox, M. 1996b. St Pancras Church Crypt: Evaluation Report. Bournemouth University (unpublished).

Cox, M. 1997. Crypt archaeology after Spitalfields: dealing with our recent dead. *Antiquity* 70 (270), 8–10.

Cox, M. and G. Stock 1995. Nineteenth century bath-stone walled graves at St Nicholas' Church, Bathampton. *Somerset Archaeology and Natural History* 138, 131–150.

DoE 1990. *Planning Policy Guidance 16 Archaeology and Planning*. HMSO, London.

Faulkner, N. 1994. On excavating the recent dead. *British Archaeological News* 18, 8.

Garratt-Frost, S. J., G. Harrison, and J. G. Logie 1992. *The Law and Burial Archaeology*. Institute of Field Archaeologists (Technical Paper 12), Birmingham.

Grauer, A. L. 1995. *Bodies of Evidence Reconstructing History through Skeletal Analysis*. Wiley-Liss, New York.

Historic Scotland 1996. *The Treatment of Human Remains in Archaeology*, version 1.1. Historic Scotland, Edinburgh.

Huggins, P. 1994. Opening lead coffins. *British Archaeological News* 17, 8.

Kirk, H. and L. Start 1998. 'The bodies of Friends': the osteological analysis of a Quaker burial ground. In M. Cox (ed.), *Grave Concerns: Death and Burial in Post-Medieval England*, 167–177. Council for British Archaeology, York.

Kneller, P. 1998. Health and safety in church and funerary archaeology. In M. Cox (ed.), *Grave Concerns: Death and Burial in Post-Medieval England*, 181–189. Council for British Archaeology, York.

Lilley, J. M., G. Stroud, D. R. Brothwell, and M. H. Williamson 1994. *The Archaeology of York*, vol. 12/3, *The Medieval Cemeteries: The Jewish Burial Ground at Jewbury*. Council for British Archaeology, York.

Molleson, T. and Cox, M. 1993. *The Spitalfields Project*, vol. 2, *The Anthropology The Middling Sort*. Council for British Archaeology (Research Report 86), York.

Morris, R. 1994. Examine the dead gently. *British Archaeological News* 17, 9.

Museums and Galleries Commission. 1992. *Standards in Museum Care of Archaeological Collections*. Museums and Galleries Commission, London.

Parker Pearson, M. 1995. Ethics and the dead in British archaeology. *The Field Archaeologist* 23, 17–18.

Reeve, J. 1997. Grave Expectations: the archaeology of crypts and burial grounds. In *Building Conservation Directory Special Report on Ecclesiastical Buildings*, 4–6.

Reeve, J. 1998. View from the metropolis: post-medieval burials in London. In M. Cox (ed.), *Grave Concerns: Death and Burial in Post-Medieval England*, 213–223. Council for British Archaeology, York.

Reeve, J. and M. Adams 1993. *The Spitalfields Project*, vol. 1, *The Archaeology. Across the Styx*. Council for British Archaeology (Research Report 85), York.

Society of Museum Archaeologists 1993. *Selection, Retention and Dispersal of Archaeological Collections: Guidelines for Use in England, Wales and Northern Ireland*. Society of Museum Archaeologists, London.

Thompson, J. 1998. Bodies, minds and human remains. In M. Cox (ed.), *Grave Concerns: Death and Burial in Post-Medieval England*, 197–201. Council for British Archaeology, York.

Waldron, T. 1994. *Counting the Dead: the epidemiology of skeletal populations*. Wiley and Sons, Chichester.

Young, S. 1998 Archaeology and smallpox. In M. Cox (ed.), *Grave Concerns: Death and Burial in Post-Medieval England*, 190–196. Council for British Archaeology, York.

12

The modern scourge: reflections on tuberculosis old and new

Charlotte Roberts

Tuberculosis wrecked hopes, broke courtships, crushed bread-
winners . . . and bereaved young families.

– Smith (1988, 1)

Tuberculosis is an infectious disease which is becoming a major
problem in both westernised and developing countries worldwide
today. A disease which is potentially recognisable in the skeleton of
those affected, the prevalence of tuberculosis has fluctuated over long
periods in our history. Since the development of effective drug therapy
to control the infection from 1944, a state of peace of mind has been
generated (unrealistically) within society in the Western world that this
disease has been, and will remain, controlled. As Smith (1988, 2) said,
'Tuberculosis is now a conquered disease in the British Isles and the rest
of the industrialised world.' However, the decades of decline in tuberculosis had begun to be reversed even by 1986; in 1987, 9,226 cases of
tuberculosis were reported in the United States and, by 1989, this figure
had risen to 23,495 (Friedland and Klein 1992); in the UK 3,002 cases of
tuberculosis were reported in the first six months of 1983 (Medical
Research Council Tuberculosis and Chest Disease Unit 1985), a figure
which has increased since that time. Tuberculosis continues to kill
millions of people in developing countries, where effective drug therapy
is potentially available but inaccessible to most. It is estimated to kill

three million people a year and in 1991 there were eight million new cases worldwide (Brown 1992, 30).

As a nurse, I remember my first hospital ward experience. One of the male patients on that medical ward in 1975 was suffering from tuberculosis and was considered a rarity compared to the large numbers of patients with senile dementia, heart and joint problems, the diseases associated with growing old. This patient was almost a novelty because his condition was unusual for that era; he died within a few weeks of being admitted to the ward, in his fifth decade of life.

TUBERCULOSIS: AETIOLOGY OF ITS DEVELOPMENT TODAY

It is only very recently that tuberculosis has reappeared as a problem, accompanied by the realisation that there is a real potential and opportunity for this disease to gain a stronghold again even in Western populations with access to health care. This reappearance has been enabled firstly because of the many people afflicted by HIV (human immunodeficiency virus) which can lead to AIDS (acquired immune deficiency syndrome) (Grmek 1990), and secondly by the poor environment in which many of these affected people live; this plays a large part in their predisposition to tuberculosis. Increased homelessness, poverty, poor diet (e.g. lack of protein), dusty occupations like pottery and textile manufacturing (inhalation of dust particles, leading to inflammation of the lung and decreased resistance to tuberculosis – Johnston 1993), substance abuse, lack of access to health care, non-compliance in drug taking, prescription of ineffective drug therapy, and increasing numbers of immigrants to cities like New York in the United States has helped the disease to develop rapidly (Annas 1993; Brown 1992); it is believed that 40% of all known tuberculous patients are HIV positive. Infancy, puberty and old age, when resistance to tuberculosis is low, are the most susceptible age groups today (Johnston 1993). However, tuberculosis can remain viable for the whole life of the host and develop into recognisable disease at any time in the right conditions. Up to the age of thirty females today are affected more than males and this may be because pregnancy and childbirth, which can suppress the immune system, makes a woman more susceptible to infection; beyond thirty years of age males are more affected.

The first reported cases of HIV were in 1981 and the virus was discovered in 1983 in France at the same time as the first cases were being reported in the UK (Adler 1991). In 1984–85 the antibody test for HIV was developed. HIV and AIDS affects an area of the immune system which plays a large part in the response of the body to infection, and their presence make a person more likely to contract other diseases such

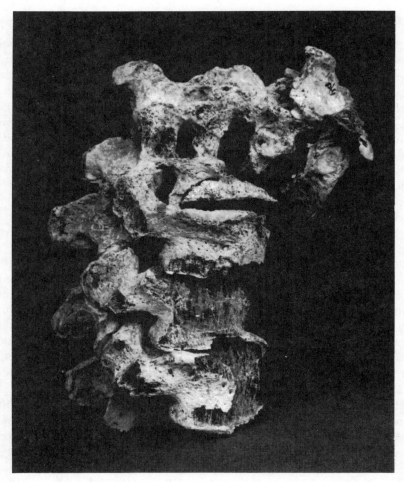

Figure 1. Spinal fragment displaying bone destruction due to tuberculosis.

as infections; coupled with particular environmental conditions, tuber-culosis as a major disease can develop rapidly within a community. In addition, it has been found that HIV can trigger tuberculosis in some-body with a latent infection and tuberculosis can precipitate the devel-opment of AIDS (Ryan 1992). In 1991 the World Health Organisation estimated that approximately 10 million people worldwide were HIV infected (Mann and Welles 1992), mostly (6 million) in Africa. In January 1990 215,144 cases of AIDS had been reported worldwide with 66.3% being in the Americas; by January 1991 366,455 AIDS cases had been documented officially. In 1987 there were 5,086 cases of AIDS re-ported in the UK and by 1991 that figure had risen to 5,604 (Brown 1992).

TUBERCULOSIS: FACTS

In humans, tuberculosis is caused by the bacteria *Mycobacterium tuberculosis* or *Mycobacterium bovis*. The two routes of infection are the respiratory tract via droplet infection from an infected human *(M. tuberculosis)* or the gastrointestinal tract from infected meat or milk from cattle *(M. bovis)*. At this stage, if the infection is not treated, the bacteria can spread to the skeleton via the bloodstream or lymphatic system. Primarily the spine (Fig. 1) and major weight bearing joints of the body are affected, with the bacteria destroying large amounts of bone and producing loss of integrity of the skeletal structure and lack of normal function.

It is probable, certainly in modern westernised societies, that tuberculosis is contracted mainly via droplet infection, i.e. human to human via the respiratory tract. However, in both westernised and developing populations, tuberculosis may spread via the gastrointestinal tract. In developing countries, unlike their western counterparts, herds of cattle are less likely to be tested for tuberculosis or their milk pasteurised. Moreover, the treatment of tuberculosis has become ineffective with many people unresponsive to anti-tuberculous drugs. Multi-drug therapy for treatment of tuberculosis has always been advocated because of a bacterial resistance problem; random mutation in the genome of the bacterium occasionally throws up a strain that resists a particular drug (Brown 1992). The tuberculosis (BCG) vaccine developed in 1921 (an accentuated form of the bovine bacillus), with its first trials in the 1950s, confers 80% protection against tuberculosis for about fifteen years (James and Studdy 1981). However, in 1992 in the UK some health authorities cut childhood vaccination programmes, believing the infection to be controlled. Even though there are antibiotics and a vaccine available to people in many countries, the world has a large-scale problem on its hands. In addition, HIV and AIDS have no effective vaccine or treatment and present an even more serious problem.

TUBERCULOSIS: AN OLD DISEASE

Although not all disease processes affect the skeleton, the major infectious diseases do. Leprosy, tuberculosis, and syphilis (one of the treponemal diseases) all leave characteristic lesions on bone and in a predictable distribution pattern around the body. These lesions are recognisable on archaeologically recovered skeletons and thus inform us about diseases among past populations. In modern populations with access to treatment, effective therapy prevents bony changes developing if the infection is treated at the soft tissue stage.

It is believed that the bovine form of tuberculosis was present at the time of cattle domestication in the Near East; contact with humans allowed the infection to spread from cattle to human. As population density increased, with the development of urban centres, so the human form of the disease developed. The introduction of a new disease into communities who had had no prior exposure to tuberculosis meant that the immune response to fight the infection was limited, resulting in rapid development of the disease. Imagine the emaciated, weak, feverish, breathless, coughing individual living nearly 1,600 years ago in Romano-British Cirencester, with no access to effective treatment and eventually suffering from progressive destruction of the spine and deformity (Wells 1982). Reflecting on this scenario in our distant ancestors is distressing, but observing the same disease in a modern patient with access to treatment is also disheartening. Access to treatment does not always mean survival. What is surprising is that the majority of skeletons displaying tuberculosis from the distant past have healed lesions which suggest that these people lived and survived with the infection. What is not known, of course, is whether tuberculosis affecting the lungs or other soft tissues finally killed the person but did not leave its mark on the skeleton.

TUBERCULOSIS: TRANSMISSION OF THE DISEASE

Did populations in the past contract the disease from other humans or from cattle? This problem cannot be easily solved; it is not known in modern populations what parts of the skeleton are specifically affected in the two routes of infection. A recent discovery of an isolated pelvis from a Lincoln cemetery with a destructive lesion consistent with tuberculosis (Boylston and Roberts 1995) perhaps supports a bovine (gastrointestinal) infection which then spread to the neighbouring skeleton. The application of molecular methods of analysis to bone may help provide valuable information about how humans contracted the disease. Some progress has been made in identifying DNA of *Mycobacterium tuberculosis* in mummified material (Salo et. al. 1994), and the next step is to try to isolate the DNA of *Mycobacterium bovis*.

Perhaps the bovine form was not prevalent, but both the human and bovine forms could have been equally present. In addition to the accepted tuberculosis destruction of the spin, hip, and knee, there is also evidence of abnormal changes on the internal (lung) surface of the ribs where they attach directly to the membrane (pleura) covering the lungs (Fig. 2). The lesions appear to be the result of inflammation, most likely from the lung tissue and, possibly, from tuberculous infection, but pneumonia may well have been the culprit. Recent work suggests that

[175]

Figure 2. Lesions on ribs.

tuberculosis is most likely to be their cause (Roberts et. al. 1994). If this proposal is correct, and the extraction of the human form of tuberculous DNA from these skeletons may be the only solution to the problem posed, then a pulmonary rather than a bovine origin could be implicated. Examination of the skeletal remains of cattle from archaeological sites could potentially help suggest how prevalent bovine tuberculosis was in the past but, unfortunately, little work has been undertaken in non-human palaeo-pathology. The problem, of course, with the study of skeletonised non-human remains is that they are almost invariably fragmentary and disarticulated, making it impossible to observe the distribution pattern of abnormal lesions.

TUBERCULOSIS: EVIDENCE IN THE PAST

Whilst the frequency of tuberculosis in the most recent past (and today) is relatively well known, its prevalence in the more distant past is difficult to determine for many reasons. Incomplete skeletons, partial excavation of cemeteries, individuals with tuberculosis and no bony changes at death, and the mere lack of work on this disease in some parts of the world means that its true frequency is hard to assess. However, large numbers of skeletons do have the sort of rib lesions described above. If accepted as tuberculous in origin, the observed frequency rate increases. For example, at two late medieval cemetery sites eight individuals (23% of 35 total burials) and fifty-four skeletons (18% of 306 total burials with ribs preserved) displayed rib lesions (Chundun 1992; Chundun 1991).

Steinbock (1976) summarised the evidence at the time of his writing for Old and New World cases of tuberculosis in skeletons and mummies. The New World evidence for tuberculosis has increased since then. Buikstra (1981), Buikstra and Williams (1991), and Larsen (1994) describe the evidence from North and South America, which suggests the existence of tuberculosis in the prehistoric Americas before Columbus travelled there in 1492; for example, the remains of an eight-year-old Nazca boy from southern Peru dated to AD 700 displayed Pott's disease (i.e. tuberculosis) of the spine, associated soft tissue change consistent with tuberculosis and even the tubercle bacillus survived in the tissues preserved. Cases from North America range in date from the fourth millennium BC to AD 1490, but further work is needed to establish a clearer idea of tuberculosis prevalence in South America. The Old World evidence is more limited because there has been little active research in biological anthropology in many countries. In the UK the majority of reports available describe Pott's disease of the spine with occasional references to tuberculous weight-bearing joints.

The earliest evidence for tuberculosis displayed in the archaeological record for Europe comes from the fourth millennium BC in Italy (Formicola et. al. 1987). In the UK the Roman-British period provides the earliest evidence (Wells 1982; Stirland and Waldron 1992) but it is not until the late medieval period that the disease becomes more frequent both in documentary and skeletal evidence. The words 'consumption' or 'pthisis' (pulmonary tuberculosis), 'scrofula' (tuberculosis of the lymph glands of the neck), or 'lupus vulgaris' (tuberculosis of the skin) conjure up a startling sight to people today who remember the many sanitoria opened for sufferers of the disease. Sanitoria were first established in Germany in the mid-1850s (Smith 1988) and there was a sudden increase in numbers of foundations by 1900. By 1911 there were eighty in England, four in Wales, twenty-one in Scotland, and seven in Ireland; these were estimated to house 2% of the estimated 300,000–350,000 cases of tuberculosis. Fresh air, a healthy diet, and appropriate drug therapy helped many sufferers earlier this century. The author's patient in 1975 did not have the 'luxury' of a hospital specifically geared to care for tuberculous sufferers. In some respects he was less fortunate and certainly did not benefit from a high altitude, fresh environment; he was in a Leeds hospital in West Yorkshire.

So what is the evidence for tuberculosis in human skeletal remains from cemeteries in the UK? How common was it? Two factors suggest that it was a common disease, certainly in the post-medieval period

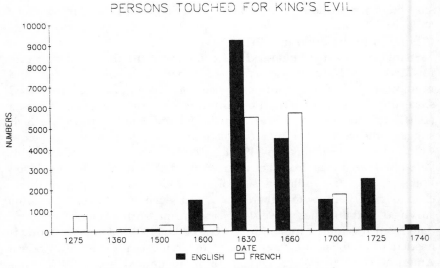

Figure 3. Persons touched for the king's evil.

when 'touching for the king's evil' (tuberculosis) was a common ritual for the king of the day (Fig. 3), and the London bills of mortality in the seventeenth century record consumption as a major cause of all deaths. Skeletal evidence in the UK is largely limited to simple case reports. At Cirencester a male skeleton suffered tuberculosis of the spine in this Romano-British cemetery of 362 individuals. At Anglo-Saxon Bedhampton, Hampshire from a total cemetery of 87 individuals, a male and female aged 17–25 years at death had spinal damage suggestive of tuberculosis, and at Addingham, Yorkshire from a total number of 58 skeletons one male (25–35 years old at death) had spinal damage indicative of tuberculosis. Another site of similar date at Raunds, Northamptonshire with a total of 356 individuals, revealed a young adult (a 17– to 25–year-old male) with knee and spinal tuberculosis. Reports on two individuals from a total of 95 skeletons from the School Street Anglo-Saxon site, Ipswich also suggests the presence of tuberculosis; two males aged about 20 years and 20–24 years at death had spinal and other bone involvement. Further evidence comes from the late- and post-medieval sites at St Oswald's Priory, Gloucester (of 487 individuals, one adult male had tuberculosis of one hip joint of Saxon date, and one female had spinal tuberculosis), Hickleton, South Yorkshire (of 68 burials, one male aged 25–30 years had spinal changes at death) and Stratford Langthorne Abbey, London (of 28 burials, one male aged over 35 years with spinal tuberculosis), Jewbury, York (of 412 burials: two males, two females, one probable male and two probable

Table 1: Prevalence (individuals) of tuberculosis from British sites.

Site	prevalence	no. of individuals affected	total burials
Romano-British			
Cirencester, Gloucestershire	0.3	1	362
Anglo-Saxon			
Addingham, Yorkshire	1.7	1	58
Bedhampton, Hampshire	2.3	2	87
Raunds, Northamptonshire	0.3	1	356
School Street, Ipswich	2.1	2	95
Medieval and post-medieval			
Ensay, Scotland	1.4	6	416
Fishergate, Yorkshire	1.5	6	402
Hickleton, Yorkshire	1.5	1	68
Jewbury, York	1.5	6	412
Spitalfields, London	0.9	2	215
St Oswalds, Gloucestershire	0.4	2	487
Stratford, London	3.6	1	28

females had tuberculosis), Fishergate, York (of 402 burials, six displayed bone changes consistent with tuberculosis: four males, three aged between 18 and 20 years and one 40–50 years displayed spinal tuberculosis and a further two children, 4–6 years and 5–8 years, had new bone formation on some of their ribs, suggesting tuberculosis), Ensay, Scotland (of 416 burials, six had evidence of tuberculosis: one male 40 years, hip, and three females 45, 40, and 18 years, two males 35 and 19 years all had spinal involvement), and finally the eighteenth/nine-teenth-century AD crypt at Spitalfields, London (of a total of 215 children excavated, two had spinal tuberculosis) (Wells 1982; Stuart-Macadam 1985; Manchester and Roberts 1987; Mays 1989; Miles 1989; Boylston 1991; Lilley et. al. 1993; Molleson and Cox 1993; Rogers 1993; Stroud and Kemp 1993).

All the figures presented here refer to the prevalence of individuals affected and not to the prevalence of tuberculosis on the basis of bones examined from each site. One cannot even assume that all bones of every skeleton were available and examined and the prevalence rates displayed in Table 1 may thus be underestimated. But, as the modern prevalence of tuberculosis of the skeleton is only a few per cent of those affected by the disease, the low prevalence in Table 1 cannot be taken to reflect the uncommon occurrence of the disease. However, when rib lesions are considered (not identified in modern cases of tuberculosis) the frequency of skeletal evidence correlates more closely with contemporary documentary sources.

TUBERCULOSIS: ABSENCE OF EVIDENCE?

Tuberculosis is believed to affect the skeleton in 3–7% of all cases of the disease and up to 50% of these individuals suffer spinal involvement (Resnick and Niwayama 1988, 2661; Steinbock 1976). There is no reason to suspect that these figures (derived from modern populations before the advent of drug therapy) cannot stand for the archaeological evidence for tuberculosis, assuming that applying the 'present' to past data is accepted. Consequently, most of the evidence for tuberculosis in antiquity comes from the spine in the form of destruction of the vertebral bodies leading to collapse and deformity of the vertebral column. However, this must represent the later stages of the disease; the earlier manifestations have rarely been recognised. A small number of individuals being affected by bone tuberculosis only means that the archaeological record is only seeing the tip of the iceberg, and determining prevalence rates over time is not possible with any degree of accuracy. In the UK, apart from lack of reported evidence, there are few freely available published reports on skeletons from cemetery sites which provide useful data which can be utilised. Absence of evidence does not mean evidence of absence in the archaeological record, and it is known that the environment necessary for tuberculosis to be established, transmitted, and maintained existed in both urban and rural groups from as early as the Romano-British period, namely the existence of domesticated cattle, crowded housing, poor diet, and increased population density. There could be a number of reasons why the archaeological record does not yield evidence of tuberculosis. It could be that many people had tuberculosis without displaying any skeletal changes. A lower frequency than might be expected may be the result of children, among whom frequency rates of tuberculosis in the past were high compared to today when all ages are affected (Resnick and Niwayama 1988, 2666) not being well represented in the archaeological record. This group does not often show any skeletal changes of disease anyway perhaps because an acute disease (tuberculosis?) caused rapid death before there was time for any bony changes. Low frequency rates may also be explained because techniques for detecting tuberculosis in archaeologically derived skeletons are not wide ranging enough; perhaps too much reliance is placed on modern clinical criteria. Returning to the question of the cause of rib lesions described at two of the cemeteries already discussed with clear evidence of tuberculosis (Raunds and Cirencester),

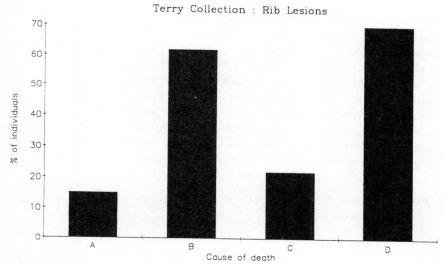

Figure 4. Rib lesions in the Terry Collection. A = non-pulmonary cause of death, B = tuberculosis, C = pulmonary disease but not tuberculosis, D = tuberculosis and another pulmonary disease.

eight and nine individuals respectively had lesions on the ribs and no other tuberculous involvement (Manchester and Roberts 1987). To support the hypothesis that rib lesions are the result of tuberculosis, a study of 1,728 'modern' skeletons from individuals with known causes of death revealed 413 with rib lesions (Fig. 4). Of the 255 who had died from tuberculosis in the whole population, 157 had rib lesions (61.6%). This was a higher proportion than for any other cause of death (Roberts et. al. 1994). More recent work supports these findings. Sledzik and Bellantoni (1994) report on a 55–year-old nineteenth-century male skeleton with rib lesions from Connecticut, USA. This individual, from historical records, was believed to have been a vampire. The New England folk belief in vampires suggests that a deceased tuberculous victim could return from the dead and cause a surviving relative to waste away. To stop this, the body of a person with tuberculosis might be exhumed and disrupted; this skeleton had its skull and femora placed on the chest of the body. Here the rib lesions may indicate tuberculosis. Another study examined 740 individuals from Plains Indians populations dated to AD 1600–1832 (Kelley et. al. 1994). Forty-six (6.2%) had rib lesions with an equal distribution of lesions in the left and right sides of the rib cage. The upper rib cage rather than the lower was affected and a mean of 4.6 ribs were involved but any number of ribs could be affected. In the Roberts et. al. (1994) study the upper rib cage was more affected and

[181]

lesions were often bilateral with any number of ribs being affected. In tuberculosis the upper ribs are usually affected and the left side more than the right so it is likely that many of the individuals in both the Kelley et. al. (1994) and Roberts et. al. (1994) studies were suffering from tuberculosis. Although studies of non-human palaeo-pathology are limited, some observers have noted the same type of rib lesion on cattle and sheep ribs suggesting pulmonary infection (tuberculosis?). It is worth noting that these often subtle rib lesions are not visible on radiographs and, therefore, new bone formation on ribs has not been recognised by modern clinicians as a diagnostic indicator of tuberculosis.

TUBERCULOSIS, HIV, AND AIDS: ASSOCIATED STIGMA AND THE LEPROSY CONNECTION

HIV and AIDS, unlike tuberculosis, but like leprosy, has precipitated the development of an attached stigma to many sufferers. Like tuberculosis, HIV and AIDS do not necessarily produce readily identifiable signs (to the untrained eye). As Drury (1994, 54) stated, 'AIDS is not a disease that has distinctive physical manifestations as leprosy', but 'both leprosy and AIDS have been regarded as plagues, a judgement on society' (ibid., 56). Leprosy and AIDS are both different and similar at the same time. The signs and symptoms of the diseases and their aetiology do not have a common link; leprosy is caused by a bacterial agent and AIDS by one of the types of HIV virus. The common factor is the parallel seen in the treatment of sufferers of both diseases; it is the fact of 'knowing' that allows stigmas to develop. Leprosy is a disease, common today and in the past, which developed an associated stigma due to mutilating features on the body. In fact many people with HIV and AIDS today are being labelled 'lepers' (Elford 1987).

Leprosy, also an infectious disease, is caused by the organism *Mycobacterium leprae*. The bacteria is inhaled from an infected human and affects the face primarily and the nervous system secondarily. Depending on the individual's resistance to the disease (immune status), bone destruction and formation is possible in certain parts of the body (face, hands, feet, and lower legs), and the skin may develop obvious lesions. Depending on the resistance of the person to the bacteria, a range of presentations are possible ranging from no external evidence of the disease to mutilating deformities of the hands, feet, and face, involving soft tissue and bone. It is the disfiguring outward signs that created such a stigma in leprosy. In medieval Europe hundreds of leprosy hospitals were founded (Roberts 1986). The aim was to remove people suffering from leprosy their normal environment into these hospitals, in other words, 'out of sight and out of mind'. They were developed to segregate

[182]

and not to cure. However, some victims who had the high resistance form of the disease would not display any outward evidence of leprosy and would, therefore, not be segregated. Evidence for skeletal leprosy is not as great as expected for the medieval period for many reasons, including lack of leprosy cemetery excavations, non-recognition of the effects of the disease, and the presence of individuals with the low resistance form of leprosy who may not have suffered any bony alteration. Leprosy is like HIV, AIDS, and tuberculosis in many respects (Volinn 1989). It has a stigma even today (Jopling 1991) yet, like tuberculosis, it may not be detected if the signs and symptoms are not obvious. Leprosy is closely linked to tuberculosis in that both are caused by bacteria of the genus *Mycobacteria* and it appears that, in Britain, leprosy decreased in prevalence in the medieval period whilst tuberculosis increased (Manchester 1991), and this may reflect a degree of cross immunity between the two diseases. It is unlikely that distinguishing between the two infections was possible in the past, but many leprosy sufferers probably succumbed to tuberculosis especially when segregated.

CONCLUSION

The author's first encounter with tuberculosis was at a time when tuberculosis was a rarity, certainly in the UK. Yet, in distant antiquity, tuberculosis was a recurring problem. Today the increase in this infectious disease is both linked to the appearance of HIV and AIDS and poor living conditions, the latter a recurrence of an environment seen in medieval Europe. Development of drug therapy to control tuberculosis, whilst undoubtedly having an effect on decreasing the frequency of the disease, appears now to be less effective. Tuberculosis as a major infectious disease is now increasing rapidly with no effective means of arresting it. There is no reliable and effective treatment for HIV or AIDS yet; perhaps a method of prevention or cure will be discovered in the future and control will be initiated for a time.

The palaeo-pathology of tuberculosis is established to a certain extent although much work is needed to fill in the gaps in terms of prevalence through time and to refine diagnostic criteria. In addition, the recording of tuberculosis in skeletal material is desperately in need of standardisation to allow true prevalence rates for tuberculosis to be determined at the population rather than the individual level. The dry bones of archaeology may commonly yield only esoteric knowledge about the past, but this disease of antiquity has turned the tables on history; tuberculosis is a modern scourge.

[183]

BIBLIOGRAPHY

Adler, M. W. 1991. *ABC of Aids* (second edition). British Medical Journal, London.

Annas, G. J. 1993. Control of tuberculosis. The law and the public's health. *New England Journal of Medicine* 328(8), 585–588.

Boylston, A. 1991. Addingham (ACH90). The Human Skeletal Report. Calvin Wells Laboratory, Department of Archaeological Sciences, University of Bradford (unpublished report), Bradford.

Boylston, A. and C. Roberts 1995. Lincoln Excavations 1972–1987. Report on the Human Skeletal Remains. Calvin Wells Laboratory, Department of Archaeological Sciences, University of Bradford (unpublished manuscript), Bradford.

Brown, P. 1992. The return of the big killer. *New Scientist* 10th Oct., 30–37.

Buikstra, J. E. (ed.) 1981. *Prehistoric Tuberculosis in the Americas*. Northwest University Archeological Program, Evanston, Illinois.

Buikstra, J. E. and S. Williams 1991. Tuberculosis in the Americas: current perspectives. In D. Ortner and A. Aufderheide (eds), *Human Paleopathology – Current Syntheses and Future Options*, 161–172. Smithsonian Institution Press, Washington D.C.

Chundun, Z. 1991. The Significance of Rib Lesions in Individuals from a Chichester Medieval Hospital. Calvin Wells Laboratory, Department of Archaeological Sciences, University of Bradford (unpublished MSc thesis), Bradford.

Chundun, Z. 1992. St Giles Hospital, Brough, North Yorkshire. Human Skeletal Report. Calvin Wells Laboratory, Department of Archaeological Sciences, University of Bradford (unpublished report), Bradford.

Drury, B. 1994. A Consideration of the Stigma Associated with Disease in Past Populations. Calvin Wells Laboratory, Department of Archaeological Sciences, University of Bradford (unpublished BSc dissertation), Bradford.

Elford, J. 1987. Moral and social aspects of AIDS: a medical student's project. *Soc. Science and Med.* 24(6), 543–549.

Formicola, V., Q. Milanesi, and C. Scarsini 1987. Evidence of spinal tuberculosis at the beginning of the fourth millenium BC from Arene Candide Cave (Liguria, Italy). *American Journal of Physical Anthropology* 72, 1–6.

Friedland, G. and R. Klein 1992. Tuberculosis and other bacterial infections. In V. T. DeVita Jr., S. Hellman, and S. A. Rosenberg (eds), *Aids, Etiology, Diagnosis, Treatment and Prevention*, 180–193. J. B. Lippincott Co., Philadelphia.

Grmek, M. D. 1990. *History of Aids. Emergence and Origin of a Modern Pandemic*. Translated by R. C. Maulitz and J. Duffing. Princeton University Press, Princeton, New Jersey.

James, D. G. and P. R. Studdy 1981. *A Colour Atlas of Respiratory Diseases*. Wolfe Medical Publications, London.

Johnston, W. D. 1993. Tuberculosis. In K. Kiple (ed.), *Cambridge World History of Human Disease*, 1059–1068. Cambridge, Cambridge University Press.

Jopling, W. H. 1991. Leprosy stigma. *Leprosy Review* 62:1–12.

Kelley, M. A., S. P. Murphy, D. R. Levesque, and P. Sledzik 1994. Respiratory disease among protohistoric and early historic Plains Indians. In D. W. Owsley and R. L. Jantz (eds), *Skeletal Biology in the Great Plains: Migration, Warfare, Health, and Subsistence*, 123–130. Smithsonian Institution Press, Washington D.C.

Larsen, C. S. 1994. In the wake of Columbus: native population biology in post-contact Americas. *Yearbook of Physical Anthropology* 37, 109–154.

Lilley, J. M., G. Stroud, D. R. Brothwell, and M. H. Williamson 1993. *The Jewish Burial Ground at Jewbury*. Council for British Archaeology for York Archaeological Trust (The Archaeology of York. The Medieval Cemeteries 12/3), York.

Manchester, K. 1991. Tuberculosis and leprosy: evidence for interaction of disease. In D. Ortner and A. Aufderheide (eds), *Human Paleopathology. Current Syntheses and Future Options*, 23–35. Smithsonian Institution Press, Washington D.C.

Manchester, K. and C. Roberts 1987. Palaeopathological Evidence for Leprosy and Tuberculosis in Britain. University of Bradford (unpublished S.E.R.C. report), Bradford.

Mann, J. M. and S. L. Welles 1992. Global aspects of the HIV epidemic. In V. T. DeVita jnr, S. Hellman, and S. A. Rosenberg (eds), *Aids, Etiology, Diagnosis, Treatment and Prevention*, 89–109. J. B. Lipinncott Co., Philadelphia.

Mays, S. 1989. The Anglo-Saxon Human Bone from School Street, Ipswich, Suffolk. English Heritage (unpublished Ancient Monuments Laboratory report 115/89), London.

Medical Research Council Tuberculosis and Chest Disease Unit. 1985. National survey of notifications in England and Wales 1983. *British Medical Journal* 291, 658–661.

Miles, A. E. W. 1989. *An Early Christian Burial Ground on the Isle of Ensay, Outer Hebrides, Scotland with a Study of the Skeletal Remains*. British Archaeological Reports (British Series 212), Oxford.

Molleson, T. and M. Cox 1993. *The Spitalfields Project*, vol. 2, *The anthropology. The middling sort*. Council for British Archaeology (Research Report 86), York.

Resnick, D. and G. Niwayama 1988. *Diagnosis of Bone and Joint Disorders*. W. B. Saunders, London.

Roberts, C. 1986 Leprosy and leprosaria in medieval Britain. *Museum of Applied Science Center for Archaeology Journal* 4 (1), 15–21.

Roberts, C., D. Lucy, and K. Manchester 1994. Inflammatory lesions of ribs: an analysis of the Terry Collection. *American Journal of Physical Anthropology* 95, 169–182.

Rogers, J. 1993. St Oswalds Priory, Gloucester. The Human Skeletons. (Unpublished manuscript.)

Ryan, F. 1992. *Tuberculosis: The Greatest Story Never Told*. Swift Publishers, Bromsgrove.

Salo, W. L., A. C. Aufderheide, J. E. Buikstra, and T. A. Holcomb 1994. Identification of *Mycobacterium tuberculosis* DNA in a pre-Columbian Peruvian mummy. *Proceedings of the National Academy of Science* 91, 2091–2094.

Sledzik, P. and N. Bellantoni 1994. Brief communication: bioarcheological and biocultural evidence for the New England vampire folk belief. *American Journal of Physical Anthropology* 94, 269–274.

Smith, F. B. 1988. *The Retreat of Tuberculosis 1850–1950*. Croom Helm, London.

Steinbock, R. T. 1976. *Paleopathological Diagnosis and Interpretation*. Charles Thomas, Springfield, Illinois.

Stirland, A. and T. Waldron 1990. The earliest cases of tuberculosis in Britain. *Journal of Archaeological Science* 17, 221–230.

Stroud, G. and R. L. Kemp 1993. *Cemeteries of St Andrew, Fishergate.* Council for British Archaeology for York Archaeological Trust (The archaeology of York. The medieval cemeteries 12/2), York.

Stuart-Macadam, P. 1985. Report on Stratford Langthorne Skeletal Collection. Level 1. (Unpublished manuscript.)

Volinn, I. J. 1989. Issues and definitions and their implications: AIDS and leprosy. *Social Science and Medicine* 29 (10), 1157–1163.

Wells, C. 1982. The human burials. In A. McWhirr, L. Viner, and C. Wells, *Romano-British Cemeteries at Cirencester,* 135–202. Excavations Committee, Cirencester.

13

A grave disturbance: archaeological perceptions of the recently dead

Angela Boyle

I *would like to take* the opportunity in this paper to examine some of the issues raised in relation to the St Nicholas' excavation project. Additionally it must be strongly emphasised that this and similar projects, such as the excavation of the crypt at Christ Church, Spitalfields (Reeve and Adams 1993; Molleson and Cox 1993; Cox 1996a and b), are never driven at the outset by the requirements of archaeological research in the fieldwork sense but rather by the wish of the church for change.

In the context of this paper the term 'recently dead' is applied to burials of the nineteenth and to a lesser extent the eighteenth century. This is because I wish to look at the factors involved in the study of well preserved (i.e. predominantly nineteenth-century) remains and to a certain extent this involves exploring the prevailing attitude regarding eighteenth- and nineteenth-century archaeology. Finch (1991, 105) rightly concludes that, despite their obvious potential for social and cultural (let alone osteological) studies, late- and post-medieval funeral monuments have been largely ignored and church archaeologists have often seemed driven by an Anglo-Saxon reductionism that condemned post-medieval evidence as disturbance (Hurst 1976, 27).

Analysis of the data from St Nicholas, Sevenoaks is still in progress and therefore any detailed conclusions are of necessity tentative. However, at the start of the post-excavation process a relatively detailed document which assessed the potential for further analysis was produced (Webber, Boyle and McAdam 1994). An interim report concerned largely with the osteological analysis has also now been written (Boyle and Keevill 1998).

The history of the excavation of the crypt at Christ Church, Spital-fields is now well documented (Adams and Reeve 1987; Adams and Reeve 1989; Cox 1989; Molleson and Cox 1993; Reeve and Adams 1993; Cox 1996a and b) and all that will be provided below is a brief summary. Pertinent aspects will however be considered throughout the article.

EXCAVATIONS AT ST NICHOLAS' CHURCH, SEVENOAKS

Excavation at St Nicholas' Church, Sevenoaks, Kent was carried out by the Oxford Archaeological Unit between August and December 1993 in advance of major building works. It was the intention of the Parochial Church Council, as part of their 'Building the Gospel' project, to build a suite of parish rooms as an undercroft below the present-day floor levels. This involved the excavation of the space below the floor to a depth of approximately 4 m destroying *all* surviving archaeological deposits. The excavation was perhaps one of the most substantial ever undertaken in an English church. The initial phase of work was further supplemented by the excavation of the vestry in March and April 1994 and a series of watching briefs, which monitored the provision of drainage and of light wells.

The church first appears in documentary sources in the *Textus Roffensis* of 1122 and not surprisingly the main thrust of the excavation was aimed at recovering evidence of the earliest church structure (potentially dating to before the Norman Conquest) and tracing its development through time. The study of the resulting human remains and associated artefacts and coffin fittings, particularly the post-medieval, was always seen as an issue of lower priority. It became possible to elucidate the structural history of the church from its inception around AD 1100 through to the present day. In addition approximately 450 burials spanning 900 years were excavated. Approximately 250 of this number belonged to the period c. 1550–1875 and 84 of these could be identified by name. Thirty-six of the named individuals were assessed and retained for further study. The retention policy was largely governed by health and safety concerns which necessitated the immediate reburial of individuals with substantial amounts of body tissue still remaining. The majority of the 84 named individuals were buried in lead coffins which were sometimes sealed, sometimes damaged and broken. Almost all were contained in brick vaults. The remainder were buried in wooden coffins, which were placed in earth-cut graves. On the whole these burials were dated to before the nineteenth century.

It was suggested (CBA 1994 Sep.) that the burials from St Nicholas were in many ways 'superior', in preservation and quality, to those at

Christ Church, Spitalfields. This comment is a sweeping one which needs careful qualification. The group from St Nicholas comprised a skeletal population which derived largely from a rural context. It is assumed that the individuals buried within the church were generally of higher status than those buried in the graveyard at St Nicholas' and the group from Christ Church, appropriately described as the 'middling sort'. Clearly a very different time-range is involved with burials dating certainly at least from the twelfth century and continuing through to the nineteenth. The latest dateable burial was that of Selina Dummelow who died in 1854.

Not all of the vaults were post-medieval. The vault located in front of the chancel may be identified with that of David Valtropkyn, who was buried in 1474. During the seventeenth century, large family vaults were built in both St Peter's chapel, belonging to the Lambarde family, and the chantry, built by Sir George Scott and later used by the Amherst family. These vaults continued in use until the nineteenth century. A further 34 vaults and brick-lined graves were present. The Burial Boards Act prohibited intramural burial in the 1850s and the law was variously re-enforced by pastoral measures. The vaults at St Nicholas' were permanently closed in 1878.

EXCAVATIONS AT CHRIST CHURCH, SPITALFIELDS

The excavation of the crypt took place in advance of extensive restoration works. Nearly 1000 burials were uncovered and of that number no less than 387 could be named. Therefore c. 40% of the archaeological contexts were dateable to within a few days of their first introduction into the crypt, and the majority of the rest closely dated within the relative chronology established for the vaults (Adams and Reeve 1989, 270). The burials a middle-class group comprised largely of Huguenots who worked in the silk industry and were interred between 1729 and 1852. The research potential at Spitalfields has since been recognised as considerable and possibly unique, providing as it did the opportunity to study a group of known age and sex whose life histories might be further illuminated by complementary documentary research.

COMMON GROUND

The assemblages have a number of features in common. Both include a number of identifiable individuals, a proportion of whom were related. Silk weaving was historically believed to be the most common occupation of the individuals buried at Christ Church. However, recent research indicates that the majority owned the silk-weaving businesses and, in fact, very few actually did silk weaving (Cox pers. comm.). At St Nicholas, silk-weaving Huguenots were represented by the Nouaille family, who were buried in a family vault which was located in the centre of the nave. Other groups included the Amhersts and the Lambardes, both of whom had family vaults, and the Petleys who tended to be buried in individual coffins in front of the chancel. Approximately 250 related individuals were identified at Christ Church. During both excavations extremely well-preserved individuals in lead coffins were encountered – the recently dead of my title – and this caused a number of complex and inter-related problems.

HEALTH AND SAFETY

A considerable amount of effort was directed at the assessment of the potential health risks likely to be encountered during the excavation of the crypt at Christ Church before the excavation started. Particular concern was attached to the possibility that spores of viable smallpox virus might survive in human tissue. As we shall see below the 'smallpox issue' is a complex one over which little consensus has yet been reached. Interestingly, a number of other factors which proved to be more insidious health risks were not initially realised. These included little air movement, high dust levels, poor visibility, restricted working areas, *and the morbid nature of the archaeological material.* Serious problems regarding the level of staff morale were encountered: many became depressed, lingering minor illnesses were experienced on a regular basis, and a number of individuals terminated their contracts prematurely (Reeves and Adams 1993, 17–20). Although it was decided prior to excavation at Christ Church, Spitalfields that the risk of smallpox infection was remote, possible smallpox pustules were discovered on the remains of a semi-desiccated body. Subsequent tests proved the sample to be non-viable. Fortunately stringent health and safety measures were already in place and these included an embargo on the removal of any excavation material from the crypt while excavation was in progress. Additionally, all surviving soft tissue had to be cremated; arrangements were made for the disposal of rubble and coffin wood while lead was hosed down. Regular blood samples were taken from everyone on the team. A further problem was the rise of lead in staff blood levels and some symptoms of mild lead poisoning were experienced during excavation though at the time they were not recognised as such. They include lassitude, constipation, abdominal discomfort and pain, anorexia, occasional nausea, sleep disturbances, irritability, pallor, and anaemia. Only staff with primary inoculations were allowed to continue work after the discovery of the smallpox lesion and it was fortunate that the entire team fell into this category.

The duration of excavation at Christ Church, Spitalfields obviously played a major role in determining the severity of the various factors and how they affected individual members of staff. The situation at St Nicholas, Sevenoaks was markedly different. Removal of the lead coffins occurred over a period of only three weeks. Most work took place within the rather more open space of the church itself. Only a select few members of the excavation team came into close contact with vault interiors, lead coffins, or their contents. They included the site director, Mike Webber, and the writer.

In the initial phases of work it was anticipated that the vaults would not be cleared until after excavation was completed (no *archaeological* provision was ever made for this aspect of the job). Additionally, and more importantly, it was never intended that the excavation team should have any involvement in this task. However, time constraints caused this situation to alter radically, and it was agreed that the clearance should take place under the auspices of specialist sub-contractors while excavation continued alongside. When the method of removal of these remains became clear it was decided that an attempt should be made to produce a basic archaeological record of the material. Only then did any of the excavation team become involved in the procedure.

An article on the risk of smallpox in excavation focused on St Nicholas' and therefore merits some detailed consideration here (CBA 1994 Oct.). The article appeared under the heading 'Disease? What Disease' and in it Dr Philip Mortimer, Head of Virology of the Public Health Laboratory Service in London, was quoted as saying 'we accept there is a notional risk of catching the disease. . . . But where there isn't any evidence [that smallpox actually still survives] you have to say that the risk does not exist. . . . Dr Susan Young [an acknowledged expert on the disease] disagreed, largely because routine childhood vaccination stopped in the 1970s and first vaccination as an adult poses a severe health risk.'

During excavations at St Nicholas' the team called upon the services of Dr Young who advised that two of the corpses exposed were suffi- ciently well preserved for the presence of smallpox to have been a possibility. She examined the corpses in question and pronounced them unaffected, as she did for the majority of other fleshed remains within lead coffins. Both of these individuals were respectively reburied on the same day that they were exposed. It was common practice for the excavation area to be cleared of people prior to the opening of sealed lead coffins, with the exception of Dr Young, who examined the corpses, and the writer, who was first checked for a primary vaccination scar. Only when corpses were pronounced clear by the doctor were the other excavators allowed to resume work. Protective clothing was worn by both Dr Young and the writer throughout the procedure. The latter along with proof of childhood vaccination against smallpox are the accepted minimum health and safety requirements of the Health and Safety Executive. In every case lead coffins were opened by specialist contractors and *not* by the archaeologists.

The closing comments in the CBA article in question are therefore somewhat alarmist and far from justified: 'the danger of the new medical thinking is that it cannot be proved wrong without tragic consequences. But if it takes root, it may at least prevent such an unhappy and wasteful experience from happening again' (CBA 1994 Oct.).

WHAT THE BONES TELL US

A letter written in response to the article outlined above asked in outraged vein: 'Are you going to learn anything that you did not know already?' (CBA 1994 Oct.). In the opinion of the present writer the answer is an unequivocal yes. The study of identifiable individuals of known age and sex provides a valuable resource for testing and corroborating the physical anthropological methods employed in the ageing and sexing of individuals (Adams and Reeve 1989, 270; Chamberlain 1994, 58). This is extremely important as there are problems with the majority of anthropological methods of age determination, which tend to underestimate the age at death of individuals in the older age ranges. It is clear that some individuals will survive into their eighties and nineties within most populations. The oldest identifiable individual excavated at St Nicholas' Church was a female named Mary Plaistow, who was 102 years old when she died. The problems with assessing ages from bones were examined in some detail employing the assemblage of named individuals from Christ Church, and the results strongly suggested that the traditional ageing methods were open to considerable error (Molleson and Cox 1993, 167–181). Waldron (1994, 90–91, note 2) has recently argued that the design of this study was epidemiologically rather unsound and unless and until further better-designed studies come to the same conclusion, biological anthropologists need not be too disheartened. Further research projects on the sample of named individuals are currently under way and it is expected that additional worthwhile data will be generated.

In her discussion of the merits of the archaeological recovery of crypt populations, Cox (1989, 277) argued that the crypt sample from Christ Church is potentially the most important collection ever recovered in Britain. So, are further crypt samples necessary? Cox (1989, 277) is not slow to admit that there are still unresolved problems.

The reality is that when one breaks down a sample of 387 into subgroups for specific purposes, the numbers are often too small to provide anything other than an indication of specific factors. . . . In order to develop fully the potential so evident in the Christ Church material more of the skeletal material being 'cleared' from many church crypts . . . is desperately needed. For this we are dependent on the church authorities and grant giving bodies, as well as the skills and methods developed by the archaeologists at Christ Church.

It should be clear, therefore, that, as far as the skeletal material is concerned, we can still learn more than what we now know after Christ Church. Preservation, which at Christ Church was variable, can play a major part in determining whether or not a sample is large enough for statistical analysis. Some workers are of the opinion that a small named sample is of very limited scientific value (e.g. Cox 1994) and to a certain extent this is so. However, small groups of named individuals are of use to workers attempting to evolve and refine new methods. For example, researchers at the University of Bradford were keen to utilise the small group from the excavations at St Nicholas' Church. Current work there involves analysing the quantity of amino-acids in teeth which is known to increase over time (Carolan, Pollard, and Gardener). Another method is morphological and aims to use skeletons of known age in order to compare skeletal changes with structural changes in the teeth and therefore elucidate the inter-relationships between the various morphological age-dependent changes (Lucy and Pollard).

The comparison of skeletal and documentary evidence places named individuals within their appropriate socio-cultural context and allows for the analysis of occupational stress, scars of parturition, dietary factors, and genetic trends. At least 250 related pairs were identified at Christ Church and at St Nicholas the majority of burials within lead coffins belonged to identifiable family groups.

At Christ Church, and also at St Nicholas', little emphasis was placed on the value of histological analyses as outlined by Garland (1987, 1988). This was largely because of health and safety requirements. Histology can offer considerable insights when attempting to understand the extrinsic and intrinsic factors which affect the processes of decay and decomposition (Adams and Reeve 1989, 270). Garland (1988) therefore sees the discard of soft tissue as a gross waste of resources.

The opportunity to compare medieval and post-medieval groups is likely to be profitable, as it was in the case of St Nicholas'. Preliminary analysis suggests a marked variation in the degree of sexual dimorphism as well as in the level of dental decay and attrition. Other interesting

[193]

avenues of research might consider demographic questions such as patterning in age and cause of death.

DOCUMENTARY EVIDENCE

The analysis of documentary sources has already been touched upon. It is clear that the lives of a number of identifiable individuals are well documented. These include Francis Austin, great uncle of novelist Jane, and Jeffrey 1st baron Amherst who secured Canada for the British Empire in 1760. In more general terms, research into the life histories of named individuals has the potential to illuminate issues of church patronage as well as many aspects of the social and economic conditions of the town in the eighteenth and nineteenth century.

THE ARTEFACTS

Writing fourteen years ago Rahtz (1981, 134–135) referred to a class of material (coffin fittings) 'which will be available for study only when comparatively recent cemeteries are dug.' He rightly commented that coffin fittings usually only turned up in uncontrolled excavations where churches were bulldozed away, or where more modern graves were sacrificed to reach 'more interesting' ones below. He concluded that coffin fittings were unlikely to be available for study in the foreseeable future. Ten years later Litten stated (1991, 198) that 'it remains painful to reflect on the quantity of valuable source material which, until recently, has been denied examination, evaluation and the concomitant post-excavation analysis, interpretation and publication.'

A brief examination confirms that the existing literature on post-medieval funerary practice in an archaeological context is minimal (Boore 1985; Watts and Rahtz 1985; Rodwell and Rodwell 1986). An exception to this is the discussion which appears, albeit on microfiche, in the report on the church of St Martin, Wharram Percy (Hurst and Rahtz 1985). Even the large assemblage of coffin furniture from Christ Church has not been dealt with in any great detail (Reeve and Adams 1993. 83–88, 144–147, M2–M3). The assemblage of coffin fittings from St Nicholas spans the entire post-medieval period and apparently includes a comparable range and of types and styles as Christ Church, albeit in smaller quantities. It has the potential to increase our knowledge of design, typology and chronological development. Additionally a study of the transition from medieval iron brackets to the elaborate lead, copper, and tin decoration would be informative. In addition a recent publication on future research directions in church archaeology has gone some way to redressing the balance (Blair and Pyrah 1996).

[194]

THE ETHICAL ISSUE

It would appear that many of the published reactions to the work at St Nicholas' are closely linked to the moral and ethical issues surrounding the excavation of the recently dead (CBA 1994 Sep.-Nov.; Philp 1995) and lack a detailed knowledge of the actual sequence of events. Correspondence was published in the *Daily Mail* (27 Dec. 1994) under the headline 'Grave Robbing' and the following quotation best conveys the mood of its writer: 'The descendants who have relatives that were lying in this crypt have seen it subjected to terrible desecration. I hope those who allowed this to happen are not rudely dug up after their short life span to make way for a cafe.' At Christ Church a number of descendants of the deceased in the crypt became very involved in the project (Adams and Reeve 1993).

It has long been acknowledged that we share a common reluctance to disturb the mortal remains of those whose religion we nominally share (Rahtz 1981, 117). Reece commented that (1982, 350): 'the intentional re-use of the same piece of ground for a second or subsequent burial when the previous occupant is known (this must happen in family vaults), struck Sidonius Apollinaris in the fifth century as disgraceful; it strikes most modern people the same way. Yet, between these two periods of disapproval the attitude was one of calculating reverence.' However, in his discussion of the prolonged use of medieval graveyards, Rahtz (1981, 120) describes the generation of charnel deposits as a regular adjunct of every inhumation, and for this reason the depiction of charnel bones in fifteenth-century funerary art became the norm (at least a further 200 individuals were represented among the charnel recovered within St Nicholas). Such images were replaced in the eighteenth century by cherubs, then willows, urns, and other 'pleasant' pictorial elements. In excavations at St Bride's church in Fleet Street, Professor W. F. Grimes (quoted in Reece 1982) came upon coffins which aroused memories in some of his visitors from the nearby law courts. He was provided with references to litigation . . . in which the church wardens claimed greatly increased burial fees from the relatives of those who insisted on using such sturdy tombs, since they would be occupying their piece of ground for well over the usual span of time, and hence preventing the expected re-use of the ground.

In his comprehensive study of the English funeral Litten comments (1991, 198) that: 'Deliberately to disturb a vault on the strength of curiosity is unnecessary, for it should not be forgotten that such places were constructed as places of private sepulchre whose occupants, at the time of purchase, probably never contemplated being disturbed by the inquisitive, and such sentiments should be respected.' This desire of the occupant to expect to remain undisturbed for all eternity does not sit particularly well with the fact that the construction of the vault itself would have caused considerable damage to any previous coffined burials in the immediate vicinity. Furthermore, because of their use as family vaults, repeated openings would have been inevitable. This, however is very different from the forcible removal of remains during an excavation.

Litten's opinions on vaults contrast markedly with his recent comments in a BBC 2 documentary (First Sight – The Last Taboo 19/1/95) which was concerned with the present-day crisis over cemetery space, particularly in the south-east. He suggested removing headstones and returning to the medieval idea of 'dig them deep and stack them high'.

The writer subscribes to the view expressed by Richard Morris (CBA 1994 Sep.):

> It could be said that our unease is irrational; why should we celebrate Boxgrove Man in one month, and confess misgivings about a Sevenoaks Victorian the next? Each was as dead as the other. . . . Within Christian tradition there is no theological argument against the disturbance of the dead . . . for a humanist or even a Protestant, 'respect for the dead' usually means respect for the beliefs and feelings of the living . . . for others it is the bones themselves that have an inalienable right to rest undisturbed. . . . Part of the reason for disquiet about Sevenoaks is that the methods adopted by specialist sub-contractors to dispose of the bodies appear to have offended against both sets of principles.

Cox argues (CBA 1994 Nov.) that throughout the post-medieval period there was an increasing concern over disturbance after death which destroyed eternal identity and prevented physical resurrection. In the eighteenth and early nineteenth century all medical education was transacted on a private basis and the only legal source of corpses for dissection was the bodies of executed criminals. This lead to a black market in which recently buried corpses were exhumed and sold to anatomists and medical students (Richardson 1988, XV). In 1832 the Anatomy Act was passed and this gave the government the right to appropriate the bodies of paupers from workhouses and hospitals. Clearly, the people buried in lead coffins would not have belonged to the group most threatened by and fearful of the Anatomy Act, i.e. the poor. Prior to the passing of the law the horror of body snatching would have affected society at all levels (for a detailed discussion of the Anatomy Act and its consequences see Richardson (1988); she sees the consequences as far reaching and believes that the act was a major factor in determining modern attitudes to death).

On a personal level, I found the experience of dealing with well-preserved remains an extremely disturbing one. Initially, this surprised me because as a biological anthropologist I spend all of my time dealing with many aspects of death whether examining skeletal material or researching burial practices of all periods. Well-preserved, i.e. fleshed remains, are still *too recognisably human* and therefore force us to consider the realities of our own deaths. This view is echoed by Margaret Cox (CBA 1994 Nov.), who considers that excavators are likely to be deeply traumatised: 'To disturb the dead is a taboo deeply ingrained in any culture where burial is the norm; and the more the dead resemble the living the more serious the breach.'

THE WAY FORWARD

The situation at St Nicholas' Church was far from a unique one as unsupervised clearance of churches, vaults, and graveyards has been going on for years. Rahtz (1985, 89) described working in 1962 alongside a Bristol Corporation gang of workmen employed in parallel to empty all the burial vaults and to remove their contents for re-burial in out-of-town municipal cemeteries.

The 'repeated investigation of burials of relatively recent date' was recently questioned (Morris, CBA 1994 Oct.). I would contend that repeated investigation has not taken place in the past and is unlikely to occur in the future, particularly merely for reasons of intellectual curiosity. An increasingly vocal evangelical tradition in the Church of England, coupled with various pressures on the physical space within churches, makes it inevitable that more churches and graveyards will be subjected to development. The real issue is whether or not archaeologists should be involved. The answer is yes *but* not for reasons of morbid curiosity. Our involvement should occur in situations where circumstances dictate that 'clearance' will take place with or without our control. Additionally more archaeological curators need to recognise the value of post-medieval cemeteries and require archaeological mitigation, preferably by excavation, to take place. If we accept that archaeological involvement is inevitable then we must also accept that there is a very real and pressing need for guidelines. It should also be emphasised that the study of recent funerary material is in essence multi-disciplinary and requires the input of archaeologists, anthropologists, art historians, social historians, histologists, and forensic scientists.

ACKNOWLEDGEMENTS

I would like to thank Graham Keevill and Jez Reeve for reading and commenting upon this paper. It should be stressed that the views expressed are entirely mine and in no way do they reflect those of the Oxford Archaeological Unit as an organisation or of the excavation director, Mike Webber.

NOTES

* This paper was originally submitted June 1995 and revised for publication May 1997.

BIBLIOGRAPHY

Adams, M. and J. Reeves 1989. It's a dirty job, but somebody's got to do it. In C. A. Roberts, F. Lee, and J. Bintliff (eds), *Burial Archaeology: Current Research, Methods and Developments*, 267–274. British Archaeological Reports (British Series 211), Oxford.

Adams, M. and J. Reeve 1989. Excavations at Christ Church, Spitalfields 1984–6. *Antiquity* 61, 247–255.

Blair, J. and C. Pyrah 1996. *Church Archaeology. Research directions for the future*. Council for British Archaeology (Research Report 104), York.

Boddington, A., A. N. Garland, and R. C. Janaway 1987. *Death, Decay and Reconstruction. Approaches to archaeology and forensic science*. Manchester University Press, Manchester.

Boore, E. J. 1985. Excavations at St. Augustine the Less, Bristol 1983–4, *Bristol and Avon Archaeology* 14, 21–33.

Boyle, A. and G. Keevill 1998. 'The the praise of the dead, and anatomie.' The analysis of the post-medieval burials at St Nicholas, Sevenoaks. In M. Cox (ed.), *Grave Concerns: Death and Burial in Post-medieval England, 1750–1850*. Council for British Archaeology, York.

Carolan, V. A., A. M. Pollard, and M. L. G. Gardener 1993. Amino Acid Racemization in Human Dentine as an Indicator of Age at Death: a Refined Procedure. University of Bradford (unpublished research outline), Bradford.

CBA (Council for British Archaeology) 1994. *British Archaeological News* Sep.-Nov. 16–18.

Chamberlain, A. 1994. *Human Remains*. British Museum, London.

Cox, M. 1989. The case for crypt excavation not crypt clearance. In C. A. Roberts, F. Lee, and J. Bintliff (eds), *Burial Archaeology: Current Research, Methods and Developments*, 275–278. British Archaeological Reports (British Series 211), Oxford.

Cox, M. 1996a. *Life and Death in Spitalfields, 1700–1850*. Council for British Archaeology, York.

Cox, M. 1996b. Crypt archaeology after Spitalfields: dealing with our recently dead. *Antiquity* 70, 8–10.

Finch, J. 1991. According to the qualitie and degree of the person deceased: funeral monuments and the construction of social identities 1400–1750. *Scottish Archaeological Review* 8, 105–114.

Garland, A. N. 1988. Histology, taphonomy and human skeletal remains. *Archaeological Forum* 2, 12–16.

Garland, A. N. 1987. A histological study of archaeological bone decomposition. In A. Boddington, A. N. Garland and R. C. Janaway (eds),

Death, Decay and Reconstruction. Approaches to archaeology and forensic science, 109–126. Manchester University Press, Manchester.

Hurst, J. G. and P. A. Rahtz 1987. *Wharram. A Study of Settlement on the Yorkshire Wolds,* vol. 3, *Wharram Percy: The Church of St. Martin.* (Society for Medieval Archaeology Monograph Series 11).

Litten, J. 1991. *The English Way of Death. The Common Funeral since 1450.* Robert Hale, London.

Lucy, D. and A. M. Pollard 1993. Outline of the research on physiological methods of age estimation using the human dentition. University of Bradford (unpublished research outline), Bradford.

Molleson, T. and M. Cox with A. H. Waldron and D. K. Whittaker 1993. *The Spitalfields Project,* vol. 2, *The Anthropology The Middling Sort.* Council for British Archaeology (Research Report 85), York.

Philp, B. 1995. Storm over excavations in Sevenoaks Church. *Kent Archaeological Review* 120, 247–248.

Rahtz, P. 1981. Artefacts of Christian death. In S. C. Humphreys and H. King (eds), *Mortality and Immortality The Anthropology and Archaeology of Death,* 117–136. Academic Press, London.

Reece, R. 1982. Bone, bodies and disease. *Oxford Journal of Archaeology* 1 (3), 347–358.

Reeves, J. and M. Adams 1993. *The Spitalfields Project,* vol. 1, *The Archaeology Across The Styx.* Council for British Archaeology (Research Report 85), York.

Richardson, R. 1988. *Death, Dissection and the Destitute.* Routledge and Kegan Paul, London.

Rodwell, W. J. and K. A. Rodwell 1986. *Rivenhall: Investigation of a Villa, Church and Village 1950–1977,* vol. 1, Council for British Archaeology (Research Report 55; Chelmsford Archaeological Trust Report 4), York.

Rodwell, W. J. and K. A. Rodwell 1993. *Rivenhall: Investigation of a Villa, Church and Village 1950–1977,* vol. 2, *Specialist studies and index to volumes 1 and 2.* Council for British Archaeology (Research Report 80; Chelmsford Archaeological Trust Report 4.2), York.

Waldron, T. 1994. *Counting the Dead. The Epidemiology of Skeletal Populations.* John Wiley and Sons, Chichester.

Watts, L. and P. A. Rahtz 1985. *St. Mary-le-Port, Bristol, Excavations 1962–3.* City of Bristol Museum and Art Gallery, Bristol.

Webber, M., A. Boyle, and E. McAdam 1994. St. Nicholas' Church, Sevenoaks Archaeological Excavations 1993. Oxford Archaeological Unit (unpublished Post Excavation Assessment and Research Design), Oxford.

14

Death at the undertakers

Lucy Kirk and Helen Start

During the autumn of 1996, excavation of a Quaker burial ground was undertaken in Kingston-upon-Thames by Archaeology South East (part of the Field Archaeology Unit, University College London). The authors of this paper were involved as osteo-archaeologists responsible for the on- and off-site analyses of the 362 individuals recovered, the results of which are discussed elsewhere (Start and Kirk 1998). The majority of burials, dating from the seventeenth to the early nineteenth centuries, were inhumations in wooden coffins with brass or iron fittings. Common to the period, but seemingly at odds with Quaker belief, lead coffins were used, sixteen of which were recovered. The presence of detailed documentary sources and legible coffin plates added further information to this rare opportunity to investigate Quaker burial practices.

The site was unique in terms of the working environment. Facilities were provided for the skeletal analysis by the Necropolis Company at their nearby offices. These facilities included a prefabricated building previously used for coffin construction, a garage in use as a coffin store, and a disused embalming room. The authors, although accustomed to dealing with the remains of the long dead, were somewhat taken aback to find themselves surrounded by the daily workings of a busy undertakers.

The following discussion is an attempt to set down and examine our reactions, whilst dealing with archaeological death, to the constant presence of recent death. Our first attempt at writing this paper was problematic and largely unsuccessful because we approached it in the wrong way, attempting to write in a traditional academic style without using personal prepositions or emotive language. This is a discussion of our personal and emotional responses to the situation. Traditional *dry* academic style was found to be too restrictive, so we have instead adopted a style of writing more suited to the subject matter and, it is hoped, more in keeping with the aims of this volume.

CEMETERY EXCAVATIONS

Due to the steady pressure on land for redevelopment, especially in urban areas, the archaeological investigation of post-medieval burial environments is becoming increasingly common. Many archaeologists have therefore excavated relatively recently buried human skeletal remains, but are they comfortable with digging up dead people? Cemeteries are approached in the same way as any other archaeological site, and skeletons are treated as just another context. Theoretically, the basic excavation and recording techniques are identical. In combination these factors promote a degree of familiarity with the site, and archaeologists are not faced with a completely alien working environment. We are not suggesting that archaeologists are not aware of the implications of what they are doing, but in theory it is possible to treat a cemetery excavation as 'just another job'. Among both archaeologists and non-archaeologists there is a perception that the archaeological removal of human remains is more respectful than the alternatives, such as the commercial clearance of skeletal material. This could stem from the careful and detailed nature of archaeological work. This idea of respect is often voiced on site during the excavation of cemetery sites with archaeologists imagining the fate of the remains if they were not the ones removing them. This justification makes us as archaeologists feel more comfortable about our work.

There are other ways in which archaeologists working on a cemetery may make themselves feel more comfortable, for example the naming of skeletons, which is a common practice familiar to many archaeologists. Assigning names to skeletons makes it easier to remember a specific context in a way that a simple number never could, but perhaps more importantly naming skeletons recognises their individuality, again promoting the idea of a respectful approach.

Many archaeologists successfully deal with the excavation of human remains in the course of their work, but it is apparent from discussions that frequently occur on site that people are uncomfortable with certain aspects of the job. Quite clearly there is an awareness that cemetery excavations do differ from other archaeological sites. Perhaps most obviously in that they are not primarily concerned with the recovery of material remains but the people who created them.

People seem to be affected in different ways by the various aspects of the excavation of skeletons. In our experience, teeth are frequently singled out for comment and are discomforing, as are juvenile remains.

Another common dislike seems to be having to face the appearance of a recognisable coffin. All these examples have in common that they make death a reality. Teeth, for example, are instantly familiar as human because they are the only skeletal element visible among the living, and link those living around us with the dead in the ground. Death of children in modern western society is relatively rare and generally felt to be tragic, and this may explain why the appearance of a child's skeleton is more shocking than that of an adult. For many people the idea of death conjures the image of a coffin, and the appearance of a coffin on site therefore provides a striking visual reminder of death. It would seem, from the variety of dislikes expressed, that everybody draws their own lines as to what they find acceptable and this is in some ways based on what makes death a reality for them.

THE QUAKER BURIAL GROUND, KINGSTON-ON-THAMES

Prior to the recent trend and necessity to excavate post-medieval cemeteries and crypts, archaeologists excavating cemetery sites expected to find only wooden coffins, which rarely survive in recognisable form. Wooden coffins predominated at Kingston, but we also uncovered a brick vault which contained, and was surrounded by, a total of sixteen lead coffins. Suddenly we were faced with whole, solid lead coffins rather than scraps of wood and iron nails. Our response to their appearance and at having to deal with them made us aware of the strong symbolism they carried. They had further significance to us as the osteo-archaeologists. Having previously only had to deal with skeletal remains, there was a strong possibility that soft tissue would survive and this presented us with a challenging situation.

Another reason why Kingston was a somewhat unusual site, and prompted the writing of this paper, is that it provided named individuals. Within the vault we were presented with three generations of one family with known familial relationships. There were also documentary records for these people giving details of their lives. The individuals named on the lead coffins were present at the Quaker society meetings, the minutes of which form part of the accessible history of the group. All these circumstances combined to make us more conscious of the past reality we were dealing with.

Quaker beliefs support simple burial style and a lack of ostentation. For this reason the presence of lead coffins had been considered as unlikely. But, being a post-medieval cemetery, the possibility was not ruled out and procedures for dealing with them had been established. However, it was not until their appearance on site that we had to make a conscious choice as to whether we would examine the contents or

[202]

have them removed for immediate reburial without investigation. Despite the potentially disturbing nature of the work, we found the decision to go ahead with excavation relatively easy. This led to the examination of our motivations as osteoarchaeologists which follows.

LIFE AT THE UNDERTAKERS

Following their removal from site, the lead coffins were opened and excavated in the garage provided by the Necropolis Company. Certain safety measures had been established for dealing with the lead coffins, and the wearing of filter masks, disposable gloves, and suits were obviously a necessary health and safety precaution. It was with some trepidation that we put these on because it further symbolised that we were doing something different and unknown. The suits, gloves, and masks also conjured up images of forensic police investigations, both fictional and non-fictional, which have strong associations with murder and very recent death. We were pleased by the exceptional preservation of skeletal material during our first experience of examining the contents of the lead coffins, but the additional presence of soft tissue and the accompanying smell was unsettling. We quickly realised that wearing the safety clothing was helping to protect our emotional peace of mind as much as our physical health. The act of putting the clothing on was part of our mental preparation for an unpleasant situation. In other words we were attempting to distance ourselves from the unpleasantness and reality of what we were doing. We decided to approach the task by applying the same archaeological techniques and principles that would be employed on any other excavation. This was prompted by our inexperience with lead coffins, and perhaps it was also an extension of the attitude adopted on the site to normalise the work. As with any other site, in this situation and previous cemetery excavations we desired professionalism and objectivity. These concepts helped us deal emotionally with the reality of digging up the remains of the dead.

This attitude enabled us to excavate the lead coffins, but as the result of interruptions to one of these excavations we realised something more was going on. When someone else came into the garage we were thrown to such an extent that we realised a strong but largely unspoken form of communication had developed between the two of us which helped us deal with our situation. Discussing it afterwards, we realised that we had each been aware of how the other was coping and this acted as a form of safety valve. In this way we prevented each other from doing something they weren't entirely comfortable with because we provided support for each other and were able to recognise in the other when we needed a break.

Most of the lead coffins were split and this affected the condition of the human remains inside them. In some cases bone and soft tissue was no better preserved than on-site. However in other cases the bone was exceptionally well preserved, and soft tissue such as decomposed brain tissue and ligamentous muscle attachments survived. The lead coffin containing Sarah Barnard was still completely sealed, and as we did not have the resources to open and excavate this coffin it was reburied intact. Following the clearing of the lead coffins, it was necessary to wash the bones. It was for this purpose that we had been provided with the disused embalming room, referred to by the undertaking staff as 'the mortuary', which contained an embalming table with running water and drainage. Clearly we were working in an environment not familiar to many archaeologists. We had transferred ourselves from the garage on the periphery, into the heart of the daily activities of a funeral directors.

Our first task was to clean the mortuary because it had been out of use for some time. Again, this was done as much for our emotional peace of mind as for any other reason. Not surprisingly the atmosphere in the mortuary was unpleasant. Popular images of mortuaries as gloomy, cold rooms, familiar to most people from the television, were instantly conjured up in our minds. The feeling of foreboding we experienced when we had to enter the mortuary did not decrease with time. Our uneasiness at the prospect of working there took the form of a physical sensation, or 'gut' feeling, including a loss of appetite, to the extent that we arranged our work schedule around it. On every wall and door there were fluorescent reminders to check the identification of the deceased. Although this should have been a comforting precaution against mistakes, we found it disturbing because it constantly reminded us of the previous use of the room where dead bodies were routinely dealt with. The desire to distance ourselves from our surroundings that we had experienced when excavating the lead coffins in the garage stayed with us, and we decided to continue wearing the protective clothing while working in the mortuary.

Small reminders of a similar kind were around us everywhere, and it was impossible not to be constantly aware of the nature of the surroundings. On the very first working day we were presented with a bunch of keys held together with a body identification tag, which we later found was standard practice. At the entrance to the embalming room stacks of boxes lent up against a disused refrigeration unit. Brass effect coffin handles had been used on several doors, including the cellar and mortuary. Within the coffin workshop the measurements of timbers used for their construction were still clearly visible on the walls, as were the labelled hooks for funeral rotas.

We were also faced with more obvious signs of the business around us. During the course of our work in the mortuary access was often required by the undertakers. This involved the delivery by private ambulance of the recently deceased to the viewing room next door. After three or four days they were transferred back through the mortuary to an awaiting hearse. The coffins were wheeled past us on such a regular basis that we became familiar with the private ambulance men. We found these interruptions disturbing because it signalled the arrival of a new body, and reminded us of our close proximity to the recently dead. However, on one occasion we were generously given a box of disposable gloves and a demonstration of the mobility of the embalming table and coffin stretcher in the corner. We appreciated the friendly manner in which these gestures had been made, but it did little to alleviate our sense of unease about our working environment.

Despite these experiences most of our time was spent analysing dry bones in the coffin workshop, where we were removed from the direct physical presence of the recently dead. However, from this vantage point we witnessed the everyday running of the funeral directors. This involved the constant flow of vehicles in and out of the yard, including relatives of the deceased, private ambulances, hearses, and vans delivering floral tributes. One morning we had difficulty gaining access to the yard because an articulated lorry was stationed near the entrance. The yard soon filled with the conversation and laughter of a dozen or so men in assorted modes of dress ranging from manual work wear to full mourning suits. The appearance of men wielding clipboards and mobile phones had created a busy and efficient atmosphere when the tarpaulin siding of the lorry was energetically drawn back to reveal stack upon stack of coffins. The scene became increasingly surreal as the coffins were unloaded and the yard was thrown into chaos with men wheeling coffins of all descriptions in every direction. As with most large deliveries of commercial goods, several quality checks were done. These involved the close inspection of all aspects of the coffins from the lining and fittings to the standard of production. Some did not pass the test with handles coming off, or torn linings and these were stacked for return to the manufacturers in the garage we used to excavate lead coffins from the site. Never had we seen anything this bizarre, and witnessing it brought home our growing awareness of death as a commercial business. We were forced to abandon our ideals regarding the death of someone close as a personal experience for everyone involved. Never had death seemed more real.

RESPONSES

Throughout the project we were faced with a situation that we were never entirely comfortable with, and one which constantly surprised us. Before the excavation began, a preliminary visit was made to the site by Lucy Kirk and the project manager, Dr Tony Pollard. Not all the facilities had been prepared for our use and they were therefore in disarray. The mortuary, for example, still contained an empty coffin, chemical bottles, and the mortuary log book. The atmosphere caused us a considerable amount of unease. Admittedly, it did not help that it was raining hard and that this part of Kingston was experiencing a power cut. This visit made a considerable impression on both of us and so much so that the practicalities of working in this environment, the establishment of which had been the purpose of the visit, was consciously avoided as a subject of conversation during the return journey.

As a result of coping with the uncomfortable feelings experienced in these surroundings we questioned how the people for whom this was normal coped with their situation. As part of this process we also questioned our own reactions both to them and their working environment.

Through our daily contact with various staff at the funeral directors, we realised that a lot of their communication was based on humour connected with death. We bore the brunt of many sarcastic comments and morbid jokes. One of their biggest sources of amusement was our insistence on wearing protective clothing, both when dealing with lead coffins and in the mortuary. They showed a certain degree of interest in what we were doing, asking numerous questions, but to a greater extent we were seen as a curiosity. At times we felt almost like a circus side show, with curious faces peering blatantly in at the window and frequent visitors. From the length of time spent talking to us and their relaxed manner it was evident that they did not realise we were not only working but under strict time pressures.

Our visitors seemed to take pleasure in attempting to shock us with horror stories, and were showing off about how hardened they were to death. We understood the nature of their humour and conversation to be an attempt to 'normalise' their daily surroundings. How else would you come to terms with their working environment? It is clear that a process of 'normalisation' had taken place because we, as outsiders who deal with death, found their behaviour morbid and to some extent shocking. Observing this behaviour, we determined that we wouldn't become hardened to it as they had, in other words we found their behaviour undesirable. The thought of indulging in the same kind of humour appalled us, we wanted to hang on to our shock and disturbance at our situation as comforting proof that we were still 'normal'. By remaining constantly aware of this thought we believed we could observe any signs of our becoming hardened, and prevent it.

Throughout the duration of work at Kingston we both experienced nightmares and disturbed sleep. Although unpleasant, this reassured us that we still found our situation abnormal and disturbing. Coffins, skeletons, bodies, and death were frequent manifestations in these dreams, which we interpreted as an understandable reaction to our surroundings. However, in some cases the actual content of the dreams eluded us and instead we simply awoke with feelings of uneasiness and fear. Through talking with the rest of the excavation team we realised that this was a shared experience. A common theme was a feeling of guilt, which we assumed was directly connected to the work we were doing. We asked members of the team if they were affected by the work and without exception they replied, 'I am not affected by it but . . .' and then proceeded to relate experiences, often including dreams, which they found disturbing. From this it was clear that everyone was affected to some extent. The way their answers were phrased made us curious as to the reasons for their initial denial. We turned these observations on ourselves and realised that this differed from our own experience.

Perhaps it is not surprising that our experiences differed from the rest of the team. They were in a normal and familiar excavation environment, whereas our work-place was totally alien to anything we had experienced before. In fact, it was the place rather than what we were doing which had the greatest affect on us and prompted our exploration of the issues discussed here. However, we believe that the recognition that our surroundings affected us made them easier to cope with and without this realisation we don't believe we could have managed.

FINAL THOUGHTS

In order to complete the skeletal analysis at the Necropolis facilities, we were aware that we had chosen to carry out tasks which even our colleagues were unwilling to do. Following his initial visit Dr Tony Pollard made it clear that he would not be willing to work in these surroundings. We felt we had to ask ourselves why we had chosen to put ourselves in this situation, what made us different? Essentially we answered these questions by examining our motivations for being osteo-archaeologists. An interest in past cultures and societies led us both to archaeology. The most vivid connection with people in the past is their physical remains and we considered this to be our primary motivation for specialising in human osteology. However, this site has made us realise that our decision to specialise was at least in part influenced by the common human fascination with death. The opportunities offered on this site including the named individuals and exceptional preservation were such that we were willing to put ourselves through these unpleasant experiences. This stemmed from a desire as osteo-archaeologists to realise the full potential of the human remains from the site, and our own interest in human skeletal remains.

It dawned on us that because of our willingness to work under these circumstances we are seen as morbid by friends and colleagues. We, however, see ourselves as normal, and the undertakers as morbid. Our experiences at Kingston have made us far more aware of how people perceive us. Having experienced the funeral directors humour and the effect it had on us, we are more careful about how we phrase things and what we say to other people about our work. Previously if we were fascinated by something, we would talk to people about it unaware that they might find it offensive or upsetting.

As a result of our experiences on this site and writing this paper we have come to see what we do in a different light. The examination of our emotional responses to our work amongst recent death led us to two important conclusions. We were forced to justify our work and motivations to ourselves. This process was beneficial to us and the rest of our team, and could be valuable to any archaeologist dealing with death. Although it is possible to treat cemetery excavations as just another job, we believe that a constant awareness of the individuality of the remains is a respectful approach and we are comfortable with our emotional responses. Secondly, we concluded that death does provoke emotional reactions and these need to be considered when we are attempting to interpret past funerary practices. This may seem obvious, but too often funerary practices are only discussed with reference to factors such as status and wealth. We accept that these play an important role, but emotions such as love and grief which are central to current funerary practices should not be underestimated in the past.

ACKNOWLEDGEMENTS

We would like to thank all the on-site staff who willingly shared their ideas and feelings with us. We are grateful for the continuing support, guidance and enthusiasm of Dr Tony Pollard and Luke Barber from Archaeology South East, Dr Margaret Cox of Bournemouth University, Jez Reeves, and Ken Whittaker from English Heritage. We would also like to thank Necropolis for their premises and helpful, friendly staff and finally Andy Hammon and Jason Sibun for their support.

REFERENCE

Start, H. and L. Kirk 1998. 'The bodies of friends': the osteological analysis of a Quaker burial ground. In M. Cox (ed.), *Grave Concerns Death and Burial in Post-medieval England, 1750–1850*. Council for British Archaeology, York.

15

The excavation of modern murder

J. R. Hunter

In the town of Franklin, Tennessee in 1977 there was some consternation when vandals looting for military memorabilia exposed the well-preserved, but headless body of a male in an old family burial ground. Parts of the soft tissue were still pink and the individual was identified as a 25- to 28-year-old male who had been dead for between six and twelve months (Bass 1984, 139). In actual fact he was 26 and later identified as one Colonel Shy, whose cause of death in a Civil War battle over a century earlier had been well documented. He was in his own grave adjacent to a headstone bearing his name and personal details. The (mis)diagnosis was the consequence of embalming, resulting in a high level of preservation which caused the authorities to view the body as the product of a modern crime.

The unusual case of Colonel Shy conveniently illustrates a point at which criminal investigation and archaeology find mutual interest, albeit for the wrong reasons. It also highlights the fact that archaeologists tend not to expect to encounter human remains bearing soft tissue and a full set of clothes, and that detectives tend to assume that any such discovery immediately presupposes foul play. In the USA such has been the frequent 'surfacing' of embalmed remains by vandalism, looting for jewellery, and processes of natural erosion that guidelines have now been produced for distinguishing between older, legal burials of the Colonel Shy type and burials resulting from more recent criminal activity (Berryman et al. 1991). One certain way of definition was shown to be the careful archaeological recovery of burial artefacts associated with the embalming process itself – notably eye caps, mouth formers, and fluid injector needles.

Ironically, Colonel Shy was one of the earliest forensic cases in the

USA to be investigated by archaeological means. At the time there was much concern within archaeological circles about the manner in which the victims of modern crime were being recovered (Morse et al. 1984), and the American literature contains a catalogue of laments. Notable examples include an incident in Illinois in which three victims were 'excavated' under the worse possible conditions by unskilled personnel and have subsequently never been identified, or a case in Texas where 17 victims were exhumed from inside a building by machine in order to counteract intense public and media interest, and because of the stench (Morse et al. 1976a). Since then the awareness of archaeology's contribution to crime scenes has increased and has been well logged (e.g. Snow 1982; Iscan 1988), although in the USA it holds, for practical reasons, a closer relationship with anthropology than in the UK where forensic archaeology is still relatively young (Hunter 1994; Hunter et al. 1995). Archaeology's forensic relevance is now well versed (e.g. Bass and Birkby 1978) and has achieved academic respectability with a comprehensive literature spanning not only field skills but also the chemistry of decomposition, and physico-chemical methods of determining the interval since death (e.g. Krogman and Iscan 1986). The first useful archaeological field guide intended for non-archaeologists in forensic pursuit is still widely alluded to (Morse et al. 1983) and has been complemented by more specialist texts on locational techniques (Killam 1990; France et al. 1992) and on recovery skills in general (Skinner and Lazenby 1983; Ubelaker 1989). Work on recent mass graves in civil rights cases has demonstrated further benefits of using archaeological methodology (Skinner 1987) and has been widely applied, for example in the Argentine where a team under the direction of Clyde Snow – *the Equipo Argentino de Anthropologia Forense* – consisting variously of anthropologists, doctors, and archaeologists, was brought in to excavate and identify commingled victims in burial pits. Similar strategies are now employed in the excavation of mass graves in Rwanda and Bosnia.

ARCHAEOLOGY AT SCENES OF CRIME

Archaeology's application at scenes of crime is far from the simple transference of theory and practical skills. The term 'forensic archaeology' is now widespread, especially in American literature, and this chapter provides a useful opportunity for outlining some of its characteristics and for examining the way in which it differs from archaeology, which has a more accepted academic basis. At a scene of crime traditional field skills are indeed applied but within a context in which other (non-archaeological) specialists are recovering different types of evidence from the same resource, and within a judicial framework which has major implications for the manner in which data is recovered, recorded, and presented. The development of forensic archaeology is a two-way exercise: police groups need to be aware of what benefits archaeology can offer, and archaeologists need to understand the objectives and constraints which govern forensic practice. This need for mutual awareness was recognised in some of the earliest courses offered in the subject (Morse et al. 1976b) and has since been the subject of more careful analysis (e.g. Snow 1982, 115). In the USA many archaeologists have been surprised to find that a crime scene involving burial, despite its overt similarities to an archaeological site, provides so many alien, rigorously controlled, and well-established processes to regulate an otherwise simple archaeological procedure. Sigler-Eisenberg's (1985, 653f) analysis of the situation makes clear some of the practical difficulties that the archaeologist may face, including the issue of 'mission', which acknowledges that the general notion of what an archaeologist is and what an archaeologist does is often cruelly misconceived. Not least of these practical difficulties is the emotional aspect of encountering recent human death, particularly of children, in an environment in which grieving relatives can generate further levels of stress.

The differences between archaeological and forensic contexts can in most respects be ascribed to differences in *protocols* and the broader issue of *objectives,* the latter clearly having an implication for what might be termed as a *research design.* British archaeologists have a certain expectancy when it comes to excavating burials. Collective experience has generated much practical advice (e.g. McKinley and Roberts 1993), legal frameworks are now better defined (Garratt-Frost 1992), and some experience has been gained in the problems encountered with soft tissue (Reeve and Adams 1993). There is a knowledge of what to do, how to do it, and what to expect. The exercise is directed towards removal of the grave fill, exposure of the human remains and associated materials, and the three-dimensional recording of all items in relation to each other and to the wider cemetery environment. Any symbolism or ritual practice is gathered by the recording of burial paraphernalia and the manner of deposition of the individual. Aspects of biological anthropology – gender, age, stature, state of health, etc. – belong to the laboratory and will be undertaken at a future date or, sadly, in some instances not at all. Each burial may have its own features of interest, but its main contribution normally lies as part of a larger understanding of the diagnostic characteristics of a particular period, population, or cultural group. This understanding will be the successful outcome of the research design. Provided that the evidence has been gathered accurately and comprehensively, the burial effectively becomes a statistical data set and is rarely used in isolation.

In forensic contexts a number of additional factors come into play; each burial is a 'one-off' rather than part of a larger statistical population and requires a set of questions which demand specific and urgent answers rather than later, more convenient, consideration. Questions which are fundamental to a police enquiry are of the type: what is the identity of the individual(s)? what was the cause and manner of death? and what is the interval since death? The last of these is a specific issue to which the archaeologist will also give priority; resolution of the question 'how old is the burial?' is a prerequisite before viable period culture study begins, but it can be answered in the broadest terms (e.g. the late Bronze Age) and still be useful. In forensic contexts the time scale will need to be tighter, measured in years, months, weeks, or even days, although the methodology can be similar. On the other hand, the first two questions are rarely considered in an academic context; in the more relaxed atmosphere of period culture study the analysis of the dead is usually (a) more limited but broadly based and (b) more conjectural. Additionally, determining the 'right' hypothesis or interpretation, although desirable, is rarely tenable and in any event is normally unprovable however much it may be tested later.

As far as individuality is concerned, the differences between the forensic and archaeological investigation of human remains and their respective requirements has been explored in some detail by Roberts (1995) and is only touched upon briefly here. Identification of the individual is not an archaeological consideration although is sometimes attempted in instances of historically documented figures with known burial places (e.g. Stirland 1990). Although archaeologists occasionally have the financial resources to enable the facial characteristics of an individual to be reconstructed, the purpose is fundamentally academic and has a high 'interest' factor with the added advantage of providing considerable popular appeal (Neave 1986). In criminal matters, however, the process is to facilitate identification, a requirement which now has the benefit of photographic superimposition techniques which received early acclaim in the Ruxton murders (Glaister and Brash 1937). Traditional forensic techniques such as radiography or odontology, which accounted for the identification of some 200 of 270 Lockerbie victims (Moody and Busuttil 1994), are based on the existence of records not available to the archaeologist. Given the decreasing number of dental visits by individuals in modern society, it may not be long before dentition ceases to be a forensic option either. Identification on a broader, racial, or cultural basis has some archaeological success, notably using blood groups for example with mummified remains (see Gruspier 1985), and potentially also with DNA. *Individuality* as such, however, is normally unfeasible in an archaeological context.

The question 'how did they die?' is also rarely answerable in an archaeological context, although in a number of cases the manner of death has been evident, notably the ligature around the neck of Lindow Man (Stead, Bourke, and Brothwell 1986), a projectile embedded in the skeleton (Bennike 1985, 210f), or a skull from a Glasgow cemetery with injuries and lead shot preserved (see Roberts 1995). Severe skeletal trauma has also been used in attempts to identify the remains of known historical figures, for example a woman who was sentenced to *peine forte et dure*, a particularly unpleasant death brought about by being crushed beneath a weighted door and having a large stone placed under the back (Roberts et al. 1992). In less severe instances it has been possible to show healed wounds and fractures or even to suggest the type of weapon that may have been used to inflict injury (Wenham 1987). In most cases, however, cause of death and the events leading to it are a matter of conjecture, no more so than in the case of 'Ötzi the Iceman' whose Neolithic demise high in the Alps has been the cause of much speculation (Spindler 1994).

Problems of identification and cause of death have been highlighted by recent exhumations of legitimate 'modern' material and have given the opportunity for archaeologists and anthropologists to take a more considered view of problems of both archaeological and forensic concern. The relatively common occurrence of localised family burial grounds, particularly in the remoter ranch environments of Nevada, has produced a number of opportunities for observation (Brooks and Brooks 1984) during redevelopment programmes when excavation is a statutory requirement. In one family burial ground it was not possible to fully identify the small number of individuals interred although they were historically documented in the late nineteenth century, nor was it possible to corroborate the documented cause of death of two of the individuals (swallowing a pin and falling from a horse respectively). To add to the concern, the body of an (unrecorded) small baby was also recovered and two further individuals (brothers), one of whom was recorded as shooting the other before committing suicide, were subsequently interpreted as the result of a double murder after an autopsy.

THE RECOVERY OF EVIDENCE

The question least likely to be asked by an archaeologist, but the one which is foremost in the minds of a crime manager (and probably the ultimate focus of the criminal investigation itself) is 'who killed the individual?' On archaeological sites the majority of burials encountered are 'legitimate' within their cultural context; in fact this legitimacy is the underlying premise that enables the manner of deposition, grave goods, and other characteristics to be used. There are no criteria that might define 'non-legitimate' graves in archaeological contexts. Burials which depart from an accepted norm in whatever way tend to be considered somehow 'special' but rarely illicit.

Attempting to solve the question 'who killed the individual?' invokes a number of ancillary questions, for example: what was the manner of death, and would it leave archaeological traces in the grave? who dug the grave and how did they dig it? what implement was used? did the perpetrator leave any traces (e.g. footprints) around or within the grave? and does the grave contain any associated materials or any part of the fill which is foreign?

The physical excavation of a forensic grave is little different from one which is purely archaeological. The investigation is carried out meticulously and involves three-dimensional recording of any items encountered even if they do not appear to be important at the time. Half-sectioning is preferable; not only does it prove the existence of a victim in the first instance, but it also provides visual proof of the infilling which may be required for evidential purposes. Significant stratigraphic features, particularly those which have a bearing on the interval since death or on sequencing, will require witnessing. Their comprehension and a general awareness of the phenomena that cause them are essential if the evidence is to be used in court. Photography of the death scene is undertaken by the specialist scene-of-crime team; it provides an exhaustive record but, unless requested, it will not provide the necessary evidence of *sequence* which archaeological recovery may be able to demonstrate.

Excavation is normally undertaken in narrow spits, typically around ten centimetres in depth, until such time as the body is reached or unless the fill dictates otherwise. The use of spits is also the most convenient way for making a broadly based record of items three-dimensionally; it is often necessary for purposes of speed or when quantities of material are being recovered. One landmark excavation involved the recovery of a victim from the bottom of a well (Levine et al. 1984) by removing the rubbish infill in thirty centimetre spits until the body was reached and recovered. By analysing the relative proportions of bottles, cans and bricks in these spits it was possible to recreate the depositional processes subsequent to the dumping of the victim.

To some extent the police investigation treads water until the body, or even part of the body, has been exposed. At that point the investigation changes gear and a number of statutory requirements, protocols, and established routines are put in place. There is often increased pressure for the rapid recovery of the victim in order to establish identification and to determine cause of death, and in order to set in train a full-scale murder enquiry. The senior investigating officer (SIO) may have to balance the fullest recovery of evidence with other factors – weather, availability of personnel, specialist support, and so on, not to mention the speedy arrest of a suspect. All those at the scene will be expected to work in unison to maximise the evidence available. Legally the body is under the control of the coroner at this point. Given that the circumstances of death are 'suspicious' the coroner will ask for the Home Office pathologist to be called. The removal of the body and its preparation for removal is the preferred role of the pathologist, whose responsibility it will be to determine a cause of death and to assist with an identification and with the calculated interval since death. The pathologist will effectively control the procedure from that point with active discussion between all those concerned, e.g. forensic scientist, archaeologist, SIO, and entomologist, regarding the different demands which have to be satisfied at this critical point.

Generally, the secure lifting of the victim for post-mortem examination takes priority over other issues. There will be occasions when, for reasons of depth, restricted access, or deteriorating state of the remains, unorthodox measures have to be taken to guarantee this integrity. These might include the excavation of an area to the side of the grave in order to allow access through the grave wall, or the fabrication of a temporary platform to be wedged between the grave sides to prevent the weight of the recovery team from damaging the victim. This author has used both methods, their success being the result of the necessary sections and plans being drawn before or during the damaging process and with the full co-operation and understanding of the other specialists involved.

In archaeological contexts, excavation is considered to have been concluded when the victim is recorded, lifted, and the fill sieved, but in a forensic situation the result of the post-mortem may necessitate additional work. Examples would include the shooting of the victim in the grave by which bullets may have penetrated below the grave bottom or the presence of toxins. It is now normal best practice for forensic scientists to take samples of earth immediately adjacent to and below the victim to test for toxic residues, although the sampling strategy does not normally take into account the grave/non-grave environments. There is also the problem of ensuring that all the human evidence is recovered. Absence of evidence, whilst a popular archaeological point for debate, is a potential forensic disaster. Evidence of absence in the recovery of human remains may have significant implications for cause of death, torture, or identification. In the exhumation of the Stewart family from a local burial ground in Nevada one of the male members was found to lack the back of the cranium at the autopsy (Brooks and Brooks 1984: 71).

[215]

It was not possible to determine whether this was *de facto*, and therefore the cause of death, or whether insufficient care had been taken during the excavation. Care is also necessary to ensure that critical tissue is not damaged in the recovery process, notably the hyoid bone, a small bone in the neck commonly fractured in cases of strangulation (Ubelaker 1992), whose state has critical implications for cause of death. Most archaeologists are unaware either of its existence or of its significance.

Within the grave itself the associated materials may be archaeologically novel – textiles, paper, man-made fibres, and plastics. The date of the burial may be given a *terminus post quem* by the presence of paper wrapping or packaging containing batch numbers; there may be cans or bottles bearing fingerprints, some of the fill may even be blood soaked. Experimentation in the USA has shown the varying degree to which different modern materials rnight survive in different types of soil environment (Morse 1983); some of the earlier Florida courses utilised 'practice' graves for decay experimentation of similar materials under controlled conditions (Morse et al. 1976b). Furthermore, the combination of a recent interval since burial and the presence of modern materials improves the chance of trace contact evidence surviving. The assumption that every contact leaves a trace (Locard 1928) underpins the theory of modern forensic science and points to the potential survival of contact evidence between victim and assassin, or between grave digger and grave. These contacts may manifest themselves in the transference of fibres or other materials or by impressions. It entails a more than usually careful removal of fill; a concerted effort is also required to avoid contamination from the excavator or specialist to the grave, its fill, or the victim. In archaeological contexts contamination is normally limited to stratigraphic or sampling integrity. At a scene of crime it is of paramount importance throughout all processes; as a matter of routine disposable overalls are worn. The Florida experiments also demonstrated that shoe prints might be recovered from the grave floor if the excavation was carried out with sufficient care. It is, however, often difficult to remove the victim simply by lifting; most pathologists are reluctant for the remains to be subjected to any further trauma before the post-mortem takes place; removal is frequently carried out by sliding a solid but pliable material (such as aluminium sheeting) below the body.

There is also the need to examine the grave wall in order to assess the method or implement used in the grave construction, for example the grab of a mechanical excavator, pick-axe, spade, or a shovel may all leave diagnostic markings depending on the local geology. Most clandestine graves are dug hurriedly. They reflect the fact that many homicides are unplanned and occur when arguments get out of hand, or when sex 'goes wrong', and when graves are dug in panic and as speedily as possible. Research in the USA has shown how predictable such burials might be in terms of (a) the extent to which the site chosen for burial is already known to the perpetrator and (b) the maximum distance those graves are likely to be from a vehicular route (Killam 1990, 15f). Such burials tend to differ from the deep, carefully cut, vertically-sided burials of the parish sexton or many of those recorded in antiquity. Viewed forensically, these differences might be used to reflect the extent to which factors of premeditation were involved in the crime – factors which have significant implications for verdicts of manslaughter or murder and on which archaeological opinion is important. Equally, if it can be shown archaeologically that the grave had been dug well in advance of the burial, for example by the identification of silted deposits on the grave floor, a similar level of premeditation can be argued.

INTERVAL SINCE DEATH

The question of the interval since death is common to both forensic and archaeological contexts, although the time scale involved will differ markedly. From a stratigraphic point of view all dating is relative and hence, in theory, the time scale becomes an irrelevance. In practice, however, most modern murder victims are recovered before any additional formation processes have occurred, and most relate directly to the modern ground surface through which they were cut. In some instances it has even been possible to take cognisance of root injury and growth in ascertaining the elapsed interval since burial (e.g. Vanezis et al. 1978; Willey and Heilman 1988). More common, however, is the use of entomological evidence for which there is now a growing literature (e.g. Erzinclioglu 1983; Rodriguez and Bass 1983). In 'older' burials, particularly where building work may have taken place involving cutting or sealing of the grave, even the simplest of stratigraphy may be critical for dating purposes. In reality many clandestine burials are only encountered during building activity or in the construction of drainage trenches, but the remains are often unwittingly removed from their context for forensic inspection. This is particularly unfortunate in that it is notoriously difficult to determine the age of 'modern' skeletal material (see Pollard 1995); as a result the retention of the burial context is paramount. From a practical point of view crimes older than seventy or so years are unlikely to be solved and are therefore rarely followed up by the police. As a result accurate dating below this range becomes all the more important. The survival of soft tissue is no guide to interval since death – a range of circumstances and environments can be responsible, as indeed can differential preservation caused by clothing, depth, waterlogging, and humidity. Decay chemistry and factors which accelerate or delay decomposition have a vast literature and owe much of their origins to the experimental work of Mant (e.g. 1987) on victims of the Second World War. Since then archaeology has produced its own examples to complement a growing forensic case load; the issue is too extensive to cover here and is well discussed elsewhere (Janaway 1995).

In archaeological contexts many burials will have an approximate contemporary context, perhaps other graves, associated features, or surviving layers which may be grouped together for phasing purposes. In other instances a burial may simply stand on its own within a longer sequence of archaeological events or within a complex burial chronology. In forensic contexts, however, the grave has often been dug into the contemporary ground surface, or has been crudely disguised by an additional layer such as branches, undergrowth or screening in outdoor circumstances, or by concrete skimming or building works indoors. This brings a whole new dimension to archaeological investigation in that it entails examination of the same environment and context in which the archaeologist is actually working. Indoors this can be reasonably well defined. For example, in a cellar burial where walls and floor may show evidence of upcast, bloodstains, transference of fibres, or other contact traces, survey controls can be established and the data logged spatially within a physically defined area. However, in the more common outdoor settings the same type of evidence is harder to secure: the boundaries are undefined and the traces are less enduring in view of climate, ground conditions, and animal activity. As a result the physical perimeters are defined arbitrarily, usually as areas restricted by plastic tape in order to preserve the scene and to control access. As far as the investigation is concerned these areas are *real* in that they delineate a specific focal area for attention, but as far as the broader context of the crime is concerned they are *artificial* in that they focus on a specific activity or event rather than on the sequence of activities which led to it. Examples of evidence within the wider environment which might have a bearing on the context of the grave include drag marks, tyre marks, fragments of clothing on bushes or trees, scattered upcast, or vegetational disturbance. In archaeological terms these all belong to the same event as the burial and therefore should belong to a common recording and interpretative process. The archaeologist, traditionally accustomed to function at a distance from the time scale of study and to work on broad chronologies, finds himself or herself uncomfortably close to the context of events being recorded and using a much tighter sub-phasing of events than is normal.

The reality of this is especially apparent with the occurrence of scattered remains when a victim has been left on the ground surface, and where a combination of decay and animal activity has caused movement of the remains, the extent of this movement generally being dependent on the time elapsed since dumping of the individual (Morse et al. 1983, table 6. 1). Scatter issues are best exampled in the so-called Green River murders in King County, Washington (Haglund et al. 1990) which involved the catalogued recovery of 40 victims discovered since 1982 with post-mortem intervals of between 2–3 days and 6 years. Although, from an archaeological point of view, the strongest relevance lies with the multiple-point recording of individual items which is directly analogous with focused EDM recording of sites and monuments, there is a significant reminder of the importance of the contemporary scene and local environment of the burial. The record involved identification and survey not only of scattered surface remains of textiles and bone, but also of the indirect evidence for human remains and decay. This included the yellowing of branches from ammonia released during putrefaction, the presence of hair or fibres in birds' nests, and the occurrence of teeth, hair, and fingernail fragments in animal faeces. Identification of these features was an important pointer to the location of some of the remains in the first instance. It is worth noting perhaps that the same investigation emphasised the importance of different specialist investigators in such circumstances: entomologists, botanists, geologists, and anthropologists (ibid., 37).

The endpoint

Although excavation of an archaeological site and the routines of a scene of crime may share some similarities, there is a fundamental difference in the manner of reporting the data recovered. Archaeological excavation occurs within an academic framework in which answers are sought to broad-ranging questions and in which hypotheses are set up for future discussion. Material and data are recorded, removed from site, studied at length, integrated, and published within the broader context of period culture at some date in the future. Although ostensibly simple, this publication process is fraught with technical, financial, and logistical difficulties (for overview see Hills 1993). Credibility is by peer judgement and by published review many months, if not years, later. Publication is undertaken as a basic principle of archaeology, given that excavation produces data which might be open to interpretation by different persons. There can never be a definitive commentary on an excavation and the findings are disseminated both formally and informally immediately after the event, and sometimes even during the process itself. The requirement to make data available is a fundamental principle of professional archaeological practice.

In a forensic excavation the framework is judicial rather than academic, although the application of the archaeological methodology has an academic pedigree. The questions which require answering are well rehearsed and although hypotheses may be set up they will be tested in the following days, if not hours, in order to support those answers. Material and data may be recorded and removed from the scene, and with a greater degree of security than on an archaeological site, but all of it will be made available. The Attorney General Guidelines of 1982 on disclosure decreed that 'unused material' should be made available to the defence; this is now interpreted as all sketches, plans, notes, photographs, as well as written or recorded comments, and any material evidence which has been recovered. Thus the freedom of selectivity enjoyed in archaeological publication becomes fundamentally unacceptable in forensic contexts. Equally unacceptable is the dissemination of data, or even the discussion of data to those outside the case in advance of Crown Court trial, an interval which can extend for months or even years. The forensic equivalent of the excavation report is the courtroom, and the peer review takes the form of a cross-examination by a skilled barrister. The archaeologist will take the role of 'expert witness' together with all the dangers that this entails (see Snow 1982; Iscan 1988). Archaeological information will have to be imparted not to a peer group, but to a lay audience (the jury) with the appropriate avoidance of terminology, jargon, and complex illustrative material. In an archaeological publication, the evidence stands alone. In the courtroom, the archaeological evidence is part of a larger body of corroborative evidence on which a successful conviction may depend. At the conclusion of the trial the judge will pronounce a verdict and that verdict will be definitive. Subject to appeal, there is no recourse to reinterpretation of the excavation findings.

These are frightening areas in which to practice excavation skills and in which to provide opinion. Worse still, and hanging over each investigation, is the 'awesomely serious' nature of the matter in hand (Skinner 1987, 273). At the end of the day, however, unlike the academic archaeologist, the forensic archaeologist can have his or her interpretation corroborated by confession. It can be more than gratifying to learn that one's interpretation of how events and sequences occurred was actually correct. Academic archaeologists will never be in a position to benefit from this, nor, on the other hand will they ever find out just how wrong they were. For the forensic archaeologist, being proved fundamentally wrong by confession is the likely end to a promising career.

Acknowledgements

The author is grateful to Charlotte Roberts and Abegail Tebbs for their support and helpful comments in the preparation of this paper.

References

Bass, W. M. 1984. Time interval since death. In T. A. Rathbun and J. E. Buikstra (eds), *Human Identification: Case Studies in Forensic Anthropology*, 136–147. Charles C. Thomas, Springfield, Illinois.

Bass, W. M. and W. H. Birkby 1978. Exhumation: the method could make the difference. *F.B.I. Law Enforcement Bulletin* July 1978, 6–11.

Bennike, P. 1985 *Palaeopathology of Danish skeletons. A comparative study of demography, disease and injury*. Akademisk Forlag, Copenhagen.

Berryman, H. E., W. M. Bass, S. A. Symes, and O. C. Smith 1991. Recognition of cemetery remains in the forensic setting. *Journal of Forensic Sciences* 36(1), 230–237.

Brooks, S. T. and Brooks, R. H. 1984. Problems of burial exhumation, historical and forensic aspects. In T. Rathbun and J. E. Buikstra (eds) *Human Identification. Case Studies in Forensic Anthropology*, 64–86. Charles C. Thomas, Springfield, Illinois.

Erzinclioglu, Y. Z. 1983. The application of entomology to forensic medicine. *Medicine, Science, and the Law* 23(1), 57–63.

France, D. L., T. J. Griffin, J. G. Swanburg, J. W. Lindemann, G. C. Davenport, V. Trammell, C. T. Armbrust, B. Kondratieff, A. Nelson, K. Castellano, and D. Hopkins 1992. A multidisciplinary approach to the detection of clandestine graves. *Journal of Forensic Sciences* 37(6), 1435–1750.

Garratt-Frost, S. 1992. *The Law and Burial Archaeology*. Institute of Field Archaeologists (Technical Paper no. 11), Birmingham.

Glaister, J. and Brash, J. C. 1937. *Medico-legal Aspects of the Ruxton Case*. E. and S. Livingstone, Edinburgh.

Gruspier, K. 1985 Paleoserology: History and New Application to the Casal San Vincenzo Skeletal Material. Unpublished M. A. Thesis, University of Sheffield.

Haglund, W. D., D. G. Reichert, and D. T. Reay 1990. Recovery of decomposed and skeletal human remains in the Green River murder investigation: implications for medical examiner/coroner and police. *American Journal of Forensic Medicine and Pathology* 11(1), 35–43.

Hills, C. 1993. The dissemination of information. In J. R. Hunter and I. B. M. Ralston (eds), *Archaeological Resource Management in the UK: an introduction*, 215–224. Alan Sutton, Stroud.

Hunter, J. R. 1994. Forensic archaeology in Britain. *Antiquity* 68, 758–769.

Hunter, J. R., C. A. Roberts, and A. Martin (eds) 1995. *Studies in Crime: an Introduction to Forensic Archaeology*. Seaby/Batsford, London.

Iscan, M. Y. 1988. Rise of forensic anthropology. *Yearbook of Physical Anthropology* 31, 203–230.

Janaway, R. C. 1995. The decay of buried human remains and their associated materials. In J. R. Hunter, C. A. Roberts, and A. Martin (eds), *Studies in Crime: an Introduction to Forensic Archaeology*, 58–86. Seaby/Batsford, London.

Killam, E. W. 1990. *The Detection of Human Remains*. Charles C. Thomas, Springfield, Illinois.

[221]

Krogman, W. M. and M. Y. Iscan 1986. *The Human Skeleton in Forensic Medicine*. Charles C. Thomas, Springfield, Illinois.

Levine, L. J., H. R. Campbell Jnr., and J. S. Rhine 1984. Perpendicular forensic archaeology. In T. Rathbun and J. E. Buikstra (eds), *Human Identification. Case Studies in Forensic Anthropology*, 87–95. Charles C. Thomas, Springfield, Illinois.

Locard, E. 1928. Dust and its analysis: an aid to criminal investigation. *Police Journal* 1, 177–92.

McKinley, J. I. and C. A. Roberts 1993. *Excavation and Post-Excavation Treatment of Cremated and Inhumed Human Remains*. Institute of Field Archaeologists (Technical Paper no. 12), Birmingham.

Mant A. K. 1987. Knowledge acquired from post-war exhumations. In A. Boddington, A. N. Garland, R. C. and Janaway (eds), *Death, Decay and Reconstruction: Approaches to Archaeology and Forensic Science*, 65–78. Manchester University Press, Manchester.

Moody, G. H. and A. Busuttil 1994. Identification in the Lockerbie air disaster. *American Journal of Forensic Medicine and Pathology* 15(1), 63–69.

Morse, D. 1983. Studies on the deterioration of associated death scene materials. In D. Morse, J. Duncan, and J. Stoutamire (eds), *Handbook of Forensic Archaeology and Anthropology*, appendix A. Rose Printing, Tallahassee, Florida.

Morse, D., D. Crusoe, and H. G. Smith 1976a. Forensic archaeology. *Journal of Forensic Sciences* 21(2), 323–332.

Morse, D., J. Stoutamire, and J. Duncan 1976b. A unique course in anthropology. *American Journal of Physical Anthropology* 45(3), 743–748.

Morse, D., R. C. Dailey, J. Stoutamire, and J. Duncan 1984. Forensic archaeology. In T. A. Rathbun and J. Buikstra (eds), *Human Identification: Case Studies in Forensic Anthropology*, 53–63. Charles C. Thomas, Springfield.

Morse, D., J. Duncan, and J. Stoutamire (eds) 1983. *Handbook of Forensic Archaeology and Anthropology*. Rose Printing, Tallahassee, Florida.

Neave, R. A. H. 1986 The reconstruction of skulls for facial reconstruction using radiographic techniques. In A. R. David (ed.), *Science in Egyptology*, 329–333. Manchester University Press, Manchester.

Pollard, A. M. P. 1995. Dating the time of death. In J. R. Hunter, C. A. Roberts, and A. Martin (eds), *Studies in Crime: an Introduction to Forensic Archaeology*, 139–156. Seaby/Batsford, London.

Reeve, J. and M. Adams 1993. *The Spitalfields Project*, vol. 1, *The archaeology. Across the Styx*. British Council for Archaeology (CBA Research Report 85), York.

Roberts, C. A. 1995. Forensic anthropology 2: positive identification of the individual; cause and manner of death. In J. R. Hunter, C. A. Roberts, and A. Martin (eds), *Studies in Crime: an Introduction to Forensic Archaeology*, 122–139. Seaby/Batsford, London.

Roberts, C. A., K. Manchester, and A. Storey 1992. Margaret Clitherow: skeletal identification of an historical figure. *Forensic Science International* 57, 63–71.

Rodriguez, W. C. and W. M. Bass 1983. Insect activity and its relationship to decay rates of human cadavers in East Tennessee. *Journal of Forensic Sciences* 28(2), 423–432.

Sigler-Eisenberg, B. B. 1985. Forensic research: expanding the concept of applied archaeology. *American Antiquity* 50(3), 650–655.

Skinner, M. 1987. Planning the archaeological recovery of evidence from recent mass graves. *Forensic Science International* (34), 267–287.

Skinner, M. and R. A. Lazenby 1983. *Found! Human Remains. A Field Manual for the Recovery of the Recent Human Skeleton.* Archaeology Press, Simon Fraser University, Vancouver.

Snow, C. C. 1982. Forensic anthropology. *Annual Review of Anthropology* 11, 97–131.

Spindler, K. 1994. *The Man in the Ice.* Weidenfeld and Nicolson, London.

Stead, I. M., J. B. Bourke, and D. Brothwell 1986. *Lindow Man. The Body in the Bog.* Guild Publishing, London.

Stirland, A. 1990. The late Sir Thomas Reynes: a medieval identification. *J. For. Sci. Soc.* 30, 39–43.

Ubelaker, D. 1989. *Human Skeletal Remains. Excavation, Analysis and Interpretation.* Taraxacum Press, Washington.

Ubelaker, D. 1992. Hyoid fracture and strangulation. *Journal of Forensic Sciences* 37(5), 1216–1222.

Vanezis, P., B. Grant Sims, and J. H. Grant 1978. Medical and scientific investigations of an exhumation in unhallowed ground. *Medicine, Science, and the Law,* 18(3), 209–221.

Wenham, S. 1987. Anatomical and Microscopical Interpretations of Ancient Weapon Injuries. Unpublished thesis submitted to the University of Leicester for the degree of BSc Medical Sciences.

Willey, P. and A. Heilman 1988. Estimating time since death using plant roots and stems. *Journal of Forensic Sciences* 32, 1264–1271.

CRUITHNE PRESS titles

Social Approaches to Viking Studies
edited by Ross Samson
hbk, 256 pp., 1991, 1-873448-00-7, £15.00

The Work of Work: Servitude, Slavery, and Labor in Medieval England
edited by Allen J. Frantzen and Douglas Moffat
hbk, 240 pp., 1994, 1-873448-03-1, £24.00

Anglo-Saxon Trading Centres and their Hinterlands. Beyond the Emporia
edited by Mike Anderton
pbk, ca 120 pp., 1999, 1-873448-04-X, £9.50

Understanding the Neolithic of North-western Europe
edited by Mark Edmonds and Colin Richards
hbk, 540 pp., 1998, 1-873448-05-8, £65.00

The Loved Body's Corruption: archaeological contributions to the study of human mortality
edited by Jane Downes and Tony Pollard
pbk, 250 pp., 1999, 1-873448-06-6, £16.50

Early Medieval Cemeteries. An introduction to burial archaeology in the post-Roman west
by Guy Halsall
pbk, 84 pp., 1995, 1-873448-07-4, £6.50

Crossing the Atlantic. Scotland and America, 1625 to the present day
edited by Douglas Gifford
pbk, ca 240 pp., 1999, 1-873448-08-2

Scottish Power Centres from the early Middle Ages to the Twentieth Century
edited by Sally Foster, Allan Macinnes, and Ranald MacInnes
pbk, 250 pp., 1998, 1-873448-09-0, £14.50

Material Harm: archaeological studies of war and violence
edited by John Carman
pbk, 256 pp., 1997, 1-873448-10-4, £19.50

Nationalism and Archaeology. Scottish Archaeological Forum
edited by John A. Atkinson, Iain Banks, and Jerry O'Sullivan
pbk, 224 pp., 1996, 1-873448-11-2, £12.50

The City and Its Worlds. Aspects of Aberdeen's History since 1794
edited by Terry Brotherstone and Donald J. Withrington
pbk, 256 pp., 1996, 1-873448-12-0, £9.95

The Tay Salmon Fisheries since the Eighteenth Century
by Iain A. Robertson
hbk, 477 pp., 1998, 1-873448-13-9, £20

Theoretical Roman Archaeology and Architecture. The third conference proceedings
edited by Alan Leslie
pbk, 216 pp., 1999, 1-873448-14-7, £18.00

Odd Alliances: Studies on Scottish Literature in European Contexts
edited by Neil McMillan and Kirsten Stirling
pbk, ca 240 pp., 1999, 1-873448-15-5

FOR TAKING NOTES

FOR TAKING NOTES